Survi

GLOBAL POLITICS ANı

Volume 67 Number 3 | June–July 2025

'Nuclear strategy, like any other strategy, should be in the first instance geared to the problem at hand … To put it bluntly: if Ukraine loses the war, the problems the West will face will be enormous and demanding; if Russia continues to fail to subjugate Ukraine, the deterrence challenge in the future will be easier.'

Lawrence Freedman, Europe's Nuclear Deterrent: The Here and Now, p. 9.

'Precisely judging an adversary's expected response with such a great variety of domains and capabilities at play is almost impossible. Risking nuclear escalation based on the expectation that national leaders will always be able to read signals and understand their opponent's resolve is a dangerous gambit.'

Anna Péczeli, Managing Escalation: America's Two-peer Nuclear Problem, p. 29.

'[Donald Trump's] incitement is usually phrased in coded, indirect or vague language, which is nonetheless clearly understood by the intended audience. This gives the speaker – or tweeter – plausible deniability by disingenuously disavowing any ulterior meaning or dismissing the incitement as a joke, effectively casting the other side as hysterical.'

Steven Simon, Trump's Century of Days, p. 67.

Survival
GLOBAL POLITICS AND STRATEGY

Volume 67 Number 3 | June–July 2025

Contents

Cover: Ludovic Marin/Pool/AFP via Getty Image

On the cover
French President Emmanuel Macron speaks at the French Air and Space Force Luxeuil–Saint-Sauveur Air Base in front of a *Rafale* aircraft on 18 March 2025.

On the web
Visit www.iiss.org/publications/survival for brief notices on new books on Deterrence, Arms Control and Nuclear History; Latin America; Europe; and Politics and International Relations.

***Survival* editors' blog**
For ideas and commentary from *Survival* editors and contributors, visit https://www.iiss.org/online-analysis/survival-online.

Strategic Shifts

Review Essay

Book Reviews

Closing Argument

Survival
GLOBAL POLITICS AND STRATEGY

The International Institute for Strategic Studies
2121 K Street, NW | Suite 600 | Washington DC 20037 | USA
Tel +1 202 659 1490 Fax +1 202 659 1499 E-mail survival@iiss.org Web www.iiss.org

Arundel House | 6 Temple Place | London | WC2R 2PG | UK
Tel +44 (0)20 7379 7676 Fax +44 (0)20 7836 3108 E-mail iiss@iiss.org

14th Floor, GFH Tower | Bahrain Financial Harbour | Manama | Kingdom of Bahrain
Tel +973 1718 1155 Fax +973 1710 0155 E-mail iiss-middleeast@iiss.org

9 Raffles Place | #49-01 Republic Plaza | Singapore 048619
Tel +65 6499 0055 Fax +65 6499 0059 E-mail iiss-asia@iiss.org

Pariser Platz 6A | 10117 Berlin | Germany
Tel +49 30 311 99 300 E-mail iiss-europe@iiss.org

Survival Online www.tandfonline.com/survival and www.iiss.org/publications/survival

Aims and Scope *Survival* is one of the world's leading forums for analysis and debate of international and strategic affairs. Shaped by its editors to be both timely and forward thinking, the journal encourages writers to challenge conventional wisdom and bring fresh, often controversial, perspectives to bear on the strategic issues of the moment. With a diverse range of authors, *Survival* aims to be scholarly in depth while vivid, well written and policy-relevant in approach. Through commentary, analytical articles, case studies, forums, review essays, reviews and letters to the editor, the journal promotes lively, critical debate on issues of international politics and strategy.

Editor **Dana Allin**
Managing Editor **Jonathan Stevenson**
Associate Editor **Carolyn West**
Editorial Assistant **Anna Gallagher**
Production and Cartography **Alessandra Beluffi, Ravi Gopar, Jade Panganiban, James Parker, Kelly Verity**

Contributing Editors

Chester A. Crocker
Bill Emmott
Franz-Stefan Gady
Bastian Giegerich
Nigel Gould-Davies
Melissa K. Griffith
Emile Hokayem
Nigel Inkster
Jeffrey Mazo
Fenella McGerty
Irene Mia
Meia Nouwens
Benjamin Rhode
Ben Schreer
Maria Shagina
Karen Smith
Angela Stent
Robert Ward
Marcus Willett
Lanxin Xiang

Published for the IISS by
Routledge Journals, an imprint of Taylor & Francis, an Informa business.

Copyright © 2025 The International Institute for Strategic Studies. All rights reserved. No part of this publication may be reproduced, stored, transmitted or disseminated, in any form, or by any means, without prior written permission from Taylor & Francis, to whom all requests to reproduce copyright material should be directed, in writing.

ISBN 978-1-041-07732-9 paperback / 978-1-003-64198-8 ebook

About the IISS The IISS, a registered charity with offices in Washington, London, Manama, Singapore and Berlin, is the world's leading authority on political–military conflict. It is the primary independent source of accurate, objective information on international strategic issues. Publications include *The Military Balance*, an annual reference work on each nation's defence capabilities; *Survival*, a bimonthly journal on international affairs; *Strategic Comments*, an online analysis of topical issues in international affairs; and the *Adelphi* series of books on issues of international security.

Director-General and Chief Executive
Bastian Giegerich

Executive Chairman
John Chipman

Chair of the Trustees
Bill Emmott

Chair of the Council
Chung Min Lee

Trustees
Caroline Atkinson
Neha Aviral
Hakeem Belo-Osagie
John O. Brennan
Florence Parly
Kasper Rørsted
Mark Sedwill
Grace R. Skaugen
Matt Symonds
Matthew Symonds

IISS Advisory Council
Caroline Atkinson
Linden P. Blue
Garvin Brown
Mark Carleton-Smith
Jong-moon Choi
Alejandro Santo Domingo
Thomas Enders
Yoichi Funabashi
Alia Hatoug-Bouran
Eyal Hulata
Badr Jafar
Bilahari Kausikan
Thomas Lembong
Peter Maurer
Florence Parly
Charles Powell
Mark Sedwill
Debra Soon
Heizo Takenaka
Marcus Wallenberg

SUBMISSIONS

To submit an article, authors are advised to follow these guidelines:

- Articles must be their authors' original work and not have been generated by any form of artificial intelligence.
- *Survival* articles are around 4,000–10,000 words long including endnotes. A word count should be included with a draft. Length is a consideration in the review process and shorter articles have an advantage.
- All text, including endnotes, should be double-spaced with wide margins.
- Any tables or artwork should be supplied in separate files, ideally not embedded in the document or linked to text around it.
- All *Survival* articles are expected to include endnote references. These should be complete and include first and last names of authors, titles of articles (even from newspapers), place of publication, publisher, exact publication dates, volume and issue number (if from a journal) and page numbers. Web sources should include complete URLs and DOIs if available.
- A summary of up to 150 words should be included with the article. The summary should state the main argument clearly and concisely, not simply say what the article is about.
- A short author's biography of one or two lines should also be included. This information will appear at the foot of the first page of the article.

Please note that *Survival* has a strict policy of listing multiple authors in alphabetical order.

Submissions should be made by email, in Microsoft Word format, to survival@iiss.org. Note that macro-enabled files will not be accepted. Alternatively, hard copies may be sent to *Survival*, IISS–US, 2121 K Street NW, Suite 801, Washington, DC 20037, USA.

The editorial review process can take up to three months. *Survival*'s acceptance rate for unsolicited manuscripts is less than 20%. *Survival* does not normally provide referees' comments in the event of rejection. Authors are permitted to submit simultaneously elsewhere so long as this is consistent with the policy of the other publication and the Editors of *Survival* are informed of the dual submission.

Readers are encouraged to comment on articles from the previous issue. Letters should be concise, no longer than 750 words and relate directly to the argument or points made in the original article.

Survival: Global Politics and Strategy (Print ISSN 0039-6338, Online ISSN 1468-2699) is published bimonthly for a total of 6 issues per year by Taylor & Francis Group, 4 Park Square, Milton Park, Abingdon, Oxon, OX14 4RN, UK. Periodicals postage paid (Permit no. 13095) at Brooklyn, NY 11256.

Airfreight and mailing in the USA by agent named World Container Inc., c/o BBT 150-15, 183rd Street, Jamaica, NY 11413, USA.

US Postmaster: Send address changes to Survival, World Container Inc., c/o BBT 150-15, 183rd Street, Jamaica, NY 11413, USA.

Subscription records are maintained at Taylor & Francis Group, 4 Park Square, Milton Park, Abingdon, OX14 4RN, UK.

Subscription information: For more information and subscription rates, please see tandfonline.com/pricing/journal/TSUR. Taylor & Francis journals are available in a range of different packages, designed to suit every library's needs and budget. This journal is available for institutional subscriptions with online-only or print & online options. This journal may also be available as part of our libraries, subject collections or archives. For more information on our sales packages, please visit librarianresources.taylorandfrancis.com.

For support with any institutional subscription, please visit help.tandfonline.com or email our dedicated team at subscriptions@tandf.co.uk.

Subscriptions purchased at the personal rate are strictly for personal, non-commercial use only. The reselling of personal subscriptions is prohibited. Personal subscriptions must be purchased with a personal cheque, credit card or BAC/wire transfer. Proof of personal status may be requested.

Back issues: Please visit https://taylorandfrancis.com/journals/customer-services/ for more information on how to purchase back issues.

Ordering information: To subscribe to the journal, please contact T&F Customer Services, Informa UK Ltd, Sheepen Place, Colchester, Essex, CO3 3LP, UK. Tel: +44 (0) 20 8052 2030; email subscriptions@tandf.co.uk.

Taylor & Francis journals are priced in USD, GBP and EUR (as well as AUD and CAD for a limited number of journals). All subscriptions are charged depending on where the end customer is based. If you are unsure which rate applies to you, please contact Customer Services. All subscriptions are payable in advance and all rates include postage. We are required to charge applicable VAT/GST on all print and online combination subscriptions, in addition to our online-only journals. Subscriptions are entered on an annual basis, i.e., January to December. Payment may be made by sterling cheque, dollar cheque, euro cheque, international money order, National Giro or credit cards (Amex, Visa and Mastercard).

Disclaimer: The International Institute for Strategic Studies (IISS) and our publisher Informa UK Limited, trading as Taylor & Francis Group ('T&F'), make every effort to ensure the accuracy of all the information (the 'Content') contained in our publications. However, IISS and our publisher T&F, our agents and our licensors make no representations or warranties whatsoever as to the accuracy, completeness or suitability for any purpose of the Content. Any opinions and views expressed in this publication are the opinions and views of the authors, and are not the views of or endorsed by IISS or our publisher T&F. The accuracy of the Content should not be relied upon and should be independently verified with primary sources of information, and any reliance on the Content is at your own risk. IISS and our publisher T&F make no representations, warranties or guarantees, whether express or implied, that the Content is accurate, complete or up to date. IISS and our publisher T&F shall not be liable for any losses, actions, claims, proceedings, demands, costs, expenses, damages and other liabilities whatsoever or howsoever caused arising directly or indirectly in connection with, in relation to or arising out of the use of the Content. Full Terms & Conditions of access and use can be found at http://www.tandfonline.com/page/terms-and-conditions.

Informa UK Limited, trading as Taylor & Francis Group, grants authorisation for individuals to photocopy copyright material for private research use, on the sole basis that requests for such use are referred directly to the requestor's local Reproduction Rights Organization (RRO). The copyright fee is exclusive of any charge or fee levied. In order to contact your local RRO, please contact International Federation of Reproduction Rights Organizations (IFRRO), rue du Prince Royal, 87, B-1050 Brussels, Belgium; email ifrro@skynet.be; Copyright Clearance Center Inc., 222 Rosewood Drive, Danvers, MA 01923, USA; email info@copyright.com; or Copyright Licensing Agency, 90 Tottenham Court Road, London, W1P 0LP, UK; email cla@cla.co.uk. This authorisation does not extend to any other kind of copying, by any means, in any form, for any purpose other than private research use.

Submission information: See https://www.tandfonline.com/journals/tsur20

Advertising: See https://taylorandfrancis.com/contact/advertising/

Permissions: See help.tandfonline.com/Librarian/s/article/Permissions

All Taylor & Francis Group journals are printed on paper from renewable sources by accredited partners.

June–July 2025

NEW IISS STRATEGIC DOSSIER

IISS | Routledge Taylor & Francis Group

ASIA-PACIFIC REGIONAL SECURITY ASSESSMENT 2025

Key developments and trends

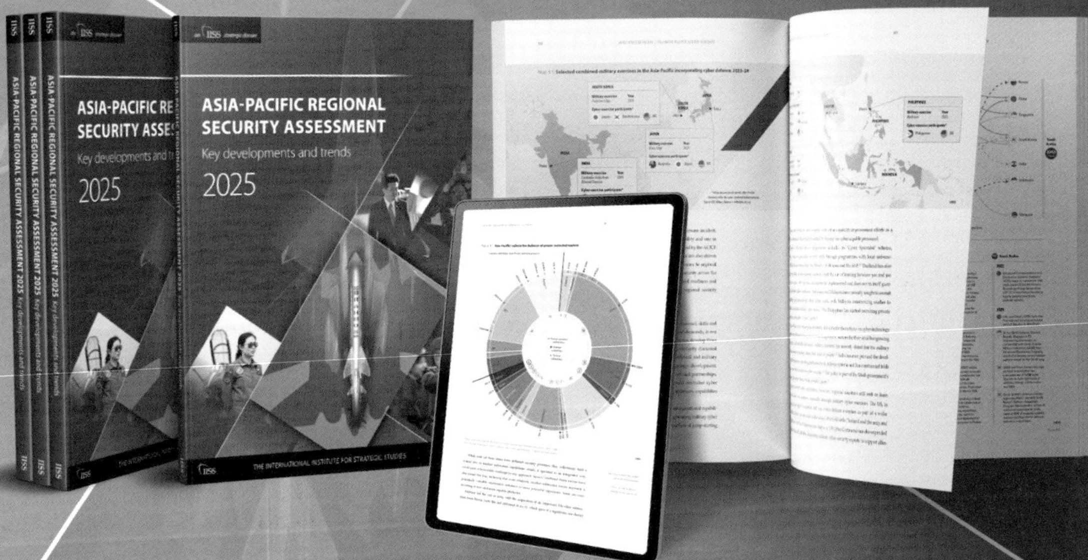

The *Asia-Pacific Regional Security Assessment* examines key regional security issues relevant to the policy-focused discussions of the IISS Shangri-La Dialogue, Asia's premier defence summit convened by the International Institute for Strategic Studies.

This twelfth edition contains an introduction and six chapters, all authored by IISS experts, which investigate important dimensions of the regional security environment, supported by maps, graphs, charts and tables.

ASIA SECURITY SUMMIT
IISS Shangri-La Dialogue

AVAILABLE ONLINE:
go.iiss.org/APRSA25

TOPICS INCLUDE:

- Defence-industrial partnerships involving regional and extra-regional powers in the Asia-Pacific
- Trump's redrawing of the international security landscape
- The implications of the growing ties between China, North Korea and Russia for Northeast Asian security
- Emerging underwater security trends
- Military cyber maturity across the Asia-Pacific
- Southeast Asia's uninhabited aerial vehicle-capability developments

The International Institute for Strategic Studies and Taylor & Francis take seriously their contribution to protecting our environment. In addition to all paper used in our journals being FSC-certified, this journal has gone plastic-free and no longer uses plastic cover lamination or polywrap for mailing.

Europe's Nuclear Deterrent: The Here and Now

Lawrence Freedman

During the Russo-Ukrainian war, nuclear escalation has been considered an ever-present possibility, though it has thus far been avoided. The war has demonstrated the ease with which nuclear threats can be made and the speed with which anxieties can be generated. In an article for this journal published in late 2023, I argued that the result had been 'pre-emptive panic' in the West. Policymakers and commentators assumed that Russian President Vladimir Putin could well employ nuclear weapons if backed into a corner. This led to unnecessary caution when it came to supporting Ukraine. Little account was taken of the many reasons why Putin would be unlikely to be the first to break the nuclear taboo. The consequences would be hard to gauge in advance, victory could not be guaranteed, vigorous responses by others, including the United States, could not be precluded, and countries friendly to Russia, such as China, would be alienated.[1]

Putin certainly looked for ways to exude nuclear menace, including tampering with nuclear doctrine. Should the war take an adverse turn, he might become even more reckless. But up to now practice has been far more restrained than rhetoric might suggest, and supposed red lines have been passed with non-nuclear means being sought to signal Moscow's displeasure and satisfy any urge to retribution. It is reasonable to suppose that in

Lawrence Freedman is Emeritus Professor of War Studies at King's College London.

Survival | vol. 67 no. 3 | June–July 2025 | pp. 7–24 https://doi.org/10.1080/00396338.2025.2508078

Putin's mind, nuclear use is best kept for the most extreme contingencies when the state faces an existential threat.

In this article I address another nuclear issue that the war has raised to make a similar point. In early 2025, the role of British and French nuclear forces was pushed to the fore in discussions about how to ensure Ukrainian security following a US-brokered peace deal. This issue became bound up with more general concerns about the status of the US nuclear umbrella.[2] The first question was whether the US would provide a 'backstop' should a force led by the United Kingdom and France seek to provide a form of security guarantee to Ukraine. This led to a second question: if the US would not provide a backstop, what might that indicate about the readiness of the US to live up to its Article 5 obligations in the event of a Russian push against NATO countries in a future war? This in turn led to a third question: with growing doubts about the US commitment to European security, could the British and French provide a substitute nuclear shield?

These questions lack answers, or at least the answers have been deliberately kept vague. It suits all actors to avoid being too explicit about what they might do in circumstances that might never arise. Short of a definitive American statement to the effect that it is abandoning NATO, neither London nor Paris will push for a more prominent role for their forces. They want the US to continue to be part of European security and will not do anything to encourage the Trump administration to believe that it could safely abandon its allies. That does not mean, however, that these forces have no role to play, especially in the context of their backing for Ukraine.

Discussions of nuclear strategy tend to move quickly to extreme contingencies. Once the issue of a possible role for British and French nuclear forces is raised, analysts soon test them against the most dire scenarios, when they will inevitably be found wanting. Yet nuclear strategy is all about providing a deterrent effect sufficient to avoid the most dire scenarios, and that can be achieved without significant changes to either declaratory policy or force structures.

Circumstances may change drastically, as we have seen with the gamble taken by Putin in launching a full-scale invasion of Russia's neighbour and the volatility of the Trump administration. This issue looked to be much more challenging in early March 2025, when the United States' outright abandonment of Ukraine seemed to be on the cards, than it did in early May, as the Trump administration tentatively began to put less pressure on Ukraine and more on Russia in its efforts to end the war. (Obviously, there is no guarantee that this pattern will continue.)

Nuclear strategy, like any other strategy, should be in the first instance geared to the problem at hand to avoid getting bogged down in speculation about potential problems to come, which may never arise and, if they do, will take a different form to how they are currently envisaged. To put it bluntly: if Ukraine loses the war, the problems the West will face will be enormous and demanding; if Russia continues to fail to subjugate Ukraine, the deterrence challenge in the future will be easier. My argument in this article, therefore, is that because of Ukraine, more weight is being placed on the deterrent role of the British and French forces, but in this specific context it is weight they can bear.

The problem

Under the Trump administration, the US footprint in Europe will shrink significantly over the coming years.[3] The question is by how much. President Donald Trump is known to have contemplated abandoning NATO altogether during his first term.[4] Despite denials that this is his current intention, it has shaken confidence in the dependability of the US as an ally in an emergency.[5] At a February 2025 press conference with British Prime Minister Keir Starmer, he said he supported NATO's Article 5 provision, adding, 'I don't think we're going to have any reason for it'.[6] European countries have chosen to take such statements literally even though they can take no real comfort, as the statements provide little guidance as to what Trump would do should he face a moment of truth. Europeans do not want a complete break with the US and wish to sustain NATO as a going concern.

However reassured they claim to be, however, they know that Trump lacks enthusiasm for the Alliance and expects them to take more responsibility for their own security. Some progress has been made in raising budgets, and there is no reason in principle why, over time, European countries cannot match and exceed Russian conventional capabilities, especially given the losses experienced by Russia since February 2022 and with its war with Ukraine yet to conclude. The challenges, both financial and organisational, that must be met to get to this position are well known and substantial, but they are not insuperable.[7] The one area where replacing the US is most difficult is the provision of a nuclear guarantee. This puts the spotlight on France and the UK as Europe's two nuclear powers. Neither has embraced the idea of substituting for the US, but they must accept that their assets may now be more important than assumed in the past.

The Russo-Ukrainian war has brought the issue to the fore. In February 2025, it seemed as if President Trump was prepared to do a quick deal with Putin to resolve the war, and that, as part of this deal, Ukraine would be denied future access to NATO. In that case, Ukraine would potentially be left unsupported should Russia renew its aggression. Ukraine's experience with security guarantees, from the Budapest Memorandum to the Minsk agreements, has not been encouraging. Aware of this, the UK and France sought to devise an alternative arrangement involving a 'coalition of the willing' that would commit to supporting Ukraine with deployed forces. To give this more credibility, they sought a 'backstop' from the Trump administration. The nature of this mechanism was never specified, but the term was assumed to refer to a nuclear guarantee. Trump deflected the issue. In the end, the lack of progress on a deal meant that the matter was left unclarified.[8]

Doubts about whether the US would seek to enforce compliance with an agreement that it had brokered were combined with the wider doubts about whether the US would honour its Article 5 obligations in the event of Russian aggression directed against NATO countries. As German Chancellor Friedrich Merz put it, there was a need to talk about nuclear sharing with European partners even while hoping that the US would not withdraw: 'We should talk with both countries [France and Britain] always, and in addition, from the perspective of supplementing the American nuclear shield, which we of course want to see maintained.'[9]

Over time, the Trump administration's position on Ukraine mellowed and it appeared more inclined to blame Moscow for the failure of its peace diplomacy. The twists and turns of its Ukraine policy explain why Paris and

London have reasons to think about hedging against the United States giving up on NATO while avoiding self-fulfilling prophecies. The question of the role of French and British nuclear forces is therefore not about a future possibility, or a new policy goal which will take time to achieve. It is not about making a point on European autonomy. It is about current strategy.

History

The normal explanation for the differences in nuclear doctrine between the UK and France, and their attitudes to the US, lies in their distinctive reactions to the humiliation of the Suez Crisis of 1956, when the Eisenhower administration refused to back their combined operation to retake the Suez Canal after Egypt had nationalised it. The British concluded that they had to stay close to the Americans, while the French sought to reduce their dependence.[10]

Arguably, for the UK, this effort was a triumph of hope over experience. Having worked together to develop the first atomic bombs, the UK's partnership with the US was terminated abruptly in 1946 with the US Congress's passage of the Atomic Energy Act. This led the UK to develop its own nuclear capabilities. In 1958, these developments were sufficient for the US to agree to renew its partnership with a treaty on nuclear cooperation.[11] The UK then decided to opt for a US delivery system – the *Skybolt* air-to-surface missile – for its nuclear bombs. But in late 1962, US secretary of defense Robert McNamara cancelled *Skybolt*. This followed a major speech in which McNamara had dismissed 'limited nuclear capabilities, operating independently' as being 'dangerous, expensive, prone to obsolescence and lacking in credibility as a deterrent'.[12] While he claimed to be referring to France rather than the UK, the cancellation of *Skybolt* looked like an effort to push the UK out of the nuclear business.

UK prime minister Harold Macmillan arranged an emergency summit with US president John F. Kennedy in December 1962. This established a lasting framework for UK nuclear forces. It would be based on American submarine-launched ballistic missiles (SLBMs), originally *Polaris* and now *Trident*, with British warheads and British nuclear-powered submarines (SSBNs). In return, as the summit communiqué stated, these British forces would be used 'for the purposes of international defence of the Western

Alliance in all circumstances'. Macmillan added a crucial qualifier: 'except where Her Majesty's Government may decide that supreme national interests are at stake'.[13] It was hard to think of circumstances in which nuclear use could be considered in which supreme national interests would not be at stake.

The 1962 agreement secured the long-term future of a UK national nuclear force, but only in close relationship with the US. This interdependence with the United States was not seen as a flaw but as a valuable feature. It was always going to be difficult to identify any circumstances in which the UK might wish to act independently in war, or to explain what difference the addition of this force would make to deterring Soviet aggression. What the deal achieved was to sustain the UK as a major player in great-power diplomacy and all the big strategic debates. A 'seat at the top table' was assumed to be the right of those with national nuclear capabilities. The close relationship with the US meant that the two governments could talk together on all nuclear matters, from arms control to possible use.

UK interdependence with the US was not seen as a flaw

In other words, the rationale was largely political. Even the supposed added value to Alliance deterrence depended on complicating Soviet choices.[14] In assessing the risks of aggression, Moscow would need to consider decision-making centres other than Washington DC, just supposing it mistakenly believed the US would not honour its Alliance obligations.

Of course, an undercurrent in the British debate was that Soviet doubts might not be mistaken and that insurance against the US abandoning Europe was necessary. This view was given little official encouragement. In 1980, for example, Francis Pym – here reflecting the views of Michael Quinlan, the most influential UK civil servant on all matters relating to deterrence – noted, only to dismiss them, alternative justifications for the nuclear force: 'Political prestige, our status in the Alliance or a comparison with France. One hears sometimes an argument made out for the concept of a "Fortress Britain" – some kind of insurance policy concept, should the United States go isolationist or the Alliance collapse.'[15]

By contrast, the politics behind the French rationale involved explicit doubts about the US commitment. The starting assumption was that alliances were inherently untenable in the nuclear age. It was unrealistic to expect one state to risk national suicide on behalf of another. While French president Charles de Gaulle did not follow this logic through to removing France from the Atlantic alliance, he did take it out of NATO's integrated military command in 1966. No other European countries followed suit, less because they were confident that should the moment come the Americans would employ nuclear weapons on their behalf, and more because they doubted that the situation would ever arise, and because the cost of acquiring their own nuclear capabilities was prohibitive. While the US and UK found ways to engage allies in NATO's Nuclear Planning Group, France stuck with its independence. Even when it returned to the integrated command, it did not join the Nuclear Planning Group.

In 1974, France did acknowledge that allies could benefit from the existence of the *force de frappe* without going so far as to make a commitment. That year's Ottawa Declaration referred to the contributions made by European members of the Alliance, 'two of whom possess nuclear forces capable of playing a deterrent role of their own contributing to the overall strengthening of the deterrence of the Alliance'.[16]

In Germany, which has eschewed its own nuclear option, there have been regular suggestions that it could benefit from a closer association with the French force. Thus, Christoph Heusgen, former security-policy adviser to chancellor Angela Merkel, suggested that Germany could engage in discussions with France to explore the possibility of joint contributions to nuclear deterrence.[17] French President Emmanuel Macron has experimented with language that hints at such a wider responsibility without quite spelling it out. For example, in a 2020 speech on deterrence, he used the Ottawa language, then added: 'France does not take part in the Alliance's nuclear planning mechanisms and will not do so in the future. But it will continue to contribute to political-level discussions aiming to strengthen the Alliance's nuclear culture.'[18]

As the issue of the wider contribution France's nuclear force might make gained more attention, in March 2025 Macron stated in a televised address that he had decided 'to open the strategic debate on the protection of our allies on the European continent by our (nuclear) deterrent'. Nonetheless, the use of France's nuclear weapons would remain only in the hands of the French president.[19] (It is not clear why this principle need be compromised by French participation in NATO's Nuclear Planning Group, as this would convey a readiness to discuss how the French force might work for the Alliance without any binding commitment.)

Thus, UK policy is to commit its forces to collective defence with the qualification that any action must still be in the national interest, while French policy is to keep its forces to promote its national interest, though acknowledging that this might include collective defence. From different starting points they end up in similar positions.

The question of whether the UK and France could work together to provide a deterrent for Europe has been raised whenever there has been uncertainty about the long-term US commitment. In 1971, it was discussed in a well-regarded IISS *Adelphi Paper*.[20] Edward Heath mentioned it when he was opposition leader in 1967. He spoke of a 'nuclear force based on the existing British and French forces which could be held in trusteeship for Europe as a whole'.[21] This required, however, a united political authority for Western Europe. When Heath became prime minister in 1970, exploratory talks with the French were limited by the restrictive terms of the 1958 agreement with the US when it came to sharing any sensitive information. The imperative behind Heath's approach, present in other discussions of European defence at this time and since, is that the completion of the 'European political project' requires a full set of military capabilities appropriate to a proper state. Without going this far, after the end of the Cold War there were deeper conversations between the UK and France as a modest precaution against major geopolitical change. The Chequers Declaration of 1995 recognised the interconnectedness of the two countries' vital interests, and the Lancaster House treaties on defence and security reinforced it in 2010.

Available forces

While existing doctrine allows both the UK and France to claim some deterrent effect on behalf of all their European allies, do they have forces to match? Because this is a here-and-now issue rather than one for the distant future, the answer has to be based on the forces currently available. There has been some discussion about other countries joining the nuclear club. Poland, for instance, has raised the issue.[22] A condition of Germany joining NATO in the mid-1950s was that it agreed not to acquire nuclear weapons, and this commitment was reiterated at the time of unification, though Germany has been a party to the Alliance's weapons-sharing agreements and, as noted, has at times been interested in sharing with France.

A combination of the legal constraints provided by the Non-Proliferation Treaty and the demanding nature of any nuclear programme means that for now, there are not going to be any more European nuclear powers. Germany has access to about 20 US nuclear warheads at the Büchel Air Base under a nuclear-sharing arrangement which allows it (with three other European countries) to use them with its own aircraft and pilots, though subject to an American veto.[23] Berlin plans to replace its ageing *Tornado* fleet with US-made F-35s. If the US did decide to abandon the Alliance and ended this arrangement, there could be even less access to nuclear capabilities than before.

The UK and French forces are operationally independent of the US. They are also much smaller and less flexible than the United States' forces. Russia is believed to have almost 4,400 warheads available, while the US has some 3,700. Against this, the UK and France have a combined stockpile of around 515 warheads. Yet numbers can mislead. Separately, and certainly in combination, the UK and French forces could survive a first strike and cause massive damage to targets in Russia.

Because of the prevalent focus on the size of the inventories, it is easy to forget the explosive power of a single warhead. UK Defence Minister John Healey has referred to the power to do 'untold damage' to adversaries such as Russia, and has insisted that the UK should not 'fight shy' of the fact it has such weapons.[24] After the full-scale invasion of Ukraine, France engaged in a form of signalling by dispatching three out of the four French nuclear-armed submarines on patrol. Noted a French analyst: 'Paris also maintained all planned nuclear exercises and missile tests, while a more risk-averse United States postponed two tests of its *Minuteman* III missile.'[25]

Both France and the UK can deliver their warheads using SLBMs. France has in addition nuclear-capable air-launched cruise missiles carried by ground- and carrier-based *Rafale* aircraft. The UK is currently building four new *Dreadnought*-class SSBNs, each with 12 missile tubes, to replace the current *Vanguard* class, which has 16 tubes. They will carry US *Trident* missiles with up to eight warheads each. There has been discussion about whether the UK should order a fifth SSBN, but it would not be operational until the 2030s. Another technical possibility would be to purchase nuclear-capable F-35As from the US and enter into a nuclear-sharing arrangement, but that would add to, rather than reduce, the dependence on the US.

The UK relies on missiles that are maintained in the United States, and its warhead and submarine programmes are integrated with America's. Should the US break with the UK, the latter would face difficulties after about six months – essentially, as SSBNs end patrols for their long refits. It would be possible to get around the end of US support only with time and considerable expense. At any rate, that, again, is not the issue of the moment, which is whether the UK's and France's nuclear forces are sufficient to influence Russia's risk calculus in the contingencies likely to be faced in the coming months and years.[26]

What role?

There are two objections to an enhanced role for British and French nuclear forces. They have been set out by Pranay Vaddi and Vipin Narang.

The first is that only the US has an arsenal of sufficient size to offer extended deterrence. They claim that 'the United States built a larger nuclear arsenal than it needed to protect the U.S. homeland, because it chose to protect allies, too'.[27] Fabian Hoffmann makes a similar point, noting that the American nuclear deterrent, 'since at least the 1960s, has evolved with an additional key objective in mind: making extended deterrence on the European continent a credible undertaking'.[28]

Neither statement is wholly true. The size of the US arsenal was not a function of a commitment to extended deterrence. It reflected the imperatives of an arms race with the Soviet Union and a desire by the US Strategic Air Command to be able to cover every possible target.

The problems of extended deterrence stem from the early days of NATO, when the 'nuclear guarantee' was first put in place even as the Soviet

Union was starting to develop means of nuclear retaliation. As it became apparent that the US could not attain a first-strike capability, it was recognised that extended deterrence was compromised. The deployment of short-range systems in Europe, which also began in the 1950s, was seen as a form of reassurance to allies, but the numbers were capped in the 1960s. Intermediate nuclear forces were introduced in the 1980s to give more credibility to extended deterrence, but were then removed as a result of the 1987 Intermediate-Range Nuclear Forces Treaty. Most US short-range forces were withdrawn after the end of the Cold War.

There was no capabilities fix to the problem of extended deterrence so long as the Soviets had a second-strike capability. The best answer was to build up conventional forces to make deterrence by denial possible, but this was considered too expensive. Instead, there was, in Thomas Schelling's terminology, the 'threat that leaves something to chance' – there could be no certainty of a US nuclear riposte to Soviet aggression, but so long as there was a possibility, deterrence was in play. The allies had reason to doubt that the US would use nuclear weapons on their behalf, but the Soviets had sufficient fear that they might to encourage caution. This has been the approach since the end of the Cold War, with the added reassurance that NATO enjoyed conventional superiority over Russia. This reassurance has weakened as Russia has built up its conventional forces, and scenarios could be envisaged in which it enjoyed local superiority – for example, in attacking one of the Baltic states.[29]

In the 1970s, claims arose, which like so many in this area were impossible to falsify, that how asymmetries in forces were perceived might influence risk-taking propensities. All this exaggerated the importance of size.[30] The basic point remained that small nuclear forces could cause an enemy catastrophic damage. British and French nuclear threats would have evident problems of credibility, but so too do American, and for that matter Russian, threats. All discussions of nuclear strategy in terms of future operational choices in the most desperate circumstances tend to the conclusion there will be only poor choices, each with their own horrific consequences. This is true for all nuclear powers, large or small, in circumstances where they might be confronting another nuclear power.

That is why discussions of nuclear strategy are framed in terms of deterring nuclear wars rather than winning them. The issue therefore becomes: what can small nuclear powers deter? This leads to Vaddi and Narang's second argument.

> London and France cannot discount they may need to threaten first nuclear use to deter a future war, an exceedingly difficult option to make credible against Russia. Furthermore, U.K. and French strategic forces are ill-equipped to threaten retaliation against Russian limited nuclear use on allied territory, as they invite an overwhelming Russian attack against their territory against which they cannot limit through offensive or defensive capabilities. Therefore, there are strong incentives for the United Kingdom and France to 'sit out' a brewing nuclear conflict with Russia to protect their own populations from strategic attacks. Russia knows this hesitation exists in a war and may then feel comfortable using nuclear weapons early in a conflict.[31]

Mark S. Bell and Fabian Hoffmann make a similar argument: 'To deter a Russian attack on frontline states in eastern Europe ... France and the United Kingdom would need to expand their low-yield, tactical-level nuclear options, and indicate a willingness to use them, including by employing them first.'[32]

If this were the case, it would preclude a role for British and French forces because they lack both the capacity and the inclination to start developing and manufacturing substantial numbers of 'tactical' systems, and while they might stick with a 'nothing can be ruled out' line on first use, in practice it would be surprising if they considered their systems to be for anything other than last resort.

There are a number of problems with presenting the lack of this specific capability as an indicator of their present disutility. It assumes that either the US will continue to be part of the Alliance, in which case the European forces would be of marginal value, or that it has withdrawn, in which case the European forces would have to perform all the tasks once expected of US forces. At the moment, there are more doubts about the US commitment than before, but in principle it remains in place and still has a residual deterrent effect. For now, though this could change, the challenge is to add deterrent value rather than provide value equivalent to that of the US.

Hoffmann has written elsewhere that, if the situation changes:

> The key question then is if France can offer a better or at least equally good extended nuclear deterrent 'product' to its European allies. Most likely, this is not the case – at least unless the French nuclear arsenal and doctrine undergo major changes, and as long as the perceived scope of the nuclear umbrella remains unchanged.[33]

The discussion becomes easier once it is accepted that the 'perceived scope' of the nuclear umbrella could be changed.

Otherwise, we have to make assumptions about a future scenario that only become valid if there has been an earlier failure in deterrence. This scenario looks forward to some future when Russia has recovered sufficiently from its war with Ukraine to be in a position to mount a large-scale attack. For this to be the case, not only would Ukraine have succumbed to its aggression, but Europeans also would have done little to improve their conventional capabilities. The next assumption is that in the event of war, Europeans would have no options other than to try to hold the line at the point of Russian attack rather than mounting counter-thrusts elsewhere or launching long-range conventional strikes deep into Russian territory. The final assumption is that 'tactical-level options' are low-risk for Russia – as if any nuclear use could ever be truly 'tactical' in its impact – and that the only response to comparatively low-level use would have to be in kind.

If we do not leap forward to a moment when Russia is sufficiently emboldened to test NATO resolve (with or without the US) by attacking bordering NATO countries, and has a political purpose in doing so, but stay with the current state of affairs, then the problem becomes more manageable.

What does this mean? Firstly, the most immediate and urgent task is to prevent the worst case from arising by ensuring that Russian aggression against Ukraine fails. If Moscow succeeds, the crisis for Europe will certainly be more worrisome and drastic.

Secondly, if Russia continues to fail in its effort to subjugate Ukraine, the present stage of the war is likely to end through a ceasefire of some sort, possibly close to that proposed by the Trump administration. This will allow for Ukrainian rearmament and a more substantial and forward European commitment to Ukraine's defence. Both will be vital to deterring Moscow from restarting hostilities, even if the US wishes to stay clear.[34]

Thirdly, the UK and France will expect to play a prominent role in such a force as part of a 'coalition of the willing'. This is the setting in which the UK and French nuclear forces first become relevant, in reminding Moscow if it starts making nuclear threats against these countries that they are both capable of substantial retaliation. Here it is worth noting that European countries have a much more direct stake in the security of their continent than does the United States. As Bruno Tertrais has observed, 'a smaller arsenal *can* deter a major power provided it has the ability to inflict damage seen as unacceptable by the other party … Most importantly … deterrence exercised by a European power might be seen as more credible than when it is exercised by a distant protector.'[35]

Fourthly, the European aim should be to strengthen all its conventional options so that the question of first use does not arise. Although many analysts were sure that Moscow was incentivised to use its low-yield weapons in desperate moments during its war with non-nuclear Ukraine, Putin held back. There were practical questions about military value and potential international responses. Even for someone such as Putin, it would be an extraordinary decision to be the first to use nuclear weapons after 80 years of restraint without confidence that he could contain the consequences.

* * *

The most credible strategy for Europe is to ensure that any decision on nuclear use is for Russia. The British and French nuclear forces may provide limited deterrence against conventional aggression, if only because the possibilities for unexpected escalation are inherent in any major war, but they provide more potent deterrence against nuclear use. They offer a degree of cover for their own forces in the event that Russia decides to re-invade

Ukraine, or if efforts to sustain Ukraine have to be stepped up because of increased Russian military pressure.[36]

None of these benefits require major changes to nuclear-force posture or declaratory policy. The most important policy conclusion is that far more must be done in the conventional sphere. Nuclear capabilities should not be considered in isolation, but as part of a wider effort by all European countries to strengthen conventional defences and pose a range of non-nuclear threats to Russia, including from long-range conventional precision-strike systems.[37]

The UK and French nuclear forces cannot be a full substitute for those of the US, and hopefully they will not need to be. They can still pose a serious risk factor that a Russian leader could not ignore.

Notes

1 See Lawrence Freedman, 'The Russo-Ukrainian War and the Durability of Deterrence', *Survival*, vol. 65, no. 6, December 2023–January 2024, pp. 7–36.

2 See Steven Erlanger, 'As Trump Stirs Doubt, Europeans Debate Their Own Nuclear Deterrent', *New York Times*, 15 March 2025, https://www.nytimes.com/2025/03/15/world/europe/nuclear-deterrent-trump.html.

3 See John Deni, 'A Drawdown of U.S. Forces in Europe Is All but Certain', *Foreign Policy*, 14 April 2025, https://foreignpolicy.com/2025/04/14/us-troops-europe-nato-drawdown-pentagon-trump-hegseth-posture-review/.

4 See Julian E. Barnes and Helene Cooper, 'Trump Discussed Pulling U.S. from NATO, Aides Say amid New Concerns over Russia', *New York Times*, 14 January 2019, https://www.nytimes.com/2019/01/14/us/politics/nato-president-trump.html. A member of the European Commission recounted that, in a meeting with the commission President Ursula von der Leyen in 2020, Trump said: 'You need to understand that if Europe is under attack we will never come to help you and to support you.' He added, 'by the way, NATO is dead, and we will leave, we will quit NATO'. Eddy Wax, 'Trump Vowed He'd "Never" Help Europe if It's Attacked, Top EU Official Says', *Politico*, 10 January 2024, https://www.politico.eu/article/donald-trump-vow-never-help-europe-attack-thierry-breton/.

5 See Matthew Lee and Lorne Cook, 'Rubio Tries to Reassure Wary Allies of US Commitment to NATO as Trump Sends Mixed Signals', Associated Press, 3 April 2025, https://apnews.com/article/nato-us-security-ukraine-russia-rubio-210c5c3856ab32570f165ea31be5e39e.

6 Franco Ordoñez, 'Trump's Commitment to Europe and Ukraine Are a Top Focus in Talks with British Leader', NPR, 27 February 2025, https://www.npr.

org/2025/02/27/nx-s1-5310656/trump-keir-starmer-russia-ukraine.

7 See Rudy Ruitenberg, 'Mind the Gaps: Europe's To-do List for Defense Without the US', *Defense News*, 25 February 2025, https://www.defensenews.com/global/europe/2025/02/25/mind-the-gaps-europes-to-do-list-for-defense-without-the-us/.

8 See, for example, Ania Nussbaum, Ellen Milligan and Andrea Palasciano, 'Elusive US Guarantees Hamper Ukraine "Coalition of Willing"', Bloomberg, 10 April 2025, https://www.bloomberg.com/news/articles/2025-04-09/elusive-us-guarantees-hamper-ukraine-coalition-of-willing.

9 'Germany's Merz Wants European Nuclear Weapons to Boost US Shield', Reuters, 9 March 2025, https://www.reuters.com/world/europe/germanys-merz-wants-european-nuclear-weapons-boost-us-shield-2025-03-09/.

10 See Beatrice Heuser, *NATO, Britain, France and the FRG: Nuclear Strategies and Forces for Europe, 1949–2000* (New York: St. Martin's Press, 1997).

11 See 'Agreement Between the Government of the United States of America and the Government of the United Kingdom of Great Britain and Northern Ireland for Cooperation on the Uses of Atomic Energy for Mutual Defense Purposes', 3 July 1958, https://treaties.un.org/doc/Publication/UNTS/Volume%20326/volume-326-I-4707-English.pdf.

12 'Commencement Address by Secretary of Defense Robert McNamara', delivered at the University of Michigan, Ann Arbor, Michigan, 9 July 1962, available from the Atomic Archive, https://www.atomicarchive.com/resources/documents/deterrence/no-cities-speech.html.

13 'Joint Statement Following Discussions with Prime Minister Macmillan – The Nassau Agreement', 21 December 1962, available from the American Presidency Project, https://www.presidency.ucsb.edu/documents/joint-statement-following-discussions-with-prime-minister-macmillan-the-nassau-agreement.

14 The development of British thinking around the idea of a second centre of decision-making is discussed in Lawrence Freedman and Jeffrey Michaels, *The Evolution of Nuclear Strategy*, 4th ed. (London: Palgrave, 2019), pp. 343–4.

15 'Nuclear Weapons', *Hansard*, vol. 977, col. 678, 24 January 1980, https://api.parliament.uk/historic-hansard/commons/1980/jan/24/nuclear-weapons#column_674.

16 'Declaration on Atlantic Relations Issued by the North Atlantic Council ("The Ottawa Declaration")', 19 June 1974, https://www.nato.int/cps/en/natohq/official_texts_26901.htm?.

17 See René Pfister, Britta Sandberg and Christoph Schult, 'A European Bomb: Debate over Nuclear Deterrence Heats Up in the EU', *Der Spiegel*, 14 April 2022, https://www.spiegel.de/international/europe/a-european-bomb-debate-over-nuclear-deterrence-heats-up-in-the-eu-a-88ab0869-67c6-4bc9-bdff-75c32340b56c.

18 La Maison Élysée, 'Speech of the President of the Republic on the Defense and Deterrence Strategy', 7 February 2020, https://www.elysee.

fr/en/emmanuel-macron/2020/02/07/speech-of-the-president-of-the-republic-on-the-defense-and-deterrence-strategy.

19 Sylvie Corbet, 'Macron Says He'll Confer with Allies on Protecting Europe with French Nuclear Deterrence', Associated Press, 5 March 2025, https://apnews.com/article/french-president-macron-tariffs-nuclear-206478d8bd7ccb20eb79b60c30af018b.

20 Ian Smart, *Future Conditional: Prospect for Anglo-French Nuclear Cooperation, Adelphi Paper* 78 (London: International Institute for Strategic Studies, 1971).

21 Edward Heath, *Old World, New Horizon: Britain, the Common Market and the Atlantic Alliance* (London: Oxford University Press, 1970), p. 73.

22 Polish Prime Minister Donald Tusk said that Poland 'is talking seriously' with France about being protected by the French nuclear umbrella. 'We must be aware that Poland must reach for the most modern capabilities also related to nuclear weapons and modern unconventional weapons … This is a race for security, not for war.' Quoted in Jan Cienski and Wojciech Kość, 'Poland Seeks Access to Nuclear Arms and Looks to Build Half-million-man Army', *Politico*, 7 March 2025, https://www.politico.eu/article/donald-tusk-plan-train-poland-men-military-service-russia/.

23 US B61 nuclear weapons are stored in secure locations in Germany, Italy, the Netherlands and Turkiye.

24 Quoted in Larisa Brown and Bruno Waterfield, 'UK Will Not Shy Away from Nuclear Weapons, John Healey Tells Russia', *The Times*, 20 March 2025, https://www.thetimes.com/uk/defence/article/nuclear-weapons-russia-john-healey-cd8bvodwn.

25 Héloïse Fayet, 'France's Tentative Overture for a European Nuclear Deterrent', *Survival*, vol. 66, no. 5, October–November 2024, p. 70.

26 See 'Does Britain's Nuclear Deterrent Have a Trump-shaped Problem?', *The Economist*, 27 February 2025, https://www.economist.com/britain/2025/02/27/does-britains-nuclear-deterrent-have-a-trump-shaped-problem; and Marion Messmer and Olivia O'Sullivan, 'The UK's Nuclear Deterrent Relies on US Support – But There Are No Other Easy Alternatives', Chatham House, 16 April 2025, https://www.chathamhouse.org/2025/03/uks-nuclear-deterrent-relies-us-support-there-are-no-other-easy-alternatives. The nuclear-cooperation agreement has been made enduring rather than subject to extension every ten years. See John Paul Rathbone and Lucy Fisher, 'US and UK Plan Indefinite Extension of Nuclear Weapons Co-operation Pact', *Financial Times*, 3 September 2024, https://www.ft.com/content/2ebca48f-e0bc-4c54-b126-244070c2cd96.

27 Pranay Vaddi and Vipin Narang, 'Building a Euro Deterrent: Easier Said than Done', *Strategic Simplicity*, 14 March 2025, https://strategicsimplicity.substack.com/p/building-a-euro-deterrent-easier.

28 Fabian Hoffmann, 'From Paris with Love: Extending France's Nuclear Umbrella over Europe', *Missile Matters – with Fabian Hoffmann*, 9 March 2025,

https://missilematters.substack.com/p/from-paris-with-love-extending-frances.

29 See David A. Shlapak and Michael Johnson, *Reinforcing Deterrence on NATO's Eastern Flank: Wargaming the Defense of the Baltics* (Santa Monica, CA: RAND Corporation, 2016).

30 For a critique, see Robert Jervis, *The Meaning of the Nuclear Revolution* (Ithaca, NY: Cornell University Press, 1989).

31 Vaddi and Narang, 'Building a Euro Deterrent'.

32 Mark S. Bell and Fabian R. Hoffmann, 'Europe's Nuclear Trilemma: The Difficult and Dangerous Options for Post-American Deterrence', *Foreign Affairs*, 31 March 2025, https://www.foreignaffairs.com/europe/europes-nuclear-trilemma.

33 Hoffmann, 'From Paris with Love'.

34 In the first instance, this is likely to involve air and sea power, and no more than token ground forces.

35 Bruno Tertrais, 'Will Europe Get Its Own Bomb?', *Washington Quarterly*, vol. 42, no. 2, Summer 2019, pp. 47–66.

36 During the Russo-Ukrainian war, Russian propagandists have often used extravagant language about the terrible things that would be done to London if it persisted with its support for Ukraine. Little notice has been taken of them.

37 See James Cameron, 'Eurodeterrent: A Vision for an Anglo-French Nuclear Force', *War on the Rocks*, 31 March 2025, https://warontherocks.com/2025/03/eurodeterrent-a-vision-for-an-anglo-french-nuclear-force/.

Copyright © 2025 The International Institute for Strategic Studies

Managing Escalation: America's Two-peer Nuclear Problem

Anna Péczeli

During the Cold War period, there was no universally accepted definition of 'escalation'.[1] Herman Kahn, who introduced one of the most influential models of escalation, defined the term as an 'increase in the level of conflict in international crisis situations'.[2] Others described escalation as including both deliberate steps to increase the intensity of a conflict and the unintended consequences of actions that were taken as a result of a misunderstanding or miscalculation of the enemy's response. As scholarly research on escalation has matured, three major mechanisms of escalation have been identified: deliberate, inadvertent and accidental. Deliberate escalation, according to a 2012 paper by Forrest Morgan, 'occurs when a party to a confrontation or conflict intentionally undertakes some action that it knows will cross one or more of an opponent's escalation thresholds'.[3] Inadvertent escalation 'occurs when one belligerent deliberately undertakes an action that it does not consider escalatory, but the action is perceived as such by an opponent'.[4] Accidental escalation is an unanticipated form of escalation that is 'the consequence of events that were not intended in the first place'.[5] Although theory distinguishes between these mechanisms, they can interact with each other, and in a crisis or war, one form of escalation might trigger another.

Anna Péczeli is a senior fellow at the Center for Global Security Research at Lawrence Livermore National Laboratory, and an affiliate at the Center for International Security and Cooperation at Stanford University. This work was performed under the auspices of the United States Department of Energy by Lawrence Livermore National Laboratory under Contract DE-AC52-07NA27344. The views and opinions of authors expressed herein do not necessarily state or reflect those of the United States government or Lawrence Livermore National Security, LLC. LLNL-JRNL-866303

 https://doi.org/10.1080/00396338.2025.2508079

On the opposite side, de-escalation should be understood as reversing escalation, which could include reducing tensions, lowering hostilities, limiting combat operations to an acceptable level, or implementing an operational pause to give way to diplomacy and a negotiated settlement. Thomas Schelling held that reaching a stalemate is a key step in the de-escalation process – a point at which one or both sides realise that they are unable or unwilling to continue the conflict at the same level of intensity, and choose to de-escalate instead.[6] But de-escalation is not necessarily about ending a crisis or terminating a war, and it should not be confused with winning.[7] On the contrary, the primary goal of de-escalation is to prevent a situation from getting worse.

De-escalation is one form of escalation management, but these terms are not the same. Escalation management is a broader concept that does not necessarily entail the improvement of a situation. For example, it could involve convincing an adversary not to escalate further. Under these circumstances, the fight goes on, but with the same scope and level of intensity.

In the post-Cold War period, the United States hoped to build partnerships with its former adversaries, and refocused its attention to other types of security challenges, such as terrorism and threats from rogue states armed with weapons of mass destruction. This may have distracted it from the rise of China and Russia's re-emergence as a strategic competitor. Due to wishful thinking about the prospects of cooperation and diminishing analytical work on the strategic concepts and intentions of adversarial countries, the United States failed to implement necessary strategic reforms to prepare for an era of renewed great-power competition.[8] Thus, the 2018 National Defense Strategy Commission found that the United States 'could lose' a regional war against its major adversaries.[9] This is largely due to the lack of a detailed understanding of the escalation dynamics that might come into play with nuclear-armed adversaries, and the lack of concepts to counter adversary escalation tactics. To remedy these problems, more needs to be done to understand how escalation might unfold in the current security environment, and new concepts are needed to support de-escalation. Kayse Jansen made a similar argument in a recent paper, introducing the concept of 'escalation manoeuvre' and suggesting that new methods are needed to navigate the complexities of today's multipolar and multidomain environment.[10]

Revisiting Cold War escalation-management strategies

Since Russia's annexation of Crimea in 2014, major-power rivalry has become the dominant feature of the security environment for the United States and its allies. Russia and China are both intent on overturning US-backed regional security orders, which significantly increases the chances of direct confrontation among the great powers and the chances of a nuclear war. This competition is unfolding in an increasingly multidomain environment in which emerging technologies have introduced several new escalatory pathways that are poorly understood and often underappreciated. In the meanwhile, the world's arms-control architecture has almost entirely collapsed and existing guardrails of competition have disappeared, increasing the risks of nuclear escalation.

During the Cold War period, three influential escalation-management strategies emerged.[11] The first was Kahn's 'escalation dominance'. He believed that escalation was likely to unfold in a gradual and linear way. In his 44-step ladder model, he focused on the structural aspects of escalation, seeking to provide a framework that represented the most likely levels of conflict.[12] He argued that states faced different escalatory pressures according to their relative strengths, and that the United States could limit the scope of wars if it acquired what he called 'escalation dominance'.[13] According to Kahn, once escalation dominance is achieved, escalatory threats become a very effective coercive tool to end a conflict on favourable terms.

The second strategy was developed by Schelling, who believed that the uncertainties associated with conflict dynamics can be used to force adversaries to change their behaviour and conform to a desired course of action.[14] In his view, increasing the risks of escalation to a point where they become intolerable for an adversary could provide a pathway to de-escalation. This strategy of 'brinkmanship' requires that states have the commitment and resolve to convince their adversary that they are willing to follow through on their threats.[15]

Despite their popularity, both strategies have their flaws. Escalation dominance was seen as unrealistic due to resource and domestic political constraints, and brinkmanship as too dangerous, since it required the United States to deliberately bring any confrontation to the brink of nuclear war as a means of de-escalation. Given these shortcomings and the sobering experience of the Cuban Missile Crisis, the United States and the Soviet Union decided to look for lower-stakes strategies, settling for the approach of conflict avoidance. While escalatory threats remained a standard feature of the Cold War period, the United States and the Soviet Union developed a shared interest in avoiding great-power confrontation by limiting themselves to proxy battles in remote regions with little direct conflict between their own troops. In comparison to escalation dominance and brinkmanship, this form of escalation management is safer, but it can only provide mutual benefits if all sides are equally committed to it.

Nuclear superiority does not guarantee coercive advantages

Although the current environment is fundamentally different from the Cold War, there are still many advocates of brinkmanship and some form of nuclear dominance.[16] Matthew Kroenig, for example, has called for a superiority–brinkmanship strategy based on the assumption that 'a robust nuclear force reduces a state's expected cost of nuclear war, increasing its resolve in high-stakes crises, providing it with coercive-bargaining leverage, and enhancing nuclear deterrence'.[17] Despite the popularity of this model in some circles, its critics have argued that nuclear superiority does not necessarily guarantee bargaining or coercive advantages, and that states often do not have a mutual understanding of the nuclear balance, and therefore might not behave according to the logic of this model.[18] China's nuclear build-up and the possibility that it might reach parity with the United States and Russia have introduced a 'three-body problem' to strategic calculations, a problem that is compounded by additional threats from rogue states (such as North Korea and Iran) and non-state actors. Nuclear competition has also expanded vertically due to the growing significance of the cyber and space military domains and the deployment of new non-nuclear strategic capabilities. Russia and China are already ahead of the United States in some areas and are pursuing many capabilities, such as new, 'exotic' nuclear-delivery systems or direct-ascent anti-satellite weapons, that the United States has no intention to match.[19] This means that there are significant asymmetries among the strategic capabilities of the three major players, and therefore achieving escalation dominance in every military domain, at every level of conflict, remains an unrealistic option.

Brinkmanship is similarly problematic. It was already considered a dangerous strategy in the more predictable and less complex Cold War environment. This tactic would be even more risky today, given that the Cold War's symmetrical, bipolar system has been replaced by growing asymmetries and multipolarity. According to Schelling, when two states have the capacity to mutually destroy each other, it is the balance of resolve that decides the outcome of coercive bargaining.[20] This implies that states with a higher risk tolerance and the willingness to take dangerous and potentially escalatory actions should eventually claim victory.[21] The main problem with this strategy in a multipolar and multidomain environment is that the chances of miscalculation are extremely high. Precisely judging an adversary's expected response with such a great variety of domains and capabilities at play is almost impossible. Risking nuclear escalation based on the expectation that national leaders will always be able to read signals and understand their opponent's resolve is a dangerous gambit. This is especially true given that our understanding of escalatory dynamics in the cyber and space domains is not as mature as in other cases. As Michael Fischerkeller has noted, 'states have little experience using cyber operations during crises, and thus no appreciable formal or informal mutual understandings exist among states of acceptable (de-escalatory or nonescalatory) cyber behaviors. This potentially increases the probability of inadvertent escalation from their use.'[22] These concerns were echoed in a Stockholm International Peace Research Institute (SIPRI) report on escalation in outer space, which concluded that 'the ways in which trends in space interact with escalation dynamics remain little understood … Potential drivers of escalation risk are centred on strategic ambiguity and unclear red lines that become more blurred due to uncertainties in the space domain.'[23] The logic of brinkmanship requires a clear understanding of adversary thresholds. It presumes that signals will be read accurately, and that escalatory threats will be perceived as intended. Without these certainties, brinkmanship becomes a suicidal strategy.

A further reason why brinkmanship is unsuitable today is the possibility of losing control. Brinkmanship as conceived by Schelling requires states to bring a conflict to the brink of war. Unforeseen circumstances, misinterpretations and domestic pressures could all propel events to spiral out of control. Not all nuclear powers give the exclusive authority to launch nuclear weapons to the head of state. Some states might pre-delegate launch authority to military commanders. Other nuclear states have allies to which they have extended security assurances, meaning that the actions of allies could tie the hands of a leader and trigger escalation. In the middle of a crisis, it might not be possible to control or coordinate with all the different centres of decision-making.

Lastly, the logic of brinkmanship is contrary to the notion of trust and cooperation. Since brinkmanship uses escalatory threats to coerce, it fosters an environment of fear and suspicion. Under these circumstances, it is very difficult to switch to diplomatic means of resolving conflicts peacefully. If a state is the target of continuous coercive threats, its leaders may not trust that the adversary will respect the terms of a settlement. This lack of trust could become the engine of more escalatory outcomes.[24]

Given all these dangers, the 2022 Nuclear Posture Review made it clear that brinkmanship is not a preferred option for the United States.[25] US adversaries, however, have shown that they are more inclined to use brinkmanship as an escalation-management tactic. In a 2020 study series, Anya Fink, Michael Kofman and Jeffrey Edmonds found that Russia generally believes that escalation management is possible up to larger-scale employment of nuclear forces, and its escalation-management approach emphasises the role of nuclear weapons.[26]

> Russia does have a strategy for escalation management, seeking to dissuade, intimidate, or achieve de-escalation at key transition points and early phases of conflict, from peacetime through large-scale and nuclear war. These stratagems work by integrating the threat to inflict damage with nonnuclear and nuclear capabilities, ideas based on 'dosed' damage,

> and applying force in a progressive manner, in an attempt to raise the adversary's expected costs well above the desired benefits.[27]

The whole world has seen Russian nuclear brinkmanship in action in its war against Ukraine. From the beginning of the war, Russia has used nuclear threats and the strategy of manipulating uncertainty to deter the West from supporting Ukraine. In doing so it has managed to constrain the scope and pace of deliveries of military equipment to Ukraine, but it has failed to deter the West from providing significant aid. This has degraded Russia's ability to use coercive threats against other nuclear-armed states. This does not mean, however, that the West should dismiss the possibility of Russian nuclear use in future conflicts.[28]

In contrast to Russia, China seems to be more sceptical that escalation could be controlled once nuclear weapons are used. Therefore, it is likely that its leaders would be reluctant to authorise even limited use. In a 2019 study, Fiona Cunningham and Taylor Fravel argued that this belief is reflected in China's nuclear operational doctrine, as well as in its force structure.[29] Yet this might change as its nuclear capabilities expand. China is working to approach nuclear parity with the United States, and this appears to be producing more assertive behaviour. In the past, Beijing has successfully used diplomatic and political pressure to coerce states to achieve its goals, which, like Russia's, are revisionist in nature. As its nuclear forces become more capable, the firewalls separating the conventional and nuclear domains might grow weaker, and China might abandon its long-standing no-first-use policy. As US nuclear superiority fades, China might display riskier behaviour in the nuclear domain as well.[30]

The third escalation-management approach used during the Cold War was conflict avoidance. While this was once an effective approach, US adversaries are becoming bolder in directly challenging Western interests. Russia has waged war on Ukraine despite the support it has received from the United States, and it is expected to grow more assertive in its efforts to re-establish its influence along the eastern flanks of NATO.[31] Conflict avoidance by the West in this situation would only benefit Russia, and might invite further aggression. As for China, the US

Department of Defense has warned that it is 'the only competitor to the United States with the intent and, increasingly, the capacity to reshape the international order'.[32]

Due to the revisionist intentions of both major US competitors, and the expectation that their foreign-policy conduct will become even more aggressive, conflict avoidance is unlikely to be a winning strategy for the United States. In fact, adversaries might be encouraged to directly confront the US by threatening its core interests or attacking its allies.

A new framework for escalation management

Although Cold War escalation-management strategies are largely unsuited to modern conflict, they offer a few enduring lessons. Firstly, as both Kahn and Schelling argued, great powers are mostly rational actors that seek to maximise their benefits and prefer to avoid a direct nuclear confrontation if they can. This does not mean, however, that they are unwilling to engage in a confrontation if their core interests are threatened. Therefore, major-power war remains a possibility, and could occur due to the deliberate escalatory actions of any of the nuclear powers. If war becomes inevitable, controlling escalation will be very difficult.[33]

Another lesson of Kahn's model is that asymmetries in capabilities matter. Escalation dynamics are likely to unfold differently between two peer competitors that have largely symmetrical capabilities than in cases where one side has a clear superiority over the other. In the first case, the literature on nuclear parity argues that peer competitors with similarly sized nuclear arsenals have a mutual interest in avoiding conflict because both sides have the capacity to inflict unacceptable levels of damage.[34] Although symmetry in capabilities is more likely to make leaders exercise caution, other factors, such as misperception or an asymmetry of stakes, could still introduce escalatory dynamics. In the second case, where there is a clear asymmetry in capabilities, opinions are divided. Proponents of nuclear superiority argue that this condition favours the superior power, because it can more effectively threaten escalation, demonstrate stronger resolve and limit damage to itself. Others claim that nuclear superiority in an asymmetric situation is not relevant, or that it is actually destabilising, because if the inferior state feels that it is facing an existential threat, backing down is not an option, and the only way it might win is by increasing the intensity of the conflict to deter the superior state.[35]

The essential lesson from Schelling's work is the importance of commitment and resolve. Most escalation-control strategies require that states threaten certain escalatory measures with the hope that adversaries will back down. For these threats to work, adversaries need to judge that the threat is credible and that the other side is willing to follow through with it. According to Schelling, commitment requires actions that make it difficult or impossible to back down in a conflict.[36] If retreat is seen as a costly choice, it is more likely that a threat will be perceived as credible. In the meanwhile, resolve is more about the determination and willpower to follow through on threats. In this regard, coherent public rhetoric and strong leadership are crucial to convince adversaries that a state is not going to abandon its goals, and is willing to run risks to achieve them.

Schelling's work on escalation also rightly emphasised that escalation management is not necessarily a contest of power, but rather one of resolve. Today, both Russia and China are confident that they can control escalation under a certain threshold and coerce the United States to back down. To a large extent, this confidence is the result of their perception that there is an asymmetry of stakes that favours them. While they acknowledge that in a regional war the United States would have important stakes such as its commitment to allies, its standing in the eyes of other allies and adversaries, and its role as a global power, these are still primarily viewed as reputational stakes, and not even necessarily short-term interests. In contrast, 'for both China and Russia', according to Brad Roberts,

> war with America right on their borders and involving attacks on their territories would invoke questions about the sovereignty and integrity of the state and the control of the regime ... The United States may be the more powerful actor, in the sense that it has more long-term power potential, but it is seen as relatively less motivated to exploit its full power potential because of an underlying asymmetry of stake.[37]

According to adversaries, this asymmetry means that they are in a better position to use coercive bargaining. They believe that, in the face of serious escalatory threats, the United States will not have the resolve to continue the conflict.

Another aspect of Schelling's work that remains relevant has to do with incorporating uncertainties into escalation-management strategies. In his brinkmanship model, Schelling effectively weaponised uncertainties and emphasised the utility of manipulating risks for de-escalation purposes. As uncertainties have only increased due to the growing number of threats and threat vectors, states must prepare to manage escalation under conditions of uncertainty. They should also explore if there are any venues to reduce the dangers associated with uncertainty through cooperative measures.

In addition to these Cold War themes, escalation-management strategies also need to account for a new set of requirements. Firstly, Cold War models primarily described escalation in a linear way, whereby sequential actions move states up or down the different levels of escalation. However, escalation can also happen horizontally. States might decide to sidestep into different theatres or domains that may not increase the intensity of the conflict but rather expand the scope of it. Along this horizontal line, some newer escalation models even consider the segregation of certain theatres and domains by allowing a situation to escalate in one specific area but keeping the overall relationship under control, or even de-escalating it.[38] This strategy is very difficult in practice, however, because competition in different theatres or domains is usually interrelated, and mistrust and hostility in one area would probably undermine cooperation in other places. Nevertheless, it is important to acknowledge that escalation is a multidimensional phenomenon that can move in many different directions.

While Cold War models described escalation as linear and predictable, today's strategic context requires a more dynamic approach. Rebecca Hersman captures this by introducing the concept of 'wormhole escalation'. She argues that escalation today is less predictable because emerging technologies introduce new threats, conventional–nuclear firebreaks are diminishing and global power has become more diffused.

While competition is intensifying and fuelling greater coercive risk-taking among nuclear powers, crisis-management tools have gradually eroded. Under these circumstances, escalation might follow a wormhole dynamic, whereby 'competing states could inadvertently enter and suddenly traverse between sub-conventional and strategic levels of conflict in accelerated and decidedly non-linear ways'.[39]

Additionally, escalation in modern conflict is context specific, which means that escalation-management strategies must be adaptable. Depending on the participants and the geographic location, certain steps or options might simply be missing in any given scenario. States can also deliberately destroy steps on the ladder by, for example, openly declaring self-restraint. In Ukraine, the United States has made it clear that it is not going to enforce a no-fly zone or send ground troops. Although critics have argued that taking options off the table only helps Russia, publicly renouncing certain options does not necessarily constrain a state's manoeuvrability. In fact, by letting Russia know that the US will not cross specific red lines, the Biden administration reduced escalatory dangers and generated more horizontal manoeuvrability under the declared thresholds.

Adapting the United States' posture and capabilities

Escalation and counter-escalation strategies play a central role in both Russia's and China's approaches to war. Both countries believe that the asymmetry of stakes favours them, and that they can use this asymmetry to coerce the United States to de-escalate. Although the US government has made progress toward a better understanding of escalation dynamics in the current security environment, a unified theory of escalation management is still missing. Here, I explore how the criteria identified above could guide the development of the necessary posture and capabilities in the United States.

Capabilities

Escalation-management strategies favour those who have a greater variety of capabilities and can use many different levers of influence. The lack of a diverse toolkit would allow adversaries to take advantage of capability gaps to coerce the US into surrender.[40] However, trying to achieve escalation dominance through nuclear superiority is, as noted, neither feasible nor advisable. Since the 1970s, the US has sought to maintain a strategic nuclear force that is 'second to none'. This guidance is still the best approach today, simply because the two alternatives (superiority or inferiority) are worse. Chasing superiority in a multipolar environment would only exhaust US resources, and might well fuel a new arms race with Russia and China. At the same time, maintaining a strategic nuclear force that is clearly inferior to Russia's or China's is also dangerous, because this would probably reinforce perceptions of US weakness and lack of resolve, embolden more risk-taking in a crisis and undermine extended-deterrence commitments, risking further proliferation.

Instead, the US should try to maintain approximate strategic equivalence, protect its current strategic advantages and seek to identify new ones.[41] As Michael Fitzsimmons has argued, the United States

> can still pursue escalation advantages without pursuing dominance. Rejecting escalation dominance need not be a prescription for abandoning extended deterrence, preemptively conceding defeat in certain scenarios, or curtailing modernization of U.S. strategic forces. To the contrary, the United States must still convince challengers that it retains the capabilities to hold their interests at risk using reliable, discriminate levels of force. This means continuing to seek robust and flexible options across a wide range of capabilities, which should include maintaining nuclear forces with a diverse set of platforms, yields, and operational characteristics.[42]

These flexible options should include advanced strategic nuclear capabilities that are adaptable and less vulnerable to adversary countermeasures, and modern theatre nuclear capabilities to fill the gaps that adversaries might hope to exploit in a limited nuclear exchange. In order to negate adversary coercive tactics, the United States should also reinforce nuclear command, control and communications systems; strengthen the resilience of its critical infrastructure; and continue to invest in its conventional forces.[43] The modernisation of adversary non-nuclear capabilities and the deployment of sophisticated anti-access/area-denial capabilities has eroded US conventional superiority, and adversaries might be tempted to attempt a quick fait accompli. Facing a possible conventional defeat would put the United States in a very inconvenient position. In such a scenario, the burden of escalation (including the crossing of the nuclear threshold) would fall on the US and its allies, unless they are ready to lose the war. To avoid such an impossible choice, the United States cannot neglect its conventional forces.

Commitment

The next requirement is building credibility through commitment. If the United States wants to control escalation in a major-power conflict and convince its adversaries to back down, it must make sure that it can formulate escalatory threats that have credibility. Developing the right capabilities to enable these threats is of course necessary, but not sufficient. Credibility also entails a need to convince adversaries that the US is willing to follow through on its threats.[44] As Schelling defined it, commitment is about making it difficult and costly to back down.[45] Since the most likely pathway to a direct nuclear confrontation with a great-power adversary is an escalating regional war, US–allied relations are at the heart of this problem. Adversaries have long sought to exploit the weaknesses of US extended-deterrence commitments and decouple the United States from its allies. Washington needs to find ways to convince its adversaries that it is not going to abandon its allies and that it is willing to run risks on their behalf. Since the early days of the Cold War, the United States has pre-positioned troops and military hardware on the territory of its allies as a signal of commitment. This is exactly the type of measure that makes abandoning these theatres costly for the US. Continuing the practices of forward-deploying nuclear forces, building missile-defence architectures and stationing US troops in allied countries are all important signals to adversaries that the United States' commitment is firm. They also lend credibility to US escalatory threats. Additionally, joint exercises, consultations and advanced-technology transfers are helpful mechanisms to underline the seriousness of US assurances.

Resolve

Resolve is another key aspect of credibility. As Schelling explained, this is about demonstrating a country's determination and willpower.[46] Key tools for doing so are public diplomacy and political continuity in rhetoric. Moscow and Beijing believe that a democratic form of government is a source of weakness because it accommodates a plurality of political views, leading to domestic divisions.[47] Through disinformation and propaganda efforts, adversaries have been working under the threshold of war to exploit political differences and undermine the functioning of Western democracies.[48] The ultimate goal of these tactics is to paralyse US and allied decision-making procedures.

Optimists argue that in times of great danger, citizens in democracies will come together and demonstrate their resolve through unity, but even if this is true, there are many advantages of forging a strong public narrative before a crisis occurs. The bipartisan Strategic Posture Commission's 2023 report has played an important role in explaining to the public why confronting Russia and China is a national priority for the United States.[49] However, there are still important political divisions regarding the seriousness of the threat, whether the US has any real need to worry about Russia, or whether Washington should maintain its alliance commitments and risk major-power war by defending allies against their revisionist neighbours. These political divisions send the wrong message to adversaries. Even if the prediction that the US public would come together in response to a major threat is correct, escalation might be completely avoided if there is no reason to doubt US resolve in the first place. Moreover, domestic divisions are harmful to the United States' ability to manage escalation. Controlling escalation through the threat of further violence will not work if adversaries believe that domestic divisions will prevent the US from following through on its threats.

Stakes

These challenges are directly tied to the issue of stakes. Adversaries often believe that there is an asymmetry of stakes that works in their favour. Since a war in their homelands would be a national priority for them, they believe that they have a higher risk tolerance and therefore can successfully coerce the United States. This could embolden them to take escalatory measures in a conflict. Overestimating their own resolve and underestimating the interests of the United State creates serious risks for miscalculation and inadvertent escalation.

Contrasting this misalignment in perceptions will require careful navigation. Firstly, in peacetime the US should do everything it can to dispel the idea that the defence of its allies is not a high priority. The US should emphasise that it considers not merely its reputation, but its role as a security guarantor, the post-war global order and the role of nuclear weapons within that order as being at stake.[50] Secondly, if it comes to a regional war with a nuclear-armed adversary, the United States is most likely to fight for the restoration of the status quo, while its adversaries would be trying to change that. Therefore, defeating adversaries at the lowest possible level of escalation, and only to the extent necessary to restore the status quo, would be the safest de-escalation strategy for the US. Given the perception of an asymmetry of stakes – no matter how misguided it might be – the United States must consider the adversary's high-level interests and thresholds. Showing restraint once US objectives are achieved is the best way to end the conflict and avoid further escalation. In contrast, if adversaries think that the US is overstepping, they are more likely to use every available tool and fight until the bitter end.[51] As Kahn noted, there are 'two traditional American biases: an unwillingness to initiate the use of moderate levels of force for limited objectives, and a too-great willingness, once committed, to use extravagant and uncontrolled force'.[52] In a major-power war, neither of these traditions would support US de-escalation objectives.

Uncertainties

The last applicable lesson of the Cold War is the importance of anticipating uncertainties. The current security environment is characterised by an abundance of uncertainties, and the US should adopt precautionary measures to prepare for them. The lack of perfect information and the opaque strategic posture of adversaries means that certain decisions will be guided by subjective perceptions and be vulnerable to miscalculations and unpredictable human emotions such as fear or vengeance. All of this will happen in a complex multidomain environment that will make it extremely difficult to understand the escalation thresholds of other parties. After all, escalation thresholds can take many forms. Thresholds that are easier to anticipate are those that have been well established in pre-war strategies, while thresholds that are more obscure or invisible to adversaries are more dangerous because they can be violated unintentionally.[53] Uncertain thresholds can also give way to purposeful manipulation between adversaries. One could, for example, strengthen a threshold to better deter adversaries from taking certain undesirable actions, or undermine the significance of a threshold to make crossing it less escalatory.[54] The Cold War strategies of escalation management presumed that states would know each other's thresholds, and that these would be largely symmetrical. Today, however, none of these conditions can be assumed.

While it is impossible to eliminate all uncertainties, the United States and its allies should work to gather as much information as possible about adversary capabilities and intentions. Understanding adversary red lines and identifying the off-ramps that might be acceptable in a coercive-bargaining process could help the West to develop a variety of options to promote de-escalation.[55] This would require better information- and intelligence-sharing, updated planning, and more realistic exercises that incorporate some of these uncertainties. The US should also continue to urge cooperation with adversaries to increase transparency and create crisis-management tools to reduce the dangers of unintended escalation.

Multidimensional escalation

The next requirement is preparing for multidimensional escalation. A key feature of modern warfare is that states have a greater variety of options to escalate. In theory, this could help to deter higher-intensity escalation, because states have more diverse response options that can allow them to continue a military engagement while also staying under a certain threshold. This suggests that in a multidomain environment, it makes sense to achieve diversity in all strategic domains, and that it might be easier, in contrast with Kahn's model, to control escalation in conflicts where both sides have a diverse toolkit. For example, Russia is a nuclear peer to the United States, but it is not a peer in any other domains, which means that its escalation-management strategies are over-reliant on nuclear options. If a war emerges between the United States and Russia, it will be extremely difficult to deter Moscow from using nuclear weapons, because those capabilities are Russia's primary means to defend its core interests. In contrast, China is an emerging peer in several different domains, which provides it with a greater variety of escalation-management options. Thus, Beijing is less likely to be dependent on nuclear options to achieve its national-security objectives.[56]

At the same time, multidomain escalation carries many dangers.[57] Deterring limited aggression by adversaries while also limiting the threat of adversary nuclear escalation requires some adjustments in planning and capabilities. John Warden recommends four concrete steps: developing a better understanding of adversary thinking on influence and nuclear use; improving US combatant-command planning; adjusting doctrine and operational concepts, and preparing the joint force to operate under the threat of nuclear escalation; and reconsidering the 'appropriate mix' of capabilities that could help the United States and its allies achieve their goals.[58]

Unpredictable escalation patterns

Expecting unpredictability and dynamic shifts in escalation patterns is directly tied to the previous two points. In today's complex security environment, regional escalation dynamics with Russia and China are going to take place under the nuclear shadow. At the same time, conflict among the great powers can evolve in unpredictable ways. There is also the potential for states with smaller nuclear arsenals to trigger a conflict that could escalate into a great-power confrontation. In addition, a conflict in one theatre might invite opportunistic aggression in another, which would require the United States and its allies to manage escalation in two parallel conflicts. These 'escalation pull' dynamics could also materialise through US extended-deterrence commitments.[59] To counter these drivers of escalation, the United States should develop a more holistic approach to burden-sharing with allies and think more strategically about resource allocation, prioritisation, planning, mobilisation and synchronisation.[60] Urging allies to strengthen strategic autonomy and develop their own capabilities for horizontal and vertical escalation can help to discourage opportunistic aggression by adversaries and complicate their risk calculus. Traditionally, the US has carried the burden of nuclear deterrence, and allies have contributed to conventional deterrence. However, the development of emerging technologies and the growing significance of the new military domains have created new opportunities for allies to acquire non-nuclear strategic options that could free up some US resources in a two-war scenario, and increase the depth of options for escalation management.[61] Allies could also take a bigger share of the burden in nuclear deterrence by acquiring more dual-capable delivery systems, undertaking conventional support roles, and deepening the cooperation in nuclear planning and coordination. All these steps would send a strong signal to adversaries and might dispel their misguided impression that the US does not have the resolve to risk a nuclear exchange to protect its allies.[62]

Developing adaptable approaches

The last requirement is developing adaptable approaches. Escalation can materialise in many different forms, and be deliberate, inadvertent or accidental. These different forms of escalation require different solutions. While deterrence is a useful tool to address the problem of deliberate escalation, it is not helpful to address the risks of inadvertent or accidental escalation. Therefore, it is important to accept that there is no one-size-fits-all solution. Instead, the US should focus on a wide array of mechanisms that range from deterrence to crisis management. The steps described above cover every aspect of strengthening deterrence, from the hardware elements (capabilities, exercises) to the software elements (rhetoric, demonstration of resolve, planning and consultations). These measures can help to undermine adversaries' confidence in their ability to control escalation, convince them that they would not achieve their objectives through coercive threats, and demonstrate that their perception of asymmetric stakes is deeply flawed.

However, avoiding deliberate escalation also requires some self-restraint. If the US goes into a conflict with limited objectives that only entail the restoration of the status quo, it should resist the temptation to overstep these goals as the conflict unfolds. If adversaries do not find the post-war settlement acceptable, they are unlikely to take an off-ramp, and more likely to resort to extreme measures. Understanding the different adversary thresholds and exercising the right mixture of pressure and restraint is key to the success of controlling deliberate escalation.

In contrast, addressing the risks of accidental escalation requires a very different set of tools. Like inadvertent escalation, accidental escalation is also unintended, yet history provides many examples of its occurrence.[63] Managing these risks depends on the potential sources of accidents, which could be technical malfunctions, system failures or human errors.[64] Measures that can help to address these risks include designing better systems, increasing safety standards, improving staff training and regularly exercising competencies. To counter the effects of adversary accidents and mistakes, the United States will need to look for ways to strengthen the resilience of its strategic assets and create active defence measures to minimise the damage such incidents could cause.

* * *

Escalation can originate from many different sources and take many different forms. Although the dangers of escalation have increased and conflict avoidance may not be a viable strategy anymore, there is a wide range of mechanisms the United States could use to promote de-escalation and avoid worst-case outcomes. Washington should approach the problem with a holistic mindset and develop a variety of adaptable tools to address the challenges of the two-peer nuclear problem.

Notes

1 According to Lawrence Freedman, escalation was generally understood as a 'growth process in warfare' during the Cold War. Lawrence Freedman, *The Evolution of Nuclear Strategy* (New York: St. Martin's Press, 1981), p. 210.

2 Herman Kahn, *On Escalation: Metaphors and Scenarios* (New York: Praeger, 1965), p. 3.

3 Forrest E. Morgan, 'Dancing with the Bear: Managing Escalation in a Conflict with Russia', Institut français des relations internationales, *Proliferation Papers*, Winter 2012, p. 22, https://www.ifri.org/en/studies/dancing-bear-managing-escalation-conflict-russia.

4 *Ibid.*, p. 25.

5 *Ibid.*, p. 26.

6 Thomas C. Schelling, *The Strategy of Conflict* (Cambridge, MA: Harvard University Press, 1960), pp. 53–80.

7 Michael Kofman, Anya Fink and Jeffrey Edmonds, 'Russian Strategy for Escalation Management: Evolution of Key Concepts', Center for Naval Analyses, April 2020, pp. 7–8, https://www.cna.org/CNA_files/PDF/DRM-2019-U-022455-1Rev.pdf.

8 See Thomas P. Ehrhard, 'Treating the Pathologies of Victory: Hardening the Nation for Strategic Competition', Heritage Foundation, 30 October 2019, https://www.heritage.org/military-strength/topical-essays/treating-the-pathologies-victory-hardening-the-nation-strategic.

9 Eric Edelman et al., 'Providing for the Common Defense: The Assessment and Recommendations of the National Defense Strategy Commission', United States Institute of Peace, 2018, p. 14, available at https://www.govinfo.gov/content/pkg/GOVPUB-D-PURL-gpo120140/pdf/GOVPUB-D-PURL-gpo120140.pdf.

10 Kayse Jansen, 'New Strategic Deterrence Frameworks for Modern-day Challenges', *Joint Force Quarterly*, vol. 112, no. 1, 2024, pp. 60–9.

11 Not everyone agreed that escalation (especially nuclear escalation) can be controlled. See, for example, Robert Jervis, *Perception and Misperception in International Politics* (Princeton, NJ: Princeton University Press, 1976); and Fred Ikle, 'Can Nuclear Deterrence Last Out the Century?', *Foreign Affairs*, vol. 51, no. 2, January 1973, pp. 267–85.

12 Herman Kahn, *Thinking About the Unthinkable* (New York: Avon Library Book, 1962); and Kahn, *On Escalation*.

13 Kahn defined escalation dominance as the 'capacity, other things being equal, to enable the side possessing it to enjoy marked advantages in a given region of the escalation ladder'. Quoted in Phil Tinline, 'Imagining Armageddon: The Mad and Dangerous Ideas of Herman Kahn', *Prospect*, August/September 2023, https://www.prospectmagazine.co.uk/politics/policy/defence-news/62117/imagining-armageddon-herman-kahn-nuclear-ladder.

14 Thomas C. Schelling, *Arms and Influence* (New Haven, CT: Yale University Press, 1966).

15 *Ibid.*

16 Supporters of nuclear superiority very often base their argument on the claim that acquiring such superiority would provide enough coercive and bargaining leverage to support victory in any crisis. David McDonough outlines the evolution of these arguments in his *Nuclear Superiority: The 'New Triad' and the Evolution of Nuclear Strategy, Adlephi* 383 (Abingdon: Routledge for the IISS, 2006). Along similar lines, Bryan R. Early and Victor Asal argue that when superior states can impose existential vulnerabilities on their competitors, the weaker states are unlikely to

take escalatory measures and thus deterrence will be upheld. Bryan R. Early and Victor Asal, 'Nuclear Weapons and Existential Threats: Insights from a Comparative Analysis of Nuclear-armed States', *Comparative Strategy*, vol. 33, no. 4, 2014, p. 316.

17 Matthew Kroenig, *The Logic of American Nuclear Strategy: Why Strategic Superiority Matters* (New York: Oxford University Press, 2018), p. 3.

18 See Matthew Kroenig, Mark Massa and Christian Trotti, 'Russia's Exotic Nuclear Weapons and Implications for the United States and NATO', Atlantic Council, Scowcroft Center for Strategy and Security, March 2020, https://www.atlanticcouncil.org/wp-content/uploads/2020/07/Russias-Exotic-Nuclear-Weapons.pdf; Abby Fanlo and Lauren Sukin, 'The Disadvantage of Nuclear Superiority', *Security Studies*, vol. 32, no. 3, 2023, pp. 446–75; David Logan, 'The Nuclear Balance Is What States Make of It', *International Security*, vol. 46, no. 4, Spring 2022, pp. 184–5; and Todd S. Sechser and Matthew Fuhrmann, 'Crisis Bargaining and Nuclear Blackmail', *International Organization*, vol. 67, no. 1, Winter 2013, p. 173.

19 See Clint Reach et al., 'Russia's Evolution Toward a Unified Strategic Operation: The Influence of Geography and Conventional Capacity', RAND Corporation, 2023, https://www.rand.org/pubs/research_reports/RRA1233-8.html; US Office of the Director of National Intelligence, 'Annual Threat Assessment of the U.S. Intelligence Community', 6 February 2023, https://www.dni.gov/files/ODNI/documents/assessments/ATA-2023-Unclassified-Report.pdf; White House, 'Fact Sheet: Vice President Harris Advances National Security Norms in Space', 18 April 2022, https://bidenwhitehouse.archives.gov/briefing-room/statements-releases/2022/04/18/fact-sheet-vice-president-harris-advances-national-security-norms-in-space/; and Kelley M. Sayler, 'Emerging Military Technologies: Background and Issues for Congress', Congressional Research Service, 22 February 2024, https://crsreports.congress.gov/product/details?prodcode=R46458.

20 Schelling, *The Strategy of Conflict*.

21 See Reid B. C. Pauly and Rose McDermott, 'The Psychology of Nuclear Brinkmanship', *International Security*, vol. 47, no. 3, Winter 2022/23, pp. 9–51.

22 Michael P. Fischerkeller, 'Cyber Signaling: Deeper Case Research Tells a Different Story', *Security Studies*, vol. 31, no. 4, 2022, pp. 772–82.

23 Nivedita Raju and Wilfred Wan, 'Escalation Risks at the Space–Nuclear Nexus', SIPRI Research Policy Paper, February 2024, pp. 1, 30, https://www.sipri.org/sites/default/files/2024-02/2402_rpp_space-nuclear_nexus.pdf.

24 See James D. Fearon, 'Rationalist Explanations for War', *International Organization*, vol. 49, no. 3, Summer 1995, pp. 379–414.

25 US Department of Defense, '2022 Nuclear Posture Review', p. 12, https://media.defense.gov/2022/Oct/27/2003103845/-1/-1/1/2022-NATIONAL-DEFENSE-STRATEGY-NPR-MDR.PDF.

26 Anya Fink and Michael Kofman, 'Russian Strategy for Escalation Management: Key Debates and Players in Military Thought', Center

for Naval Analyses, April 2020, https://www.cna.org/cna_files/pdf/DIM-2020-U-026101-Final.pdf; and Kofman, Fink and Edmonds, 'Russian Strategy for Escalation Management'.

27 Michael Kofman and Anya Loukianova Fink, 'Escalation Management and Nuclear Employment in Russian Military Strategy', *War on the Rocks*, 19 September 2022, https://warontherocks.com/2022/09/escalation-management-and-nuclear-employment-in-russian-military-strategy-2/.

28 See Janice Gross Stein, 'Escalation Management in Ukraine: "Learning by Doing" in Response to the "Threat that Leaves Something to Chance"', *Texas National Security Review*, vol. 6, no. 3, Summer 2023, http://dx.doi.org/10.26153/tsw/47414.

29 Fiona S. Cunningham and M. Taylor Fravel, 'Dangerous Confidence? Chinese Views on Nuclear Escalation', *International Security*, vol. 44, no. 2, Autumn 2019, pp. 61–109.

30 See Michael Tkacik, 'Will China Embrace Nuclear Brinkmanship as It Reaches Nuclear Parity?', *Diplomat*, 5 August 2023, https://thediplomat.com/2023/08/will-china-embrace-nuclear-brinkmanship-as-it-reaches-nuclear-parity/; and Fiona S. Cunningham, 'The Unknowns About China's Nuclear Modernization Program', *Arms Control Today*, vol. 53, no. 5, June 2023, pp. 6–14.

31 See Defense Threat Reduction Agency, 'Nuclear Stability and Escalation Risks in Europe', July 2023, available at https://www.fpri.org/article/2023/09/nuclear-stability-and-escalation-risks-in-europe/; and Michael Kofman et al., 'Russian Approaches to Competition', Center for Naval Analyses, October 2021, https://www.cna.org/reports/2021/10/russian-approaches-to-competition.

32 US Department of Defense, 'Military and Security Developments Involving the People's Republic of China', Annual Report to Congress, 2023, p. I, https://media.defense.gov/2023/Oct/19/2003323409/-1/-1/1/2023-MILITARY-AND-SECURITY-DEVELOPMENTS-INVOLVING-THE-PEOPLES-REPUBLIC-OF-CHINA.PDF.

33 See Maximilian Hoell et al., 'Escalation, De-escalation, and Intra-war Deterrence: Workshop Summary', Center for Global Security Research, 3–4 April 2024, https://cgsr.llnl.gov/content/assets/docs/Intrawar-Deterrence-Workshop-Summary.pdf.

34 See Jacek Kugler and Frank C. Zagare, 'The Long-term Stability of Deterrence', *International Interactions*, vol. 15, nos 3–4, 1990, pp. 255–78; and McDonough, *Nuclear Superiority*.

35 See Bernard Brodie, *The Atomic Bomb and American Security* (New Haven, CT: Yale Institute of International Studies, 1945); Robert Jervis, *The Illogic of American Nuclear Strategy* (Ithaca, NY: Cornell University Press, 1984); and Fanlo and Sukin, 'The Disadvantage of Nuclear Superiority'.

36 Schelling, *The Strategy of Conflict*.

37 Brad Roberts, 'On Theories of Victory, Red and Blue', Center for Global Security Research, Livermore Papers on Global Security no. 7, June 2020, p. 44, https://cgsr.llnl.gov/content/assets/docs/CGSR-LivermorePaper7.pdf.

38 See Tim Sweijs, Artur Usanov and Rik Rutten, 'Back to the Brink: Escalation

and Interstate Crisis', Hague Centre for Strategic Studies, March 2016, https://www.researchgate.net/publication/298771091_Back_to_the_Brink_Escalation_and_Interstate_Crisis.

39 Rebecca Hersman, 'Wormhole Escalation in the New Nuclear Age', *Texas National Security Review*, vol. 3, no. 3, Autumn 2020, http://dx.doi.org/10.26153/tsw/10220.

40 See Erik Gartzke, Jeffrey M. Kaplow and Rupal N. Mehta, 'The Determinants of Nuclear Force Structure', *Journal of Conflict Resolution*, vol. 58, no. 3, 2014, pp. 481–508.

41 See Anna Péczeli et al., 'Long-term Competition and Nuclear Deterrence: Workshop Summary', Center for Global Security Research, 5–6 December 2023, https://cgsr.llnl.gov/sites/cgsr/files/2024-08/Workshop-Summary-Long-Term-Competition-and-Nuclear-Deterrence.pdf.

42 Michael Fitzsimmons, 'The False Allure of Escalation Dominance', *War on the Rocks*, 16 November 2017, https://warontherocks.com/2017/11/false-allure-escalation-dominance/.

43 Daniel A. McGinnis-Welsh, 'Disentangling from Nuclear Superiority–Brinkmanship Theory: Combating a Legacy of Bootstrapping Toward Armageddon', *Journal of Indo-Pacific Affairs*, vol. 7, no. 3, May–June 2024, pp. 188–205, https://www.airuniversity.af.edu/JIPA/Display/Article/3768365/disentangling-from-nuclear-superiority-brinkmanship-theory-combating-a-legacy-o/.

44 See Fearon, 'Rationalist Explanations for War'.

45 Schelling, *The Strategy of Conflict*.

46 *Ibid*.

47 See Roberts, 'On Theories of Victory, Red and Blue'.

48 See Craig Douglas Albert et al., 'Weaponizing Words: Using Technology to Proliferate Information Warfare', *Cyber Defense Review*, vol. 8, no. 3, Autumn 2023, pp. 15–31.

49 Madelyn R. Creedon et al., 'America's Strategic Posture: The Final Report of the Congressional Commission on the Strategic Posture of the United States', October 2023, available at https://www.ida.org/research-and-publications/publications/all/a/am/americas-strategic-posture.

50 This requires a strong rhetoric about the importance of alliances, but pre-positioning assets and creating tripwires are also helpful to dispel adversary misperceptions.

51 See Morgan, 'Dancing with the Bear'.

52 Quoted in Michael Krepon, 'Herman Kahn', Arms Control Wonk, 10 September 2009, https://www.armscontrolwonk.com/archive/402459/herman-kahn/.

53 See Forrest E. Morgan et al., 'Dangerous Thresholds: Managing Escalation in the 21st Century', RAND Corporation, 8 July 2008, https://www.rand.org/pubs/monographs/MG614.html.

54 See Sweijs, Usanov and Rutten, 'Back to the Brink'.

55 See Hoell et al., 'Escalation, De-escalation, and Intra-war Deterrence'.

56 *Ibid*.

57 See Caitlin Talmadge, 'Emerging Technology and Intra-war Escalation Risks: Evidence from the Cold War, Implications for Today', *Journal of Strategic Studies*, vol. 42, no. 6, 2019, pp. 864–87; and James N. Miller, Jr, and Richard Fontaine, 'A New Era in

U.S.–Russian Strategic Stability: How Changing Geopolitics and Emerging Technologies Are Reshaping Pathways to Crisis and Conflict', Center for a New American Security, September 2017, https://s3.amazonaws.com/files.cnas.org/documents/CNASReport-ProjectPathways-Finalb.pdf?mtime=20170918101504.

58 John K. Warden, 'Conventional–Nuclear Integration in the Next National Defense Strategy', Center for a New American Security, 26 October 2020, https://www.cnas.org/publications/commentary/conventional-nuclear-integration-in-the-next-national-defense-strategy.

59 Although US extended-deterrence commitments carry the danger of pulling the US into a conflict, there are ways to design alliances so that the threat of entrapment is limited. See Neil Narang and Rupal N. Mehta, 'The Unforeseen Consequences of Extended Deterrence: Moral Hazard in a Nuclear Client State', *Journal of Conflict Resolution*, vol. 63, no. 1, 2019, pp. 218–50; and Michael Beckley, 'The Myth of Entangling Alliances: Reassessing the Security Risks of U.S. Defense Pacts', *International Security*, vol. 39, no. 4, 2015, pp. 7–48.

60 See Jacek Durkalec et al., 'Extended Deterrence and the Two-war Problem: Workshop Summary', Center for Global Security Research, 6–7 April 2022, https://cgsr.llnl.gov/content/assets/docs/Workshop_Extended_Deterrence_and_Two_War_Problem_CGSR_Summary.pdf.

61 See Rupal N. Mehta, 'Extended Deterrence and Assurance in an Emerging Technology Environment', *Journal of Strategic Studies*, vol. 44, no. 7, 2021, pp. 958–82.

62 See Durkalec et al., 'Extended Deterrence and the Two-war Problem'.

63 See Morgan, 'Dancing with the Bear'; and Morgan et al., 'Dangerous Thresholds'.

64 See Eric Schlosser, *Command and Control: Nuclear Weapons, the Damascus Accident, and the Illusion of Safety* (New York: Penguin Books, 2014).

Copyright © 2025 The International Institute for Strategic Studies

Arms Control Under Nuclear Asymmetry

Inwook Kim and Seung Joon Paik

The arms-control literature, premised predominantly on the rough nuclear parity between the United States and the Soviet Union during the Cold War, is at odds with today's nuclear asymmetry. Contemporary nuclear rivalries now feature stark disparities in power, technology and doctrine. The risks of nuclear conflict are proliferating and intensifying, with critical hotspots in Ukraine, the Korean Peninsula, South Asia, Taiwan and potentially even the Middle East. US President Donald Trump's implicit embrace of a 'madman' strategy for crisis management amplifies these risks.[1] The revival of arms control is more urgent than ever, but the question remains whether and how it can be achieved.

Arms-control regimes are broadly divided into structural and behavioural types. While both entail the threshold challenge of striking agreements with military adversaries, they differ markedly in means and objectives. Structural arms control regulates the size and composition of nuclear forces to create strategic stability, while behavioural arms control establishes common rules of interaction that mitigate the risk of nuclear war during crises. Nuclear asymmetry raises the costs of structural arms control to the point where neither strong nor weak states may find it appealing. The strong state must bear large adjustment costs and endure severe political

Inwook Kim is an Associate Professor in the Department of Political Science and Diplomacy at Sungkyunkwan University. **Seung Joon Paik** is a Research Fellow at the Korea Institute for National Unification.

Survival | vol. 67 no. 3 | June–July 2025 | pp. 49–62 https://doi.org/10.1080/00396338.2025.2508081

backlash, while the weak state must incur high monitoring costs. Under these conditions, behavioural arms control becomes more urgent. Nuclear disparities make nuclear first use during crises more tempting, elevating the risk of escalation. Anticipatory behavioural measures can help ensure crisis controllability.

The Cold War naval arms-control experience demonstrates this dynamic. Asymmetry in naval power hindered structural agreements, yet fostered behavioural measures such as the 1972 Incidents at Sea Agreement (INCSEA) between the United States and Soviet Union. Under today's nuclear asymmetry, comparable mechanisms could offer a way forward.

Structural and behavioural arms control

Arms control refers to a set of measures, agreements and policies aimed at managing the proliferation, deployment and use of nuclear weapons, with the ultimate goal of reducing the likelihood of nuclear conflict. Historically, structural arms control has stabilised relationships between nuclear states by either capping or reducing arsenals. Behavioural arms control has bolstered crisis stability by regulating operational conduct.

Structural arms control looks to establish a stable and predictable balance of power by limiting the size and types of nuclear arsenals. It prioritises retaliatory-strike capabilities over first-strike capabilities, relying on the deterrent effect of assured retaliation to discourage deliberate first strikes. This framework emerged during the Cold War, as the superpowers sought to avert an arms race predicated on first-strike capability. Agreements such as the Strategic Arms Limitation Treaty (SALT I) and the Strategic Arms Reduction Treaty (START) reflect this approach, preserving nuclear parity while capping offensive and damage-limitation capabilities to reduce the perceived threat of a first strike.

Behavioural arms control, by contrast, establishes norms and rules of engagement to reduce the risks of inadvertent escalation, particularly during crises. Rather than limiting capabilities, behavioural controls create mechanisms for crisis management, communication and de-escalation. The arrangements focus on routinised and reliable communication and transparency in operational conduct, recognising that the absence of clear protocols can lead to misperception and miscalculation. Key examples of behavioural arms control include the Direct Communications Link established in 1963, the Accidents Measures Agreement of 1971 and the Nuclear Risk Reduction Center established in 1987.

Enter nuclear asymmetry

As noted, the nuclear symmetry that defined Cold War arms-control theory is no longer the prevailing characteristic of adversarial nuclear relationships. It is worth exploring this shift more deeply. The US and Russia still maintain the world's largest nuclear arsenals, rooted in Cold War legacy structures, but arms-control efforts have struggled to keep pace with contemporary shifts. China's nuclear forces, rapidly rising through aggressive modernisation and expansion, represent a third major pole. The country's growing nuclear triad and counterforce capabilities are transforming global deterrence dynamics.[2] The United Kingdom's and France's more limited nuclear-weapons programmes feature relatively static force structures aimed at supporting NATO's deterrent vis-à-vis Russia.

Smaller nuclear states increasingly influence regional and global security. India and Pakistan's nuclear rivalry, in combination with conventional asymmetry and territorial disputes, has reduced stability in South Asia. North Korea's advancing nuclear arsenal is challenging US alliances and global non-proliferation efforts, while Israel's policy of nuclear ambiguity is fuelling latent competition in the Middle East, most notably with Iran.

The prevalence of nuclear asymmetry necessitates a clear definition of the concept. The phenomenon can be defined as an imbalance between nuclear adversaries in terms of size, technology and doctrine. Size encompasses the number of warheads and delivery systems. Technology involves advanced scientific and engineering capabilities, such as control over nuclear-explosive power, extended range, accuracy, adaptability to various launching platforms and integration with supportive systems including radar, satellites and missile defence. Doctrine pertains to the purposes, strategies and conditions for nuclear use, as well as nuclear-force posture. Smaller nuclear states often diverge from superpowers in their postures, contributing to doctrinal asymmetries.[3]

As nuclear asymmetry deepens, the military and political costs of establishing structural arms control become more pronounced. Orchestrating mutual vulnerability – a key element of mutual deterrence, which is needed to sustain structural arms control – is nearly impossible under asymmetry. Strong states must either concede significant first-strike capability or allow weaker states to enhance their retaliatory forces, which strong states consider unacceptable. Additionally, strong states cannot afford to tailor their nuclear forces and doctrines to a single weak nuclear state when also facing more powerful rivals.

Asymmetry could be preserved under structural arms control if strong states were accorded greater nuclear capabilities. But such arrangements are equally unappealing to weak states, as they codify their vulnerability and impede efforts to bridge capability gaps. This dynamic partly explains China's reluctance to engage in trilateral arms-control negotiations with the more powerful US and Russia.[4] Overall, nuclear asymmetry makes a balance in capabilities that is agreeable to all stakeholders difficult, if not impossible, to strike.

In addition, monitoring compliance becomes especially challenging under nuclear asymmetry. Monitoring aims to detect and deter cheating, but also risks revealing sensitive military information to adversaries. Measures to strengthen monitoring capacity (mainly via transparency) can weaken military capabilities, and vice versa. This transparency–security trade-off makes structural arms control rare enough to begin with.[5] Under nuclear asymmetry, the problem becomes even more acute. The survivability of the weak state, already lacking a credible retaliatory capability, becomes even lower if it is compelled to expose sensitive information such as numbers of warheads, and delivery systems and their whereabouts, to the strong state. In such circumstances, the weak state is often dissuaded from engaging in arms-control negotiations altogether.

Furthermore, effective arrangements call for a participating government to acknowledge an adversary's status as a nuclear power, which could invite domestic pushback. Nuclear asymmetry amplifies these costs for the strong state. Entering into a structural arms-control agreement with North Korea – thus conceding its status as a nuclear state and alarming segments of the US population – would be harder for the United States to justify than making one with China. Structural arms control thus emerges as a politically untenable strategy for a strong nuclear state.

Behavioural arms control, however, becomes a more pressing priority under nuclear asymmetry because of a heightened risk of inadvertent escalation during military crises. Military crises exert intense psychological pressure on the weak state's leaders, forcing rapid decisions on nuclear use based on limited credible information.[6] In particular, the weak state, facing the strong state's overwhelming first-strike capability, confronts a severe 'use it or lose it' dilemma with respect to its nuclear assets.[7] Its fear heightens the weak state's sensitivity to the strong state's military movements, expanding the risks of misperception and miscalculation. In turn, perceiving the weak state's temptation to strike first, the strong state may feel pressure to pre-emptively neutralise the weak state's nuclear forces. Nuclear deterrence becomes more fragile.

Weak states face a 'use it or lose it' dilemma

The need to 'lengthen the fuse' and 'create time for diplomacy' increases the urgency and plausibility of behavioural arms control under nuclear asymmetry.[8] Hotlines, for instance, enable rapid and direct communication between senior decision-makers, helping to control sources of inadvertent escalation such as nuclear accidents, unauthorised launches and technical malfunctions.[9] They could also serve as symbolic tools for 'altercasting' – that is, designating officials to focus on mutual desires for peace and draw on the trust, however delicate, that the hotline generates during crises.[10] Advance-notification agreements can prevent misinterpretations of routine missile or nuclear tests as acts of aggression, as they did when Russia test-fired its *Sarmat* intercontinental ballistic missile (ICBM) two months into the Russia–Ukraine war.[11] Behavioural arms control might include regular reviews of nuclear-related conduct, which could minimise the possibility that an innocent act during military crises will be misconstrued as a hostile one and prompt a nuclear exchange. These measures are relatively low in cost and serve the mutual interest of avoiding unintended wars.[12]

Naval arms control during the Cold War

The Cold War naval arms-control experience offers valuable insight into the impact of asymmetry on the effectiveness of structural and behavioural arms control. During that period, command of the sea was a crucial strategic imperative for both superpowers, stoking an aggressive naval arms race. Yet, unlike the parallel competition in nuclear weapons, the naval rivalry had evolved in a distinctly asymmetrical manner across the customary parameters: size, technology and doctrine.

From the outset of the Cold War, the United States enjoyed clear naval superiority, fielding the largest and most advanced fleet in the world, which included numerous aircraft carriers, advanced submarines and state-of-the-art surface vessels. The Soviet Navy initially consisted of outdated and lighter vessels, which struggled to match US capabilities. Although Soviet naval-modernisation efforts in the 1950s and 1960s narrowed the gap, US naval supremacy remained unequivocal throughout the Cold War.

Doctrinal divergence further complicated naval arms control. The US Navy adopted an offensive doctrine focused on projecting superior maritime power 'as far forward as possible' to 'seek out and destroy' adversaries and rapidly reinforce allies.[13] By contrast, the Soviet Navy emphasised 'defence, deterrence, and reaction'.[14] This asymmetry made it difficult to design structural arms-control frameworks that satisfied both parties.[15]

The Soviet Union proposed several structural measures akin to the Five-Power Treaty of 1922, which had established tonnage limits among major naval powers. These proposals reflected Moscow's interest in reducing the financial and operational burdens of countering US forward-deployed naval forces.[16] For the Soviet Union, structural naval arms control offered a way to avoid costly investments in air defences, anti-submarine-warfare capabilities and land-based aircraft. Washington, of course, consistently rejected these proposals. Any US concessions that could narrow the capability gap between the two navies would undermine American dominance and power projection to regions of vital national-security interest such as Europe, the Middle East and East Asia. As a result, key players in the US national-security establishment deemed structural arms control untenable.[17]

In contrast, INCSEA demonstrated that behavioural arms control could succeed even under conditions of pronounced asymmetry. By the 1960s, the growing frequency of dangerous naval encounters had raised concerns about inadvertent escalation. Notable incidents, such as the 1968 crash of a Soviet Tu-16 bomber while it was buzzing the US aircraft carrier *Essex* in the Norwegian Sea, underscored the risks of unregulated naval interactions. There was, in the words of US Admiral Elmo Zumwalt, 'an extremely dangerous, but exhilarating, running game of chicken … all the time' between the two navies that 'might be … impossible to control'.[18] Several factors exacerbated these risks: technological advances afforded each side overwhelming first-strike advantages; warships were high-value nuclear targets; and young naval officers tended to have an 'assertive inclination'.[19] To manage the heightened risks, analysts on both sides recognised the need for behavioural arms control.[20]

The United States first proposed INCSEA in 1967 and, after two rounds of negotiations in 1971 and 1972, the agreement was signed on 25 May 1972. The agreement established 'rules of the road' to minimise unintended escalation by regulating dangerous manoeuvres, harassment, signalling, communication, advance notifications and review processes.[21] In 1973, its provisions were extended to cover non-military vessels. While overshadowed by grander structural agreements like SALT I and START, INCSEA reduced the frequency of naval clashes by approximately 60%.[22] Over time, mutual compliance fostered a 'professional and workmanlike' relationship between the two navies, institutionalising INCSEA norms and reinforcing its utility in avoiding dangerous incidents at sea.[23]

Two points warrant emphasis. Firstly, INCSEA faced remarkably little resistance from negotiation to implementation. Except for disagreements over provisions related to submarines and distance formulas – which the US Navy refused to negotiate, citing their disproportionate benefit to the Soviet Union – both navies were sincere in designing effective measures to prevent dangerous incidents and constrain escalation. The only significant American reservation was that INCSEA might symbolically suggest parity between the US Navy and the Soviet Navy.[24] However, as Sean Lynn-Jones observed in 1985, this concern was misplaced. INCSEA focused solely on operational conduct and left substantive US naval supremacy unchallenged. Under initiatives such as the Reagan administration's aspirational 600-ship programme, the US continued to expand its fleet, which was to include 15 carrier battle-groups, four battleship surface-action groups and 100 attack submarines.[25]

Secondly, although INCSEA focused on behavioural measures, it existed alongside structural arms-control efforts in areas of relative symmetry. For instance, Article III of the SALT I agreement, also signed in May 1972, capped the United States' submarine-launched ballistic-missile (SLBM) launch tubes at 710 and modern ballistic-missile submarines at 44, the Soviet Union's SLBM launch tubes at 950 and modern ballistic-missile submarines at 62.[26]

In sum, while structural arms control was deemed infeasible under conditions of pronounced naval disparity, behavioural measures like INCSEA succeeded by addressing immediate risks without challenging the underlying balance of power. These lessons remain eminently relevant.

Promises and challenges

Nuclear asymmetry clearly complicates efforts to forge strategic stability by regulating nuclear forces through structural arms control. On top of that, the distribution of nuclear power has evolved from the relatively simple bipolarity of the Cold War to more complex tripolarity. The diversification of nuclear capabilities and advances in technology further challenge efforts to measure equivalency and define mutual vulnerability. Unsurprisingly, structural arms control is falling out of favour. The United States and Russia, architects and long-time advocates of structural arms control, have either suspended or withdrawn from major agreements such as the Anti-Ballistic Missile Treaty, the Intermediate-Range Nuclear Forces Treaty and START.

Behavioural arms control has arguably become 'arms control's last lifeline' and expanded into broader relationships.[27] The creation of hotlines, for example, has accelerated since the late 1990s, with agreements established between Russia and China (1998), the US and China (1998), Russia and NATO (2003), India and Pakistan (2004), India and China (2010), Taiwan and China (2015), and Japan and China (2018). Notably, all but one such arrangement – between Greece and Turkiye, initiated in 2020 – involve at least one nuclear-armed state, highlighting behavioural arms control's perceived utility in managing nuclear crises in particular.[28]

Behavioural measures, though, are susceptible to underuse or even abuse. States might pointedly ignore them as part of their crisis-bargaining strategy. Refusing to communicate can signal a willingness to accept greater risk, potentially providing leverage.[29] Governments might also fear that adhering to behavioural procedures could confer 'credence and legitimacy' on adversaries' activities in contested areas, such as the South China Sea.[30] States could worry that behavioural regimes could inadvertently encourage military adventurism or provocations by creating a perceived safety net. And costly delays in response can arise from bureaucratic processes. Deciding whether and how to react to hotline calls could require lengthy consultations to achieve internal consensus, leaving 'no room for individually directed, real-time talk between rival generals' during fast-paced military crises.[31]

Despite these challenges, interest in behavioural arms control is showing signs of revival, spurred by the resurgence of great-power competition among the United States, Russia and China. A noteworthy recent example is the United States and China's agreement to refrain from delegating nuclear-launch authority to artificial intelligence (AI).[32] Simulations have consistently demonstrated a propensity in AI systems for escalation and nuclear use, often exceeding the risk tolerance of human decision-makers.[33] Additionally, the belief that AI can facilitate rapid and decisive victories could nourish misguided temptations to escalate, further underlining the desirability of robust behavioural safeguards.[34] Meanwhile, though Russia suspended the only remaining structural arms-control regime, New START, in February 2023, the US–Russia Nuclear Risk Reduction Center has survived the war in Ukraine. Continuing to serve as a notification channel for ballistic-missile launches, the centre has mitigated the risk of misperception during active military hostilities.[35]

The need for behavioural constraints is particularly salient in cases of nuclear asymmetry, notably in the US–North Korean relationship. Despite its rapid modernisation and diversification of its nuclear assets, Pyongyang remains highly vulnerable due to the overwhelming power imbalance favouring the United States. North Korea fears counterforce or 'decapitation' strikes by the US, and it has recently revised its nuclear doctrine to authorise nuclear first use and the delegation of nuclear-launch authority to military commanders, and fielded tactical nuclear weapons. While such measures are typically intended to bolster deterrence, they also significantly increase the risk of inadvertent escalation.[36] A crisis similar to that of late 2017 – when North Korea conducted nuclear tests, ICBM tests and continuous intermediate-range ballistic-missile tests over Japan in the context of escalating rhetorical threats between Pyongyang and Washington[37] – could arise.

Diminishing crisis stability and dimming prospects for denuclearisation have made behavioural regimes more appealing to Washington and Pyongyang. In March 2024, a US National Security Council official suggested considering 'interim steps on [the] pathway to denuclearization … to reduce the risk of misperception and inadvertent escalation on the peninsula'.[38] In January 2024, Pyongyang warned that 'any tiny spark may trigger an enormous physical clash between the two hostile countries', suggesting the risk of nuclear escalation.[39] While it is unclear whether the US and North Korea will ever be in a position to discuss risk-reduction measures, these statements suggest shared recognition of the need for restraint and careful management of tensions.

* * *

Some experts view arms-control measures as a consequence of friendly political relations.[40] But historical evidence suggests that they are often adopted in the aftermath of military crisis. The Cuban Missile Crisis in October 1962, for instance, led to the establishment of the Washington–Moscow hotline in June 1963.[41] Burgeoning nuclear risks pose grave threats to global security but could also encourage states to adopt mutually acceptable codes of conduct to mitigate them. Such low-cost behavioural measures could in practice build trust. The history of hotline diffusion shows that one successful transaction can inspire broader and deeper engagement. As the world grapples with escalating nuclear risks, marked by growing asymmetry and complexity, this interconnectedness may offer a pathway towards a more secure future.

Notes

1 See, for example, Daniel W. Drezner, 'Does the Madman Theory Actually Work?', *Foreign Policy*, 7 January 2025, https://foreignpolicy.com/2025/01/07/madman-theory-international-relations-unpredictability/; Jonathan Stevenson, 'The Madness Behind Trump's "Madman" Strategy', *New York Times*, 26 October 2017, https://www.nytimes.com/2017/10/26/opinion/the-madness-behind-trumps-madman-strategy.html; and Zachary B. Wolf, 'Trump Veers Toward the "Madman Theory" While His Aides Are Trying to Sound Sane', CNN, 6 February 2025, https://www.cnn.com/2025/02/06/politics/donald-trump-madman-theory-gaza/index.html.

2 See, for example, Alexey Arbatov, 'Controlling Nuclear Arms in a Multipolar World', *Survival*, vol. 66, no. 6, December 2024–January 2025, pp. 87–102; and Linde Desmaele, 'US Security Assurances and Nuclear Tripolarity', *Survival*, vol. 66, no. 2, April–May 2024, pp. 143–56. On unilateral steps the US could take to address new risks while preserving the future viability of structural arms control, see Douglas Barrie and Timothy Wright, 'Not More, But More Assured: Optimising US Nuclear Posture', *Survival*, vol. 66, no. 4, August–September 2024, pp. 7–28.

3 See Vipin Narang, *Nuclear Strategy in the Modern Era: Regional Powers and International Conflict* (Princeton, NJ: Princeton University Press, 2014).

4 See Tong Zhao, 'Practical Ways to Promote U.S.–China Arms Control Cooperation', Carnegie Endowment for International Peace, 7 October 2020, https://carnegieendowment.org/posts/2020/10/practical-ways-to-promote-us-china-arms-control-cooperation?lang=en.

5 See Andrew J. Coe and Jane Vaynman, 'Why Arms Control Is So Rare', *American Political Science Review*, vol. 114, no. 2, May 2020, pp. 342–55.

6 See Richard Ned Lebow, *Nuclear Crisis Management: A Dangerous Illusion* (Ithaca, NY: Cornell University Press, 1987).

7 See Mark S. Bell and Julia Macdonald, 'How to Think About Nuclear Crises', *Texas National Security Review*, vol. 2, no. 2, February 2019, pp. 40–64.

8 See Michael Krepon et al., 'Has Arms Control Worked?', *Bulletin of the Atomic Scientists*, vol. 45, no. 4, May 1989, pp. 27–45.

9 See Desmond Ball, 'Improving Communications Links Between Moscow and Washington', *Journal of Peace Research*, vol. 28, no. 2, May 1991, pp. 135–59.

10 See Eszter Simon and Agnes Simon, 'Trusting Through the Moscow–Washington Hotline: A Role Theoretical Explanation of the Hotline's Contribution to Crisis Stability', *Journal of Global Security Studies*, vol. 5, no. 4, October 2020, pp. 658–74.

11 See Caitlin Talmadge, 'Putin Just Tested a New Long-range

Missile. What Does That Mean?', *Washington Post*, 23 April 2022, https://www.washingtonpost.com/politics/2022/04/23/russia-sarmat-missile-test-arms-control/.

12 See Ulrich Kühn and Heather Williams, 'A New Approach to Arms Control', *Foreign Affairs*, 14 June 2023, https://www.foreignaffairs.com/united-states/new-approach-arms-control; and Lynn Rusten and Mark Melamed, 'The Three-competitor Future: U.S. Arms Control with Russia and China', *Arms Control Today*, March 2023, https://www.armscontrol.org/act/2023-03/features/three-competitor-future-us-arms-control-russia-and-china.

13 Desmond Ball, 'Nuclear War at Sea', *International Security*, vol. 10, no. 3, Winter 1985–86, pp. 3–31.

14 Clyde A. Smith, 'Constraints of Naval Geography on Soviet Naval Power', *Naval War College Review*, vol. 27, no. 5, September–October 1974, pp. 46–57.

15 See J.R. Hill, *Arms Control at Sea* (Abingdon: Routledge, 2024), pp. 98–9.

16 See Richard W. Fieldhouse (ed.), *Security at Sea: Naval Forces and Arms Control* (New York: Oxford University Press, 1990), pp. 13–16.

17 See *ibid.*, p. 12.

18 Quoted in Ball, 'Nuclear War at Sea', p. 6.

19 See, respectively, Sean M. Lynn-Jones, 'A Quiet Success for Arms Control: Preventing Incidents at Sea', *International Security*, vol. 9, no. 4, Spring 1985, pp. 154–84; Ball, 'Nuclear War at Sea', p. 8; and David F. Winkler, *Cold War at Sea: High-seas Confrontation Between the United States and the Soviet Union* (Annapolis, MD: Naval Institute Press, 2000).

20 See David F. Winkler, *Incidents at Sea: American Confrontation and Cooperation with Russia and China, 1945–2016* (Annapolis, MD: Naval Institute Press, 2017), pp. 72–82.

21 See Lynn-Jones, 'A Quiet Success for Arms Control'.

22 Ball, 'Nuclear War at Sea', p. 8.

23 Lynn-Jones, 'A Quiet Success for Arms Control', p. 178.

24 See *ibid.*, p. 179.

25 See Norman Polmar, 'The U.S. Navy: Toward a 600-ship Fleet', *Proceedings*, vol. 108, no. 948, February 1982, https://www.usni.org/magazines/proceedings/1982/february/u-s-navy-toward-600-ship-fleet.

26 See Arms Control Association, 'Strategic Arms Limitation Talks (SALT I)', https://www.armscontrol.org/treaties/strategic-arms-limitation-talks.

27 Kühn and Williams, 'A New Approach to Arms Control'.

28 Steven E. Miller, 'Nuclear Hotlines: Origins, Evolution, Applications', *Journal for Peace and Nuclear Disarmament*, vol. 4, sup. 1, May 2021, pp. 176–91, https://www.tandfonline.com/doi/full/10.1080/25751654.2021.1903763#abstract.

29 See Christian Ruhl, 'Beijing Is Unavailable to Take Your Call: Why the US–China Crisis Hotline Doesn't Work', *Bulletin of the Atomic Scientists*, 24 June 2024, https://thebulletin.org/2024/06/beijing-is-unavailable-to-take-your-call-why-the-us-china-crisis-hotline-doesnt-work/.

30 Julian Borger, 'Hotlines "Ring Out": China's Military Crisis Strategy Needs Rethink, Says Biden Asia Chief', *Guardian*, 6 May 2021, https://www.theguardian.com/world/2021/may/06/hotlines-ring-out-chinas-military-

crisis-strategy-needs-rethink-says-biden-asia-chief-kurt-campbell.

31 Avery Goldstein, 'First Things First: The Pressing Danger of Crisis Instability in U.S.–China Relations', *International Security*, vol. 37, no. 4, Spring 2013, pp. 49–89. See also Ellen Knickmeyer, '"It Just Rang": In Crises, US–China Hotline Goes Unanswered', Associated Press, 11 February 2023, https://apnews.com/article/politics-united-states-government-lloyd-austin-china-9d1b7c9aa40b22d0bda497ba29be8d9b.

32 See Asma Khalid, 'Biden and Xi Take a First Step to Limit AI and Nuclear Decisions at Their Last Meeting', NPR, 16 November 2024, https://www.npr.org/2024/11/16/nx-s1-5193893/xi-trump-biden-ai-export-controls-tariffs.

33 See Max Lamparth and Jacquelyn Schneider, 'Why the Military Can't Trust AI', *Foreign Affairs*, 29 April 2024, https://www.foreignaffairs.com/united-states/why-military-cant-trust-ai.

34 See Michael E. O'Hanlon, 'Artificial Intelligence, International Security, and the Risk of War', Brookings Institution, 19 November 2024, https://www.brookings.edu/articles/artificial-intelligence-international-security-and-the-risk-of-war/.

35 See Polina Lytvynova, Hanna Palamarenko and Charles Maynes, 'Putin Says Russia Tested a New Intermediate-range Ballistic Missile on Ukraine', NPR, 21 November 2024, https://www.npr.org/2024/11/21/nx-s1-5199704/russia-ukraine-war-ballistic-missile.

36 See Ankit Panda, 'Missiles, Preemption, and the Risk of Nuclear War on the Korean Peninsula', Arms Control Association, March 2024, https://www.armscontrol.org/act/2024-03/features/missiles-preemption-and-risk-nuclear-war-korean-peninsula.

37 See, for example, 'The North Korea Crisis', IISS *Strategic Comments*, vol. 23, no. 31, September 2017.

38 Quoted in 'Biden Administration's North Korea Policy', Center for Strategic and International Studies, 3 March 2024, https://www.csis.org/analysis/biden-administrations-north-korea-policy.

39 Quoted in 'Commentary: The Moment of Tragic Self-destruction Draws Near', Korean Central News Agency, 15 January 2024.

40 See, for instance, Colin S. Gray, *House of Cards: Why Arms Control Must Fail* (Ithaca, NY: Cornell University Press, 1992).

41 See Miller, 'Nuclear Hotlines', p. 177.

Copyright © 2025 The International Institute for Strategic Studies

Commentary

Trump's Century of Days

Steven Simon

Presidents of the United States are elected to four-year terms. They can occupy the office for a total of two terms. Donald Trump has spoken publicly about a third term, probably to further scandalise his opponents and delight his base, but it wouldn't surprise most observers if he were serious about circumventing or simply ignoring a constitutionally mandated term limit set 80 years ago. Trump is 79, still golfs and appears vigorous for a man his age; his father made it to his nineties. Yet he'd be 83 at the start of his hypothetical third term, and he already shows a loss of mental and verbal acuity. It's fair to say that Trump's personal dominance over American politics has at most another three years to run.

In a way that perhaps only Albert Einstein could explain, this is cold comfort, because the Trump administration has figured out how to manipulate political relativity and slow time. Only a little older than the canonical 'first hundred days', Trump's presidency already seems as though it is in its 100th year. He has engendered this illusion in an extremely short period by spewing scores of executive orders and extortionist demands, orchestrating defiantly illegal manoeuvres, dramatically reversing long-accepted strategic principles, rejecting firm scientific knowledge and economic experience, and ignoring a 100-year-old consensus on the inescapable need for an administrative state. Just keeping track entails

Steven Simon is a Distinguished Fellow and Visiting Professor at Dartmouth College and senior fellow at the Quincy Institute for Responsible Statecraft. He spent 20 years in the US government, holding senior positions in the State Department and at the National Security Council.

Survival | vol. 67 no. 3 | June–July 2025 | pp. 63–72 https://doi.org/10.1080/00396338.2025.2508084

the kind of sleep deprivation that George W. Bush authorised as torture when applied to enemy combatants in the 'war on terror'.

The Trump administration has been able to accomplish all it has so quickly because a prominent right-wing think tank, the Heritage Foundation, compiled in advance an annotated register, known as Project 2025, of thousands of initiatives already worded and framed for use as executive orders.[1] An executive order, in the American system, is typically an instruction to executive-branch agencies and departments to take or refrain from taking specific actions until such time as the order is rescinded. These are not laws but administrative directions. Suffice it to say, a president could get a lot of mileage out of these orders, unless they were countermanded by the courts or Congress.

Bait and switch

While Trump trumpeted prosperity for all during his campaign, as president he has articulated a considerably less equitable objective: the United States' return to the Gilded Age (1865–1902). During that time, tariffs were high, regulation was low, corrupt practices were unimpeded, the country – except for the formerly enslaved and their offspring – was overwhelmingly white, Christianity was the unofficial state religion, labourers were mere fodder, and the rich took what they wanted at home while their government took what it wanted overseas. For the Trumps of that era, life was good. For most, it emphatically was not.

This would not appear to be a winning campaign platform, but the Democrats made serious mistakes, relied on out-of-touch and uninspiring candidates, and were plagued by high inflation and party infighting. The Republicans made deft use of immigration and Democratic preoccupations with race and gender, which, though substantively justifiable if sometimes excessive, did not resonate with most voters. Unlike the Republican Party, the Democratic Party is a coalition whose members need to be accommodated by the leadership at the national level in general elections. Progressive agenda items are generally out of sync not only with American public opinion, but also with rank-and-file Democrats themselves. Thus, the Democrats face something close to a structural impediment to victory in presidential elections. Yet they do win, or, as in the 2024 popular vote, come very close. Trump won by just 1.5 percentage points, scarcely a landslide or a mandate. This is a useful reminder for readers outside the United States that not all Americans have lost their minds. As it becomes clear to voters that the president's desire to restore the United States to an earlier, crueller era is abjectly unresponsive to the broadly accepted source of the electorate's rage – that is, the neo-liberal orgy that seduced greedy elites and abandoned the middle class – Trump will lose popularity. Indeed, he already is.[2]

The clock is ticking, however. The administration is doing things that will be difficult to reverse and, in the interim, generate much mayhem. The duration of this interim and the scale of mayhem are matters of urgent debate. Historians and political scientists tend to differ, with important exceptions within both disciplines.

Historians, like Timothy Snyder, look for analogies and extrapolate trajectories from them. They're prey to proximity, heuristic and other cognitive biases, and seem immune to the lure of American exceptionalism. If you know a great deal about the Weimar Republic, they argue, then you know where the United States is headed.[3]

Political scientists, apart from dedicated comparativists, generally stay focused on patterns of political behaviour that recur in a specifically American context.[4] Weimar might be interesting, but is it truly relevant? They're more likely to assess the future in terms of a reversion to the mean, while acknowledging striking uncertainties about the path back. Thus, the collapse of the Republican Party owing to a MAGA/non-MAGA split is virtually assured, and the presumed beneficiary will be its Democratic rival. Democrats themselves will have learned the lessons of their own defeats. Whether these lessons dictate a return to the centre or a more dramatic move to the left is at this point unknowable. But the direction it takes will affect the prospects of whatever kind of party emerges from the wreckage on the other side of the aisle. Meanwhile, there will be midterm elections in 18 months which could give Democrats control of the House of Representatives. This won't bring the administration to its knees, but will limit its freedom of manoeuvre, particularly on the federal budget.

It appears that the courts will eventually have to clean up the detritus of Trump's transgressive performance. Although prominent legal scholars do not take this for granted, there are signs that the federal judiciary could come through.[5]

Not all political scientists are quite this sanguine. Dartmouth College just published its latest Bright Line Watch survey results, which measure academic and public opinion on the state of American democracy. This round reflected the sharpest single drop in experts' confidence in the viability of American democracy since the programme was initiated in 2017. In the public surveys, the most unsettling disclosure was the apparent readiness of 7–10% of the respondents for political violence in the current environment. Especially noteworthy is the greater Democratic support.[6] Perhaps this shouldn't be a surprise, since Democrats are the losers and under serious pressure.

The prerogative state

The emerging view is of a country sliding toward competitive authoritarianism along contemporary Hungarian lines. Elections will still take place, but the opposition will find it difficult to organise and mobilise supporters, and face a range of hurdles to making its case to voters. Opposition candidates might be disqualified or eliminated. The list of suppressive options available to an authoritarian leader is long. The incumbent weakens checks and balances, and delegitimates opponents.

The Trump administration, for example, is instrumentalising the Federal Communications Commission to threaten the media, using control over appropriated funds to intimidate universities and public radio and television, eliminating mainstream-media access to press briefings, compelling law firms that had worked for Democrats to do vast amounts of pro bono work for Republican organisations, and dispatching the Department of Justice to investigate allegedly disloyal Republicans and former Democratic officials. It has taken at least one judge into custody, vilified others and exposed them to attack, stripped Democratic former officials of their security clearances and protective details, removed Democrats from the governing bodies of important institutions and advisory boards, and made the case both rhetorically and operationally that the president can order the deportation of individuals and their incarceration in brutal foreign prisons if he deems it expedient. The decision to do so, in the president's view, is his alone and not within the jurisdiction of the courts, and therefore not subject to judicial review, as the White House has adamantly defied court orders to return deportees to the United States. In general, if someone wishes to oppose the Trump administration, he or she would be imprudent not to consider the possible consequences.[7]

Ernst Fraenkel, a German-Jewish lawyer who practised in Germany until 1938, first described the model for this kind of control in 1941. He argued that in Germany there were parallel states: a 'normative state' whose legal governance was conventional in a range of fields from criminal law to contract enforcement; and a 'prerogative state' that was either unburdened by the law entirely, or devised and applied a specific set of laws meant to suppress opposition and preserve regime power.[8] While most Germans would never encounter the face of the prerogative state, those who did were in serious trouble: isolated, stripped of protection and entirely at the mercy of a punitive system. The deportation orders Trump is experimenting with fit all too neatly into the concept.

The other disturbing tool deployed by the president is stochastic terrorism – that is, incitements to political violence that are statistically likely to result in bloodshed but contemplate only random perpetrators. Trump might suggest that the country would be better off without a particular judge. He knows that there are many Americans who would respond positively to this message, so many that the odds of someone acting on the message are quite high. But where, when and by whose hand the attack would take place is not predictable.[9]

The incitement is usually phrased in coded, indirect or vague language, which is nonetheless clearly understood by the intended audience. This gives the speaker – or tweeter – plausible deniability by disingenuously disavowing any ulterior meaning or dismissing the incitement as a joke, effectively casting the other side as hysterical. Specific iterations of the general approach, however, have been astonishingly direct, employing inflammatory phraseology such as 'enemy of the people', 'un-American', 'treasonous', 'traitor', 'enemy from within' and the newly refurbished epithet 'communist'. He called for the execution of General Mark Milley, former chairman of the Joint Chiefs of Staff, and withdrew Milley's security detachment. He is also in the habit of condemning prosecutors and judges with whom he has tangled as motivated by personal animus. A substantial cohort of Trump's base regards him as sacred and not unlike a messianic figure, who, as Trump himself has said, returned to be their 'retribution'.[10] To these true believers, condemnation of Trump the man conveys something tantamount to blasphemy and would be especially provocative.

In this warp, violence prompted by Trump's language, or undertaken in response to it by outraged left-of-centre actors, would set the stage for more serious assertions of presidential power. (A conventional Islamist attack, enabled by the administration's devastation of its security services, would also do the trick.) The Weimar case inexorably intrudes on this scenario. In February 1933, the Reichstag building in Berlin was consumed by flames. The Nazis blamed the Communists. Within weeks, Adolf Hitler issued the Reichstag Fire Decree, which cancelled civil liberties and allowed warrantless searches and indefinite detention. The decree authorised the dissolution of political parties and detention of individuals without charge – especially, of course, Communists.

Disruption and incoherence

Recognising that the United States of 2025 is not the Germany of 1933, one can nonetheless imagine how a Trump administration would exploit a violent episode to consolidate his control and call the viability of an election process into question. To facilitate its ruthless border and immigration policy, the administration has reconfigured domestic law enforcement, oriented the army for domestic operations, practised rounding up hundreds of people, constructed camps run by security contractors to house and feed them, and placed control of key agencies – the departments of Homeland Security and Defense, and the FBI – in the hands of fierce political loyalists who appear to have little competence and even less regard for the Constitution. The fact that a Weimar-esque eventuality is even a matter for speculation is disconcerting to many Americans.

For American Jews, the situation is especially vexing because the administration is setting them up as a lightning rod to divert criticism of the administration's assault on universities (a tactic of Hungarian Prime Minister Viktor Orbán) while deporting dissenters. The subtext is, the Jews made me do it. On the perennial question of dual loyalty, Trump said in 2019, 'I think any Jewish people that vote for a Democrat, I think it shows either a total lack of knowledge or great disloyalty'.[11] More recently, in the run-up to the 2024 election, he told a Jewish audience: 'If I don't win this election – and the Jewish people would really have a lot to do with that if that happens because if 40%, I mean, 60% of the people are voting for the enemy – Israel, in my opinion, will cease to exist within two years.'[12] Given Trump's enthusiasm for admirers of Hitler, these statements must be troubling to many American Jews.

In foreign affairs, it is difficult to infer a strategy from the administration's actions. Tariffs have been its chief strategic instrument. They are generally thought to be highly consequential in part because their effects will be so hard to unwind once US trading partners – the transaction costs they are willing to bear being finite – make all the adjustments Washington is forcing on them. Trump's approach consists of audacious forays followed by swift retreats and then measured or partial advances. No method is apparent, likely because there isn't one. A similar pattern has emerged with respect to the Russo-Ukrainian war in Trump's progression from Vladimir Putin acolyte and Volodymyr Zelenskyy humbler to Zelenskyy deal-maker and Putin scold. This too will likely undergo further gyrations as White House interest in peacemaking founders on the shoals of Putin's expansionism and Ukraine's will to survive. Trump's on balance pro-Putin posture will probably persist for at least another year.

Meanwhile, Trump has exiled his first national security advisor, Michael Waltz, one of the two prominent China hawks in the administration, to New York to preside over a thoroughly marginalised US United Nations mission. Although he was implicated with Secretary of Defense Pete Hegseth in the 'Signalgate' operational-security debacle, Waltz's main offence was apparently discussing options for attacking Iran in a phone call with Israeli Prime Minister Benjamin Netanyahu without Trump's knowledge.[13] Trump has been clear about his desire to avoid a war with Iran in attempting to resuscitate the Obama administration's 2015 nuclear deal, which he ripped up in 2018, and about his disinterest in Israel's views on the matter. Despite this turn of events, the White House and Congress strongly support Israel's blockade and destruction of Gaza.

Overall, there are three salient factors affecting Trump's foreign policy. Firstly, he's not worried about his re-election prospects, because he either believes he can just stay in the White House or intends to leave on schedule. Secondly, he's a beneficiary of the American voting behaviour identified by Gabriel S. Lenz in his 2012 book *Follow the Leader?* In a nutshell, voters choose candidates on the basis of their perceived confidence, language and ideology, and adapt their policy preferences to suit these qualities.[14] This penetrating if depressing insight may enlighten those perplexed by a Republican president nuzzling his Russian counterpart, equivocating about the transatlantic relationship, pursuing a protectionist trade policy, complimenting a jihadist leader on his strong past, expressing a deep regard for Iran and an interest in a nuclear deal while dismissing Israel's concerns, and disregarding the budget deficit, all while facing no crippling blowback from his own party. Trump is the leader and Republican voters will follow him – which, of course, leaves Congress all dressed up with no place to go. Those who look back on the record of failed US military interventions from Vietnam through Libya, including most Democrats, are compelled to endorse Trump's full-throated condemnation of such wars, however much they might object to the messenger.[15] The last element shaping his foreign policy is simple greed. During the first Middle East trip of his second term, he mostly struck private business deals and solicited bribes, no doubt rationalised as service fees from wealthy sheikhs. He has made billions for his and US Special Envoy to the Middle East Steve Witkoff's families, but has not done much else.

* * *

While Trump's grip on American politics and governance may appear vice-like, he lacks a genuine democratic mandate. His audacious, breakneck lawlessness makes his power seem greater than it may actually be. If he has an ideology, it is incomprehensible. The appeal of Trumpism is essentially personalist and, insofar as he has no clear successor of comparable charisma, limited by his advanced age and evident mental deficits. On the merits, Trump's retrograde vision of America as an oligarchs' paradise appears unsustainable in light of its incongruity with Americans' core grievances, its subversion of the United States' geopolitical primacy, and the resistance of US institutions, which seems likely to intensify with time. Yet remedying the damage his second term is doing to American confidence and standing, after a destructive-enough first term, will take a new national consensus and its steady implementation. The process could take decades. In the meantime, by dint of cynicism, ignorance and avarice, he is steering the United States' putatively mature democracy toward authoritarianism and, therefore, the potential end of the American project.[16] America, as it is commonly understood, now looks perishable.

Notes

1 See Heritage Foundation, 'Project 2025', https://heritage.org/conservatism/commentary/project-2025.

2 See, for example, Tyler Pager and Ruth Igielnik, 'Trump's Approval Rating Has Been Falling Steadily, Polling Average Shows', *New York Times*, 23 April 2025 (updated 25 April 2025), https://www.nytimes.com/2025/04/23/us/politics/trump-approval-rating.html.

3 See, for example, Timothy Snyder, *On Tyranny: Twenty Lessons from the Twentieth Century* (New York: Crown, 2017); and Timothy Snyder, 'The Reichstag Warning', *NYR Daily*, 26 February 2017, https://www.nybooks.com/online/2017/02/26/reichstag-fire-manipulating-terror-to-end-democracy/.

4 See, for example, Zachary Callan and Philip Rocco (eds), *American Political Development and the Trump Presidency* (Philadelphia, PA: University of Pennsylvania Press, 2024); and Steven Levitsky and Daniel Ziblatt, *How Democracies Die* (New York: Broadway Books, 2018).

5 See Noah Feldman, 'The Last Bulwark', *New York Review of Books*, vol. 72, no. 8, 15 May 2025, pp. 38–9.

6 See Bright Line Watch, 'Accelerated Transgressions in the Second Trump Presidency', February 2025 Survey, https://brightlinewatch.org/accelerated-transgressions-in-the-second-trump-presidency/.

7 See Steven Levitsky, Lucan Way and Daniel Ziblatt, 'How Will We Know When We Have Lost Our Democracy?', *New York Times*, 8

May 2025, https://www.nytimes.com/2025/05/08/opinion/trump-authoritarianism-democracy.html.

8 See Ernst Fraenkel, *The Dual State: A Contribution to the Theory of Dictatorship*, trans. E.A. Shills (Oxford: Oxford University Press, 2017).

9 See James Angove, 'Stochastic Terrorism: Critical Reflections on an Emerging Concept', *Critical Studies on Terrorism*, vol. 17, no. 1, February 2024, pp. 21–43; David Corn, 'Donald Trump: Stochastic Terrorist', *Mother Jones*, 1 May 2024, https://link.motherjones.com/public/35215969; and Bryn Nelson, 'How Stochastic Terrorism Uses Disgust to Incite Violence', *Scientific American*, 5 November 2022, https://www.scientificamerican.com/article/how-stochastic-terrorism-uses-disgust-to-incite-violence.

10 Quoted in, for instance, David Smith, '"I Am Your Retribution": Trump Rules Supreme at CPAC as He Relaunches Bid for White House', *Guardian*, 4 March 2023, https://www.theguardian.com/us-news/2023/mar/05/i-am-your-retribution-trump-rules-supreme-at-cpac-as-he-relaunches-bid-for-white-house.

11 Quoted in, for instance, Dareh Gregorian, 'Trump: Jewish People Who Vote Democratic Show "Great Disloyalty"', NBC News, 20 August 2019, https://www.nbcnews.com/politics/donald-trump/trump-jewish-people-who-vote-democrat-show-great-disloyalty-n1044621.

12 Quoted in, for instance, Alec Hernández et al., 'At a "Fighting Antisemitism" Event, Trump Says Jewish Voters Will Bear "a Lot" of Blame if He Loses', NBC News, 19 September 2024, https://www.nbcnews.com/politics/donald-trump/trump-says-jewish-voters-will-bear-lot-blame-loses-fighting-antisemiti-rcna171938.

13 See Michael Birnbaum et al., 'Inside Waltz's Ouster: Before Signalgate, Talks with Israel Angered Trump', *Washington Post*, 3 May 2025, https://www.washingtonpost.com/politics/2025/05/03/waltz-trump-israel/.

14 See Gabriel S. Lenz, *Follow the Leader? How Voters Respond to Politicians' Policies and Performance* (Chicago, IL: University of Chicago Press, 2012).

15 See White House, 'In Riyadh, President Trump Charts the Course for a Prosperous Future in the Middle East', 13 May 2025, https://www.whitehouse.gov/articles/2025/05/in-riyadh-president-trump-charts-the-course-for-a-prosperous-future-in-the-middle-east/.

16 See Levitsky, Way and Ziblatt, 'How Will We Know When We Have Lost Our Democracy?'.

Copyright © 2025 The International Institute for Strategic Studies

Commentary

DOGE and the Future of US Foreign Aid

Heidi Jane M. Smith

The Department of Government Efficiency (DOGE), helmed by unelected billionaire Elon Musk with US President Donald Trump's blessing, is restructuring US foreign-aid programmes not in response to financial constraints but rather to serve populist ideology. Acutely indicative of this reality is DOGE's attempt to shut down the Inter-American Foundation (IAF) – a small but highly effective independent agency whose long and distinguished record exemplifies the best of American foreign assistance: lean, community led and diplomatically smart. Long considered a model for advancing sustainable international development, the IAF is now caught between class-based resentment and corporate disdain.[1] Its plight is a test of the American state's ability to protect functional arms of the federal government against partisan efforts to discredit, defund or replace them.

The United States is not the only country grappling with the politics of foreign aid. The United Kingdom has witnessed comparable attacks on its aid sector. The merger of its Department for International Development into the Foreign and Commonwealth Office in 2020 was widely seen as a downgrading of aid expertise. Canada too has restructured its aid apparatus under domestic austerity pressure. Across the member states of the Organisation for Economic Co-operation and Development (OECD), there is growing interest in 'private-sector partnership models' that prioritise

Heidi Jane M. Smith is a research professor in public policy at Universidad Iberoamericana in Mexico City, affiliated faculty at George Mason University, and a former Inter-American Foundation staff member.

Survival | vol. 67 no. 3 | June–July 2025 | pp. 73–80 https://doi.org/10.1080/00396338.2025.2508085

investor returns over developmental outcomes. Yet these countries have not experienced the levels of ideological hostility and disruption that have arisen in the United States, where foreign aid has become a proxy for domestic legitimacy. Foreign-aid agencies are no longer judged on their results abroad but on their symbolic value at home. The fate of the IAF is now bound up with debates over the deep state, public trust and the future of professional governance itself.

A cultural and ideological wedge

I began working at the IAF during the week of 11 September 2001. That morning, my job – and the world – irreversibly changed. I did not expect my starting salary at a small federal agency in Washington DC would exceed what my father was earning as a public-university professor in a state college in Minnesota. That made for awkward family conversations, but it also offered an early lesson in political symbolism: that public service – particularly in the federal bureaucracy – was becoming a cultural wedge issue. Today, the wage gap has become political fodder in a campaign that sees not so much inefficiency as betrayal in government. The aid worker, the regulator, the diplomat – they are no longer regarded as professionals advancing US interests but as elites disconnected from the 'real America'.

That disconnect has been weaponised. In February 2025, President Trump signed executive order 14217, 'Commencing the Reduction of the Federal Bureaucracy', triggering a large-scale bureaucratic purge that specifically targeted foreign-assistance agencies including the IAF and the US Agency for International Development (USAID).[2] The stated goal was efficiency. But the deeper purpose was ideological: to dismantle the architecture of multilateralism, diplomacy and cooperative development. This has happened alongside other deregulatory measures, such as pausing the Foreign Corrupt Practices Act and reviewing its anti-kleptocracy provisions with an eye to softening or eliminating them – measures that once would have been unthinkable. These are not isolated blips; they are coordinated moves towards the privatisation of US power, now formalised through a sweeping State Department reorganisation that centralises authority around trade and security, and sidelines diplomacy, development and multilateral engagement in favour of a transactional, corporate-first, commercially driven approach to engagement.[3]

Established by Congress through the Foreign Assistance Act of 1969, the IAF was designed to function independently of the traditional bureaucracy anchored by the State Department and USAID.[4] It was a legislative response to frustration with Cold War-era, top-down development efforts that often ignored local realities. The IAF would take the opposite approach: small grants, directly extended to grassroots organisations, with minimal overhead and strong local ownership. According to its founding legislation, the IAF was intended to 'support self-help efforts designed to enlarge the opportunities for individual development' of the people of Latin America and the Caribbean.[5]

For more than 50 years, the IAF has done just that and done it efficiently, in 2024 supporting more than 425 local organisations a year with a $47 million annual budget, a team of fewer than 40 professionals and a low 8.6% overhead factoring in co-investments from communities. Its programmes reached more than 4.6m people across Latin America and the Caribbean. Over 70% of its grantees reported improved perceptions of the United States.[6] These are not vanity metrics. They are concrete dividends of a foreign policy rooted in respect and collaboration.

The IAF provides a powerful counter-narrative to inferences of American coercion. But it is ideologically incompatible with the United States' emerging global posture. A foreign-aid agency that empowers local partners, bypasses corrupt intermediaries and functions with a degree of transparency CharityWatch would applaud is a poor fit for those who believe that only private actors like Musk and DOGE-affiliated ventures can solve the world's problems. The attack on the IAF is not about its cost or its performance. It is about what it represents: a professional public sector that still works.

What we are witnessing is not a correction but a reckoning about who gets to shape America's image and identity. The Trump administration is framing political backlash against federal employees as a populist response to inequality, signalling a class war within the public sector. Broadly speaking, teachers in Minnesota and aid officers in Washington serve the same public mission of improving the public good. But only the latter, superficially targeted for having higher salaries, are labelled overpaid, out of touch and expendable.

Congress has not been silent. On 24 February 2025, several members sent a letter to Trump reminding him that the executive branch did not have the authority to eliminate agencies created by statute.[7] On 5 March, Democratic members of the Senate Committee on Foreign Relations publicly urged the administration to reconsider its decimation of the IAF and USAID.[8] In *Cristosal Human Rights v. Marocco*, a US district court in Washington DC temporarily blocked the executive order, ruling that DOGE's funding cuts violated constitutional provisions requiring Congress to authorise major budgetary decisions.[9] The ruling is a reprieve, not a resolution. New legislation is under consideration that could sunset or restructure foreign-aid agencies such as the IAF.

There is more at stake than a few million dollars in grants and a handful of federal jobs. The fundamental issue is whether the United States will continue to operate under a rules-based, institutionally grounded system of foreign assistance, or pivot fully to a foreign policy dictated by branding, venture capital and market logic. If aid becomes another arm of corporate power, then accountability, strategy and public interest will atrophy. Foreign aid was never meant to be glamorous. Its impact is slow, often quiet and rarely photogenic. But the institutions behind it – agencies like the IAF – have helped build lasting goodwill in Latin America and around the world. As rival and emerging powers start to win friends through infrastructure, connectivity and strategic patience, the US cannot afford to abandon the few tools it has left that actually work.

A bureaucratic survivor

The current effort to dismantle the IAF is not the first. During Ronald Reagan's administration – a period defined by Cold War geopolitics, rising anti-communism and the rollback of Great Society programmes – the IAF came under fierce attack from prominent conservatives for funding groups that engaged in grassroots activism, community organising and indigenous empowerment, which they associated with left-wing ideology. The Reagan administration at least partially co-opted the agency.[10]

The IAF came through the turbulence intact for several reasons. Firstly, bipartisan support from key members of Congress, including moderate Republicans and foreign-affairs leaders, helped shield the agency. They argued that the IAF's localised, non-state approach was in fact consistent with conservative principles of self-reliance, minimal government, decentralised finance and cost-effective aid. Secondly, testimonials from Latin American grantees and US ambassadors demonstrated that the IAF was an effective tool of soft power, enhancing the credibility of US engagement in the region against a backdrop of widespread suspicion towards US intervention.

Most importantly, the IAF adapted under pressure. The agency tightened oversight protocols, refined its grant-selection criteria and made a concerted effort to emphasise its alignment with US strategic objectives in Latin America. By the late 1980s, the agency had weathered the storm and entered a period of quiet resilience. It continued its work, albeit more cautiously, throughout the 1990s and early 2000s, often overlooked but steadily effective.

As it did in the 1980s, the IAF now finds itself targeted not because it has failed but because it embodies a model of governance that resists ideological capture. It is decentralised, independent and rooted in bottom-up partnerships – traits that challenge both populist narratives and centralised control. Its survival may once again depend on the bipartisan recognition that impact rather than ideology determines the effectiveness of government institutions.

The institutionalisation of aid

The most striking feature of the current landscape is the emergence of corporate-led foreign-aid models. The DOGE network is emblematic. Aligned with figures such as Musk, this digital-libertarian movement advocates the radical decentralisation of governance functions. Their proposals include blockchain aid delivery, micro-incentivised behaviour change and the replacement of public oversight with sterile algorithms.[11]

In theory, these models promise efficiency. In practice, they lack institutional grounding. Who is held accountable when a decentralised autonomous organisation fails to deliver food assistance? Who audits a smart contract when its data input is manipulated? The public sector exists for a reason: to balance accountability, legality and legitimacy in environments where markets alone cannot operate.

The IAF's model is not just more transparent, it is more democratic. Its decisions are reviewed by a board of directors appointed by the president and confirmed by the Senate. It is subject to annual audits, congressional oversight and independent evaluation. This is not inefficiency, it is institutional legitimacy. And in the long run, legitimacy is more strategic than speed.

Reframing foreign aid as national strategy

To defend and preserve the IAF and similar institutions, foreign aid must be seen not as charity but as national strategy. It is not just an expression of goodwill but also a pillar of global influence. It projects values, builds alliances and strengthens the international order on which US prosperity depends. There is nothing new in this characterisation: it was the very *raison d'être* of the Truman administration's Marshall Plan, arguably the most strategically successful foreign-assistance programme ever, and a core rationale for the notion of soft power crystallised by Joseph Nye in 1990.[12]

Somewhat ironically, China understands and appreciates this. Through its Belt and Road Initiative, Beijing has embedded itself in infrastructure, telecommunications and logistics across the Global South. Russia's Wagner Group, for its part, has weaponised aid as a means of political control. Gulf states have used humanitarian diplomacy to expand ideological and economic reach. In this context, the United States cannot afford to abandon its own effective instruments of engagement. The IAF is not a mere legacy programme or a sentimental favourite. It is a living example of development done right. The agency delivers positive social and economic results, builds goodwill and supports democratic norms in a region where authoritarianism is resurging. The deliberate erosion of the administrative state and the sidelining of bureaucratic expertise reflect a broader decline in democratic norms. This diminishing role of accountable institutions weakens international confidence in US governance and threatens to accelerate the country's loss of global influence.[13]

* * *

Agencies like the IAF are valuable not just for what they do, but also for what they represent: a US government that is principled, pragmatic and present. In considering the future of US engagement abroad, policymakers should resist the urge to caricature the key issue as a battle between elites and outsiders. Public workers across the US and within the federal bureaucracy are stewards of a democracy that still, at its best, can perform effectively. Absent that conviction, the United States will lose hard-earned allies and perhaps gain enemies. As the political climate grows more volatile, and market-driven models become more seductive, it is imperative to preserve government institutions that continue to work. That means defending public servants from ideological attacks, rejecting the false dichotomy between innovation and expertise, and understanding that government per se is not the problem.

Notes

1 For broader cultural analyses of the 'bureaucratic elite' narrative, see Robert F. Durant, *Building the Compensatory State: An Intellectual History and Theory of American Administrative Reform* (Abingdon: Routledge, 2021); and Suzanne Mettler, *The Government–Citizen Disconnect* (New York: Russell Sage Foundation, 2018).

2 See White House, 'Commencing the Reduction of the Federal Bureaucracy', 19 February 2025, https://www.whitehouse.gov/presidential-actions/2025/02/commencing-the-reduction-of-the-federal-bureaucracy/.

3 See White House, 'Pausing Foreign Corrupt Practices Act Enforcement to Further American Economic and National Security', 10 February 2025, https://www.whitehouse.gov/presidential-actions/2025/02/pausing-foreign-corrupt-practices-act-enforcement-to-further-american-economic-and-national-security/; and Harvard Law School Forum on Corporate Governance, 'Takeaways from the Pause on Foreign Corrupt Practices Act Enforcement', 24 February 2025, https://corpgov.law.harvard.edu/2025/02/24/takeaways-from-the-pause-on-foreign-corrupt-practices-act-enforcement/.

4 See, for example, US Agency for International Development, 'OIG Oversight: Inter-American Foundation', Office of Inspector General, https://oig.usaid.gov/IAF-English.

5 The relevant legislation can be found in the US Code, Title 22, section 290f (b).

6 Inter-American Foundation, '2023 Year in Review', https://www.iaf.gov/wp-content/uploads/2024/01/2023_YearReview_508-compliant.pdf.

7 See Joaquin Castro et al., letter to President Donald Trump, 24 February 2025, https://castro.house.gov/imo/media/doc/inter-american_foundation_letter.pdf.

8 See, for example, US Senate Committee on Foreign Relations, 'Ranking Member Shaheen Remarks at Hearing on Advancing American Interests in the Western Hemisphere', 5 March 2025, https://www.foreign.senate.gov/press/dem/release/ranking-member-shaheen-remarks-at-hearing-on-advancing-american-interests-in-the-western-hemisphere.

9 See, for instance, Zach Schonfeld, 'Judge Blocks Trump's Takeover of Inter-American Foundation', *Hill*, 4 April 2025, https://thehill.com/regulation/court-battles/5233012-inter-american-foundation-trump-blocked/.

10 See Francis X. Clines, 'Administration Scores a Quiet Coup', *New York Times*, 28 December 1983, https://www.nytimes.com/1983/12/28/us/administration-scores-a-quiet-coup.html.

11 See Olga Kharif and Stephanie Lai, 'Musk Exploring Blockchain Use in US Government Efficiency Effort', *Fortune*, 25 January 2025, https://fortune.com/2025/01/25/elon-musk-blockchain-department-of-government-efficiency-doge-crypto-bitcoin/; Adam Rogers, 'Elon Musk's Time Machine', *Business Insider*, 21 April 2025, https://www.businessinsider.com/elon-musk-doge-cuts-federal-worker-firings-government-plan-2025-4; and 'Musk Reportedly Weighs Blockchain to Track Federal Spending', PYMNTS, 26 January 2025, https://www.pymnts.com/blockchain/2025/musk-reportedly-weighs-blockchain-to-track-federal-spending/.

12 See Joseph S. Nye, Jr, 'Soft Power', *Foreign Policy*, no. 80, Autumn 1990, pp. 153–71.

13 See Scott R. Anderson et al., 'The Implications of a USAID Shutdown', Brookings Institution, 4 February 2025, https://www.brookings.edu/articles/what-comes-after-a-usaid-shutdown/.

Copyright © 2025 The International Institute for Strategic Studies

Commentary

The Sahel Coup Belt and the Return of Praetorianism

Naman Habtom and Julian G. Waller

Military coups have hardly been rare. They were the predominant means of succession during the Roman Empire's less happy centuries and became common occurrences again in the nineteenth and twentieth centuries. During the interwar and Cold War years, anti-communist groups often relied on coups to preclude the political ascension of radical left-wing ones.[1] That said, civilian control over the military is presumptively preferred, and a military coup implies dysfunctional antagonism between political and military elites, and a breakdown in civil–military relations.[2] In his foundational work *The Soldier and the State*, Samuel P. Huntington posited that 'the one prime essential for any system of civilian control is the minimizing of military power'. He also acknowledged the inherent tension between military and civilian control: 'The subjective definition of civilian control presupposes a conflict between civilian control and the needs of military security.'[3]

Military intervention and insurgency were features of politics in the Sahel after the first wave of decolonisation in the 1960s. Since the end of the Cold War, however, many states in the region have maintained their internal political order through relatively stable, if often poorly performing, authoritarian regimes, usually with the superficial trappings of

Naman Habtom is a foreign- and security-policy researcher, writer and editor who is currently a visiting researcher at the University of Luxembourg. **Julian G. Waller** is a research analyst at the Center for Naval Analyses (CNA) and a professorial lecturer in political science at George Washington University. He is a co-author of *Autocrats Can't Always Get What They Want: State Institutions and Autonomy Under Authoritarianism* (University of Michigan Press, 2024).

Survival | vol. 67 no. 3 | June–July 2025 | pp. 81–91 https://doi.org/10.1080/00396338.2025.2508086

electoral democracy.[4] Yet military rule has re-emerged in a quick succession of coercive regime changes, breaching the theoretically more stable political pattern that had emerged since post-Cold War democratisation. In the four-year stretch between 2020 and 2024, successful coups occurred in Chad, Mali, Guinea, Burkina Faso, Niger and Gabon, and attempts were made elsewhere.[5] This phenomenon can be understood as a return of an older form of post-colonial regime politics: praetorianism.

Huntington, along with several French theorists, popularised the notion of praetorianism in the 1950s and 1960s.[6] Concisely put, the praetorian state is one in which political groups fight one another directly for power rather than through mediating institutions, and in which military organisations hold a significant advantage against non-military ones due to their relative cohesion, aggressive self-conception and freedom from effective control. Military elites, who have greater autonomy and coherence relative to other social structures, are in turn ultimately motivated by guardianship concerns, along with other more prosaic and material interests, to engage in politics in a decisive and interventionist manner.[7]

The median age in the coup belt is very low, averaging around 20 years old, meaning that the vast majority of the population have few, if any, memories of earlier military governments. Coup-born regimes between 1990 and 2012 in the francophone Sahel region tended not to last long. Mali had two such governments, in 1991–92 and 2012, that lasted 15 months and less than one month respectively. Between January 1990 and July 2000, coup-born regimes in Africa (mostly in Central and Western Africa) lasted on average 20.4 months, while between July 2000 and December 2012, the average duration was a mere 11.4 months.[8] Survey data suggests that, as memories of earlier military governments have faded, support for democracy has declined and openness to military intervention in politics has grown among young constituencies.[9]

Drivers of praetorianism

Praetorianism in its present incarnation in the Sahel has three main drivers. The first is the armed forces' widespread perception of themselves as national guardians.[10] This attitude has crystallised in the middle and middle-upper tiers of the officer corps in a range of francophone African states, as it did in post-colonial governments in the 1960s and 1970s.[11] It has also gained traction among the urban poor and middle classes.[12]

Latin American military juntas have often been non-ideological or defined themselves by their opposition to a particular ideology, such as communism. In francophone Africa, however, guardianship itself – protecting the country from its direct enemies, such as Islamist rebels, or its indirect ones, such as incompetent or self-interested civilian rulers – has risen to the level of ideology. This is in line with earlier patterns of militarism in post-colonial Africa, termed by one scholar as the 'ideology of discipline'.[13] After ousting civilian Nigerien president Mohamed Bazoum, for example, General Abdourahamane Tiani did not declare himself the new president of Niger, but rather 'president of the National Council for the Safeguard of the Homeland', arguing that his civilian predecessor betrayed the people's trust in failing to safeguard the nation.[14]

The second driver is the populations' abiding multigenerational resentment of foreign influence, especially France's post-colonial presence and perceived de facto hegemony, reinforced by youth bulges that crowd out prior attitudes of deference and negative memories of previous military regimes.[15] External actors can provoke resentment through their mere presence. In francophone Africa, political rulers' high levels of dependency on France have induced militaries and large segments of the public to view civilian elites as captured by the French, or at least enabling France to remain dominant.[16] Entrenched inequalities intensify resentment, while militaries offer greater social mobility to those who join. Military officers motivated by resentment are liable to feel sufficiently empowered to actually do something about it.[17]

The new military leaders in the Sahel region, as well as much of the citizenry, have framed coups as responses to French neo-colonialism, symbolised by a large French military presence in their countries. In Burkina Faso, Mali and Niger, the expulsion of French forces has been explicitly characterised as a reclamation of national sovereignty. Following French President Emmanuel Macron's announcement that French troops would leave Niger, its new rulers issued a statement noting that they were 'celebrating this new step towards Niger's sovereignty' and describing the French military's exit as 'a historic moment'.[18] Indigenous civilian governments' willingness to enable French neo-colonialism has also engendered resentment towards them. In his speech at the second Russia–Africa Summit in 2023, Burkina Faso's interim President Ibrahim Traoré condemned 'African heads of state who contribute nothing to these people who are fighting, but who sing the same song as the imperialists, calling us militias, calling us men who don't respect human rights'.[19]

While France's chequered colonial past makes it particularly vulnerable to local military criticism, its military's poor performance in protecting local populations has also contributed. Amadou Harouna Maïga, a Nigerien civil-society leader who favours continued French support, acknowledged that in the wake of the coup cascade, France's 'presence has in no way brought any change to the security situation, despite the ultra-sophisticated modern means at its disposal'.[20] Burkina Faso offers a striking example. The country was once seen as 'an island of stability in an otherwise unstable and troubled region', but it surpassed both Afghanistan and Iraq to top the Global Terrorism Index in 2023.[21] Seizure of power, of course, does not necessarily reduce resentment. Following Bazoum's ouster in Niger, the new rulers insisted on the departure of French military forces and the French ambassador. Macron, however, refused to recognise the new government and resisted pressure to withdraw militarily or diplomatically. While he eventually relented, his initial disregard of the military's wish not only deepened its resentment but also strengthened popular disdain for all things French.

The third factor is contemporary geopolitics. Increased uncertainty about the international system and the flagging position of Western states and institutions have created new political opportunities for resentful praetorian actors with a smaller risk of backlash.[22] During the Cold War, Western powers – in the Sahel, mainly France – had the leverage to engineer the forcible dislodging and replacement of popular *souverainiste* figures like Burkina Faso's Thomas Sankara and the Congo's Patrice Lumumba in favour of more compliant and pro-Western leaders. Since then, worsening security situations under pro-French civilian governments have discredited them as well as Paris in the eyes of Sahelian military officers.

Since the 2000s, the United States has to an extent assumed France's historical supervisory role in the region. Despite its superior resources, America's perception of itself as indispensable has fuelled resentment comparable to that felt towards France. Russia and China have emerged as counter-hegemonic forces. Thus, as Cameron Hudson puts it, 'in this new multipolar world, it seems that the United States, still arguably the richest and most powerful country in the world, needs Niger, one of the world's poorest and weakest countries, more than Niger needs it'.[23] While the Sahelian states are not hedging in the traditional sense – that is, shifting between geopolitical blocs – the advent of multipolarity has afforded them greater room for manoeuvre.

In July 2023, the military overthrew Bazoum, the French insisted that Bazoum be reinstated, and the junta then expelled the French. Niger's military cooperation with the United States continued. By March 2024, however, Niger's military government had become equally offended by America's attempts to control its foreign affairs and cancelled the arrangement whereby approximately 1,000 US troops were deployed in-country and maintained and operated an air base there. According to a spokesperson for the new Nigerien government, what occasioned this divorce was 'the condescending attitude accompanied by the threat of retaliation' from the United States, which had lodged concerns about Niger's 'potential relationships with Russia and Iran'.[24]

A new partner

France and the United States were in some ways natural partners for Sahelian states, not least due to the dynamics of decolonisation. France's decades of post-colonial involvement in the Sahel made military-to-military partnerships easily implementable. The United States is the world's premier military power and after 9/11 took greater strategic interest in Sub-Saharan African states for counter-terrorism reasons, which coincided with regional states' security interests.[25] France's complacency and incapacity, and America's imperious heavy-handedness, have simply made them less appealing partners, while Russia – by way of the state-supported if mercenary Wagner Group – has become a more attractive alternative.[26]

Among other things, Wagner has been more willing than France or the United States to put its personnel at risk in defence of African states and interests.[27] In July 2024, dozens of Wagner fighters were killed alongside Malian soldiers by Tuareg rebels.[28] More broadly, Russia has aligned itself tightly with new military governments and their theme of anti-colonial guardianship, keying on counter-hegemonic pushback in its own strategic discourse, as well as its messaging to the Global South in general and the African continent in particular.[29] At the July 2023 Russia–Africa Summit, Dmitry Medvedev, deputy chairman of the Security Council of Russia, stated that his government intended to 'pursue avenues that would liberate sovereign states from their colonial heritage'.[30] A year later, Medvedev published an article lauding anti-imperialist and Marxist-inspired pan-Africanists Sankara and Kwame Nkrumah while arguing that Russia and the Global South shared the cause of combatting Western neo-colonialism.[31] For Nigerien supporters of the coup, Russian President Vladimir Putin seemed 'like … an African' who understood 'the damage of colonial rule' and 'how it crushed our culture and the lives of the people of the Sahel'.[32]

Neither Russia nor Russian-backed groups have played a direct role in recent African military coups, but they haven't had to. Had one or more early coup attempts been thwarted, the recent wave might not have occurred and the incumbent rulers might actually have been strengthened.[33] But each provisionally successful coup has demonstrated the plausibility of a coup and rendered the concept more legitimate.[34] At the outset of the Nigerien crisis of 2023–24, the Economic Community of West African States (ECOWAS) threatened armed intervention to restore the Bazoum government, which in turn prompted the military leaders of Mali and Burkina Faso to pledge their support for Niger's new government, galvanised by shared animosity towards France and ECOWAS, which they perceived as dominated by the West. Even so, the regional proximity of Russia and its proxies – Wagner having effectively refocused on Africa in the wake of its short-lived June 2023 rebellion[35] – and their willingness to aid post-coup governments have likely altered the calculus of military leaders contemplating coups, who may be more willing to act with the prospect of external support.

* * *

While relative power imbalances can stave off military takeovers, instability or poor governance can amplify a putatively subordinate military's impulse towards guardianship. In fact, resentment and a revived sense of national guardianship have resonated even with relatively stable civilian African governments. In late 2024, both Senegal, customarily the West's favoured francophone partner in West Africa, and Côte d'Ivoire, historically a singularly close West African partner of France's, demanded the withdrawal of French troops from their respective territories.[36] The civilian-controlled Central African Republic may be a potential road map for African states that advances anti-colonial and guardianship objectives and still avoids coups. Moscow's backing has helped the government repel rebels while casting off French influence.[37]

The trade war and the security crises in Europe and the Middle East are likely to draw great-power attention and energy away from Sub-Saharan Africa. Competing priorities for France and the United States – the latter of which appears to be severely circumscribing and marginalising the State Department's Africa portfolio – will likely preclude them from decisively reasserting themselves in the region.[38] While Russia and its proxies could continue to fill the demand for outside support there, Moscow's preoccupations elsewhere could just as well diminish its motivation, capacity, utility and influence to stay deeply engaged, as they have in Syria. African military leaders are likely to continue to self-identify as national guardians and to remain resentful of colonial baggage, but may lack easy resort to effective outside assistance. While this situation may very well lead to some restraint, it suggests that regime dynamics will remain fluid for the foreseeable future.

Notes

1 See Brian Loveman, '"Protected Democracies" and Military Guardianship: Political Transitions in Latin America, 1978–1993', *Journal of Interamerican Studies and World Affairs*, vol. 36, no. 2, July 1994, pp. 105–89; and R. Blake McMahon and Branislav L. Slantchev, 'The Guardianship Dilemma: Regime Security Through and From the Armed Forces', *American Political Science Review*, vol. 109, no. 2, May 2015, pp. 297–313.

2 See James Burk, 'Theories of Democratic Civil–Military Relations', *Armed Forces and Society*, vol. 29, no. 1, Fall 2002, pp. 7–29; and David Pion-Berlin and Danijela Dudley, 'Civil–Military Relations: What Is the State of the Field', in Anders Sookermany (ed.), *Handbook of Military Sciences* (Cham: Springer International Publishing, 2020), pp. 1–22.

3 Samuel P. Huntington, *The Soldier and the State* (Cambridge, MA: Belknap Press, 1981), p. 84.

4 See Michael Bratton and Nicolas van de Walle, 'Neopatrimonial Regimes and Political Transitions in Africa', *World Politics*, vol. 46, no. 4, July 1994, pp. 453–89; and Yonatan L. Morse, 'From Single-party to Electoral Authoritarian Regimes: The Institutional Origins of Competitiveness in Post-Cold War Africa', *Comparative Politics*, vol. 48, no. 1, October 2015, pp. 126–43.

5 On regime cascades and diffusion under permissive environmental conditions, see, for example, Henry E. Hale, 'Regime Change Cascades: What We Have Learned from the 1848 Revolutions to the 2011 Arab Uprisings', *Annual Review of Political Science*, vol. 16, May 2013, pp. 331–53; and Kurt Weyland, 'Patterns of Diffusion: Comparing Democratic and Autocratic Waves', *Global Policy*, vol. 7, no. 4, 2016, pp. 557–62.

6 See Samuel P. Huntington, *Political Order in Changing Societies* (New Haven, CT: Yale University Press, 1968).

7 See Amos Perlmutter, 'The Praetorian State and the Praetorian Army: Toward a Taxonomy of Civil–Military Relations in Developing Polities', in Norman Provizer (ed.), *Analyzing the Third World: Essays from Comparative Politics* (Abingdon: Routledge, 2017 [1978]).

8 See Issaka K. Souaré, 'The African Union as a Norm Entrepreneur on Military Coups d'États in Africa (1952–2012): An Empirical Assessment', *Journal of Modern African Studies*, vol. 52, no. 1, March 2014, pp. 69–94.

9 See 'Afrobarometer Data Show Worrying Trends for Democracy in Africa, Prof. Gyimah-Boadi Warns', *Afrobarometer*, 16 June 2023, https://www.afrobarometer.org/articles/afrobarometer-data-show-worrying-trends-for-democracy-in-africa-prof-gyimah-boadi-warns/.

10 See Hazem Kandil, 'Military, Security, and Politics in Regime Change: Explaining the Power Triangle', in *Oxford Research Encyclopedia of Politics* (Oxford: Oxford University Press, 2021).

11 See Samuel Decalo, *Coups and Army Rule in Africa: Studies in Military Style* (New Haven, CT: Yale University Press, 1976).

12 See Mirjam de Bruijn and Jonna Both, 'Youth Between State and Rebel (Dis)Orders: Contesting Legitimacy

from Below in Sub-Sahara Africa', in Isabelle Duyvesteyn (ed.), *Rebels and Legitimacy: Processes and Practices* (Abingdon: Routledge, 2018), pp. 111–30; and Prince Bright Majiga, 'The Proliferation of Popular Protests and Coups d'États in Africa', in Dan Kuwali (ed.), *The Palgrave Handbook of Sustainable Peace and Security in Africa* (Cham: Springer International Publishing, 2022), pp. 181–95.

13 Samuel Fury Childs Daly, *Soldier's Paradise: Militarism in Africa After Empire* (Durham, NC: Duke University Press, 2024).

14 'Niger's General Abdourahamane Tiani Declares Himself Leader After Coup', France 24, 28 July 2023, https://www.france24.com/en/live-news/20230728-niger-s-general-abdourahamane-tchiani-declared-new-leader-following-coup-state-tv.

15 See Lance Y. Hunter, Josh Rutland and Zachary King, 'Leaving the Barracks: Military Coups in Developing Democracies', *Politics and Policy*, vol. 48, no. 6, November 2020, pp. 1,062–103.

16 See Frank Gerits, 'La France en Afrique: Pourquoi Les Politiques de Macron Ont Accru La Méfiance et La Colère', *Conversation*, 7 September 2023, https://theconversation.com/la-france-en-afrique-pourquoi-les-politiques-de-macron-ont-accru-la-mefiance-et-la-colere-212988.

17 See Edward N. Luttwak, *Coup d'État: A Practical Handbook*, 2nd ed. (Cambridge, MA: Harvard University Press, 2016); and Perlmutter, 'The Praetorian Army and the Praetorian State'.

18 'Niger: le régime militaire "célèbre une nouvelle étape vers la souveraineté"', *Le Point*, 25 September 2023, https://www.lepoint.fr/monde/niger-le-regime-militaire-celebre-une-nouvelle-etape-vers-la-souveraincte-25-09-2023-2536722_24.php#11.

19 '"A Slave Who Cannot Assume His Own Revolt Does Not Deserve to Be Pitied", Says Ibrahim Traoré of Burkina Faso', *Peoples Dispatch*, 2 August 2023, https://peoplesdispatch.org/2023/08/02/a-slave-who-cannot-assume-his-own-revolt-does-not-deserve-to-be-pitied-says-ibrahim-traore-of-burkina-faso/.

20 Garé Amadou, 'Why Nigeriens Are Protesting Against France's Anti-jihadist Campaign', *New Humanitarian*, 28 February 2023, https://www.thenewhumanitarian.org/news-feature/2023/02/28/why-niger-protest-france-anti-jihadist-campaign-interviews.

21 Viljar Haavik, Morten Bøås and Alessio Iocchi, 'The End of Stability – How Burkina Faso Fell Apart', *African Security*, vol. 15, no. 4, October 2022, pp. 317–39; and Institute of Economics and Peace, 'Global Terrorism Index 2024', February 2024, https://reliefweb.int/report/world/global-terrorism-index-2024.

22 See Alexander Cooley and Daniel H. Nexon, 'The Real Crisis of Global Order: Illiberalism on the Rise', *Foreign Affairs*, vol. 101, no. 1, January/February 2022, pp. 103–18; and G. John Ikenberry, 'Three Worlds: The West, East and South and the Competition to Shape Global Order', *International Affairs*, vol. 100, no. 1, January 2024, pp. 121–38.

23 Cameron Hudson, 'How the United States Lost Niger', *Foreign Policy*, April 2024, https://foreignpolicy.com/2024/04/02/us-niger-sahel-military-deal-russia-china/.

24 Nick Turse, 'The U.S. Is Building a Drone Base in Niger that Will Cost More than $280 Million by 2024', *The Intercept*, 21 August 2018, https://theintercept.com/2018/08/21/us-drone-base-niger-africa/; and US Department of Defense, 'Deputy Pentagon Press Secretary Sabrina Singh Holds an Off-camera, On-the-record Press Briefing', 18 March 2024, https://www.defense.gov/News/Transcripts/Transcript/Article/3710176/deputy-pentagon-press-secretary-sabrina-singh-holds-an-off-camera-on-the-record/.

25 See, for example, Jonathan Stevenson, 'Africa's Growing Strategic Resonance', *Survival*, vol. 45, no. 4, Winter 2003–04, pp. 153–72.

26 See Naman Karl-Thomas Habtom, 'The Potential Consequences for Africa of an FTO Designation of the Wagner Group', *Lawfare*, March 2023, https://www.lawfaremedia.org/article/potential-consequences-africa-fto-designation-wagner-group.

27 See John Lechner, 'Why Wagner's Operations in Africa May Be Far from Over, Despite Mali Setback', *Moscow Times*, 12 August 2024, https://www.themoscowtimes.com/2024/08/12/why-wagners-operations-in-africa-may-be-far-from-over-despite-mali-setback-a85886.

28 See Tim Lister, Avery Schmitz and Darya Tarasova, 'Dozens of Russian Mercenaries Killed in Rebel Ambush in Mali, in Their Worst Known Loss in Africa', CNN, 29 July 2024, https://www.cnn.com/2024/07/29/africa/russian-mercenaries-wagner-killed-mali-intl-latam/index.html.

29 See Dzvinka Kachur, 'Manifestations of Russian Formal and Informal Strategies in Southern and Eastern Africa, 2000–2022', *South African Journal of International Affairs*, vol. 29, no. 4, December 2022, pp. 509–34.

30 Quoted in James Pogue, 'Wagner in Africa', *Granta*, April 2024, https://granta.com/wagner-in-africa/.

31 See Dmitry Medvedev, 'The Humanity Should Get Rid of the Colonial System Heritage. Colonial Powers' Time Is Up', *Rossiyskaya Gazeta*, 14 June 2024, available at https://mid.ru/en/foreign_policy/historical_materials/1956884/.

32 Floriana Bulfon, 'Why Niger Left the West and Embraced Russia', *New Lines Magazine*, 4 September 2024, https://newlinesmag.com/reportage/why-niger-left-the-west-and-embraced-russia/.

33 See Naman Karl-Thomas Habtom, 'When Failed Coups Strengthen Leaders', *War on the Rocks*, July 2023, https://warontherocks.com/2023/07/when-failed-coups-strengthen-leaders/.

34 See Sohaib Mahmoud and Mohamed Taifouri, 'The Coups d'État of the Sahel Region: Domestic Causes and International Competition', Arab Center, September 2023, https://arabcenterdc.org/resource/the-coups-detat-of-the-sahel-region-domestic-causes-and-international-competition/.

35 See, for example, Kimberly Marten, 'Whither Wagner? The Consequences of Prigozhin's Mutiny and Demise',

Survival, vol. 65, no. 5, October–November 2023, pp. 45–64.

36 See Chris Ewokor and Alex Therrien, 'Ivory Coast Says French Troops to Leave West African Nation', BBC, 31 December 2024, https://www.bbc.com/news/articles/c5y7zz99jlxo.

37 See John Lechner, 'Are Russian Mercenaries Bad for the Central African Republic?', Responsible Statecraft, 11 April 2023, https://responsiblestatecraft.org/2023/04/11/are-russian-mercenaries-bad-for-the-central-african-republic/.

38 See Edward Wong, 'Trump Administration Draft Order Calls for Drastic Overhaul of State Department', *New York Times*, 20 April 2025, https://www.nytimes.com/2025/04/20/us/politics/trump-state-department-overhaul.html.

Copyright © 2025 The International Institute for Strategic Studies

Noteworthy

In contempt

'It is difficult in some cases to get to the very heart of the matter. But in this case, it is not hard at all. The government is asserting a right to stash away residents of this country in foreign prisons without the semblance of due process that is the foundation of our constitutional order. Further, it claims in essence that because it has rid itself of custody that there is nothing that can be done.

This should be shocking not only to judges, but to the intuitive sense of liberty that Americans far removed from courthouses still hold dear.

The government asserts that Abrego Garcia is a terrorist and a member of MS-13. Perhaps, but perhaps not. Regardless, he is still entitled to due process. If the government is confident of its position, it should be assured that position will prevail in proceedings to terminate the withholding of removal order … Moreover, the government has conceded that Abrego Garcia was wrongly or "mistakenly" deported. Why then should it not make what was wrong, right?

The Supreme Court's decision remains, as always, our guidepost. That decision rightly requires the lower federal courts to give "due regard for the deference owed to the Executive Branch in the conduct of foreign affairs." … That would allow sensitive diplomatic negotiations to be removed from public view. It would recognize as well that the "facilitation" of Abrego Garcia's return leaves the Executive Branch with options in the execution to which the courts in accordance with the Supreme Court's decision should extend a genuine deference. That decision struck a balance that does not permit lower courts to leave Article II by the wayside.

The Supreme Court's decision does not, however, allow the government to do essentially nothing. It requires the government "to 'facilitate' Abrego Garcia's release from custody in El Salvador and to ensure that his case is handled as it would have been had he not been improperly sent to El Salvador." … "Facilitate" is an active verb. It requires that steps be taken as the Supreme Court has made perfectly clear … The plain and active meaning of the word cannot be diluted by its constriction, as the government would have it, to a narrow term of art. We are not bound in this context by a definition crafted by an administrative agency and contained in a mere policy directive … Thus, the government's argument that all it must do is "remove any domestic barriers to [Abrego Garcia's] return," … is not well taken in light of the Supreme Court's command that the government facilitate Abrego Garcia's *release from custody in El Salvador.*

"Facilitation" does not permit the admittedly erroneous deportation of an individual to the one country's prisons that the withholding order forbids and, further, to do so in disregard of a court order that the government not so subtly spurns. "Facilitation" does not sanction the abrogation of habeas corpus through the transfer of custody to foreign detention centers in the manner attempted here. Allowing all this would "facilitate" foreign detention more than it would domestic return. It would reduce the rule of law to lawlessness and tarnish the very values for which Americans of diverse views and persuasions have always stood.

Survival | vol. 67 no. 3 | June–July 2025 | pp. 92–94 https://doi.org/10.1080//00396338.2025.2508087

The government is obviously frustrated and displeased with the rulings of the court. Let one thing be clear. Court rulings are not above criticism. Criticism keeps us on our toes and helps us do a better job … Court rulings can overstep, and they can further intrude upon the prerogatives of other branches. Courts thus speak with the knowledge of their imperfections but also with a sense that they instill a fidelity to law that would be sorely missed in their absence.

"Energy in the [E]xecutive" is much to be respected … It can rescue government from its lassitude and recalibrate imbalances too long left unexamined. The knowledge that executive energy is a perishable quality understandably breeds impatience with the courts. Courts, in turn, are frequently attuned to caution and are often uneasy with the Executive Branch's breakneck pace.

And the differences do not end there. The Executive is inherently focused upon ends; the Judiciary much more so upon means. Ends are bestowed on the Executive by electoral outcomes. Means are entrusted to all of government, but most especially to the Judiciary by the Constitution itself.

The Executive possesses enormous powers to prosecute and to deport, but with powers come restraints. If today the Executive claims the right to deport without due process and in disregard of court orders, what assurance will there be tomorrow that it will not deport American citizens and then disclaim responsibility to bring them home? And what assurance shall there be that the Executive will not train its broad discretionary powers upon its political enemies? The threat, even if not the actuality, would always be present, and the Executive's obligation to "take Care that the Laws be faithfully executed" would lose its meaning.

[…]

Today, both the United States and the El Salvadoran governments disclaim any authority and/or responsibility to return Abrego Garcia … We are told that neither government has the power to act. The result will be to leave matters generally and Abrego Garcia specifically in an interminable limbo without recourse to law of any sort.

The basic differences between the branches mandate a serious effort at mutual respect. The respect that courts must accord the Executive must be reciprocated by the Executive's respect for the courts. Too often today this has not been the case, as calls for impeachment of judges for decisions the Executive disfavors and exhortations to disregard court orders sadly illustrate.

It is in this atmosphere that we are reminded of President Eisenhower's sage example. Putting his "personal opinions" aside, President Eisenhower honored his "inescapable" duty to enforce the Supreme Court's decision in *Brown v. Board of Education II* to desegregate schools "with all deliberate speed." … This great man expressed his unflagging belief that "[t]he very basis of our individual rights and freedoms is the certainty that the President and the Executive Branch of Government will support and [e]nsure the carrying out of the decisions of the Federal Courts." … Indeed, in our late Executive's own words, "[u]nless the President did so, anarchy would result."

[…]

Now the branches come too close to grinding irrevocably against one another in a conflict that promises to diminish both. This is a losing proposition all around. The Judiciary will lose much from the constant intimations of its illegitimacy, to which by dent of custom and detachment we can only sparingly reply. The Executive will lose much from a public perception of its lawlessness and all of its attendant contagions. The Executive may succeed for a time in weakening the courts, but over time history will script the tragic gap between what was and all that might have been, and law in time will sign its epitaph.

It is, as we have noted, all too possible to see in this case an incipient crisis, but it may present an opportunity as well. We yet cling to the hope that it is not naïve to believe our good brethren in the Executive Branch perceive the rule of law as vital to the American ethos. This case presents their unique chance to vindicate that value and to summon the best that is within us while there is still time.

In sum, and for the reasons foregoing, we deny the motion for the stay pending appeal and the writ of mandamus in this case. It is so ordered.'

In a ruling dated 17 April 2025, the United States Court of Appeals for the Fourth Circuit rejects the US government's appeal against an order of the Supreme Court to 'facilitate' the return of Kilmar Armando Abrego Garcia, a Salvadoran immigrant to the US who had been granted protection from deportation but who was removed from the country and jailed in El Salvador in March 2025, to the United States.[1]

'There is before the Court an application on behalf of a putative class of detainees seeking an injunction against their removal under the Alien Enemies Act. The matter is currently pending before the Fifth Circuit. Upon action by the Fifth Circuit, the Solicitor General is invited to file a response to the application before this Court as soon as possible. The Government is directed not to remove any member of the putative class of detainees from the United States until further order of this Court … Justice Thomas and Justice Alito dissent from the Court's order. Statement from Justice Alito to follow.'

In a ruling dated 19 April that was issued after midnight and before Justice Samuel Alito could complete his dissent, the United States Supreme Court bans the deportation of some Venezuelan migrants, whom the US government wished to remove from the country under the 1798 Alien Enemies Act, until further notice.[2]

Sources

1 United States Court of Appeals for the Fourth Circuit, *Kilmar Armando Abrego Garcia, et al. v. Kristi Noem, et al.*, no. 25-1404, 17 April 2025, https://storage.courtlistener.com/recap/gov.uscourts.ca4.178400/gov.uscourts.ca4.178400.8.0.pdf; and Gil Guerra, 'The Kilmar Abrego Garcia Case, Explained', *Dispatch*, 19 April 2025, https://www.niskanencenter.org/op-ed-the-kilmar-abrego-case-explained/.

2 United States Supreme Court, *A.A.R.P., et al. v. Trump, President of U.S., et al.*, no. 24A1007, 19 April 2025, https://www.supremecourt.gov/orders/courtorders/041925zr_c18e.pdf; and Andrew Chung et al., 'US Supreme Court Temporarily Blocks Deportations of Venezuelan Migrants Under Wartime Law', Reuters, 21 April 2025, https://www.reuters.com/world/us/us-supreme-court-temporarily-blocks-deportations-venezuelan-migrants-under-2025-04-19/.

Copyright © 2025 The International Institute for Strategic Studies

Knock-on Risks to NATO's Space-based War-fighting Capabilities

Ian Bowers and Henrik Stålhane Hiim

NATO is taking an increasingly adversarial rhetorical stance against China. In the Alliance's 2022 Strategic Concept, NATO members pledged to work together to 'address the systemic challenges posed by the [People's Republic of China] to Euro-Atlantic security and ensure NATO's enduring ability to guarantee the defence and security of Allies'.[1] Since then, NATO's approach has hardened further, driven in large part by China's provision of material support for Russia's war effort in Ukraine.[2] In turn, NATO has taken concrete steps to bolster its standing in the Indo-Pacific region through its Individually Tailored Partnership Programme and by inviting the leaders of Australia, Japan and South Korea to attend NATO summits.[3] At the military level, however, NATO remains focused on and structured for deterrence and defence in Europe. It has no real footprint in Asia and, beyond heightened cooperation and contact, there is little enthusiasm – let alone spare military capacity – for expanding its operational portfolio to include East Asia.[4]

Debates about China and the challenge it poses to Euro-Atlantic security tend to focus on either indirect or political, strategic-level developments. Policymakers and analysts frequently point not only to China's continued support for Russia but also to the risk of a two-front scenario in which Russia engages in opportunistic aggression in Europe after war between the

Ian Bowers is a senior researcher at the Norwegian Institute for Defence Studies, focusing on contemporary and future military operations, sea power and the Korean Peninsula. **Henrik Stålhane Hiim** is a professor at the Norwegian Institute for Defence Studies and head of its Centre for International Security, focusing on Chinese security policy, nuclear weapons and East Asian security.

Survival | vol. 67 no. 3 | June–July 2025 | pp. 95–108 https://doi.org/10.1080/00396338.2025.2508089

United States and China erupts in Asia, and to China's ongoing challenge to the international order.[5] While these are deep and legitimate concerns, a conflict in Asia – most likely over Taiwan – could have a much more direct operational impact on Euro-Atlantic security than many appreciate.

In a high-intensity war, China will target US war-fighting systems and the US capabilities that enable them. NATO relies heavily on these, in particular on a critical set of space-based command, control, communications, computers, intelligence, surveillance and reconnaissance (C4ISR) capabilities that serve the European theatre as well as the Indo-Pacific one. A conflict in East Asia could therefore lead to a significant degradation of NATO's war-fighting capabilities – not because of the physical redeployment of US assets from Europe to Asia, but because of the knock-on disruption of NATO's own command-and-control capabilities.

The Alliance's exposure to such risks is the result of deliberate choices. NATO members have long counted on the United States to provide space-based C4ISR capabilities. Until quite recently, there has been little incentive for NATO to develop greater redundancy in key capabilities across the Alliance. Russia's full-scale invasion of Ukraine in 2022 and the re-election of Donald Trump, who is deeply sceptical of the Alliance's value, as US president have substantially increased that incentive. Yet although some European NATO members are now boosting their space capabilities and the Alliance itself is incorporating the commercial space industry into its plans, investment remains limited.

At the same time, NATO's space dependency – and thus its risk exposure – is growing. Ongoing force-development efforts, including the gradual transition to multidomain operations (MDO), will require increasing inter-operability – long a NATO objective – to unprecedented levels, particularly in terms of gathering and then sharing data among platforms, units, commands and countries. To achieve it, NATO will, to a greater or lesser degree, depend on extant and future space-based C4ISR capabilities, controlled mainly by the United States. Reducing this dependency will be very challenging. For European NATO allies to build a parallel set of capabilities would be extremely costly and technologically demanding, and might impede efforts to improve inter-operability. Nevertheless, European

NATO members and possibly the Alliance itself need to build some redundancy into their C4ISR systems to preclude the degradation of the Alliance's ability to defend Europe.

NATO and the space domain

The space domain is becoming more and more integral to contemporary war-fighting operations.[6] As the vice chairman of the US Joint Chiefs of Staff said in early 2024, 'space has emerged as our most essential warfighting domain – integral to our national security, our coalition interoperability and our global stability'.[7] The United States, NATO, US-allied countries in East Asia, and adversaries including Russia and China have all incorporated space into their military doctrines.[8] The Ukrainian military's use of commercial space-based platforms for communications; intelligence, surveillance and reconnaissance (ISR); and positioning, navigation and timing (PNT) illustrates their essential importance.[9]

Military technologies require increasing amounts of data, which means the possession, security and resilience of space assets are operational and strategic imperatives. Any military or alliance seeking to maximise its war-fighting potential must continuously invest in space-related technology, including ISR, PNT, satellite communications, high-speed network connections, multiple redundant ground stations, advanced computing to process incoming data, and the ability to launch new satellites at short notice.[10]

In 2019, NATO declared space an operational domain, on a par with more traditional war-fighting domains such as land and air. Two years later, the Alliance recognised that attacks 'to, from or within space' could trigger an Article 5 collective response.[11] Consequently, NATO has supported the development of several supporting institutions, including a Space Centre at Ramstein Air Base in Germany and a Space Centre of Excellence in France. These two facilities help coordinate NATO space activities and the sharing of space-related information and knowledge across the Alliance.

Like nearly all of NATO's capabilities, its space assets are owned by member states – and to an increasing degree commercial companies – rather than the Alliance itself. NATO accesses its members' satellite capabilities through two mechanisms. Under the first, 'allocate and commit', a specific capability is provided to the Alliance for NATO commanders to use as they see fit. Under the second, 'managed access service', NATO requests a specific service that a member state provides and oversees. With the latter arrangement, which applies to most NATO capabilities, NATO does not have automatic access to members' capabilities, since each member state has its own political strategic and operational requirements.

For communications, NATO currently has an agreement known as NATO SATCOM Services 6th Generation, whereby six Alliance members provide the requisite services. The United States provides the communications capabilities needed for nuclear command and control and for super-high-frequency communications. France, Italy, Luxembourg, Spain and the United Kingdom accord NATO similar capabilities – excluding extremely high-frequency communications – via about 12 satellites.[12]

Although other countries contribute space assets for purposes such as ISR, NATO remains heavily reliant on the United States.[13] Currently, the US military operates approximately 246 satellites for early warning, ISR, data transfer and communications. The NATO ally with the second-highest number of military-operated satellites is France with 14 (five for satellite communications, three for electronic and signal intelligence, and six for ISR).[14] Canada, Germany, Italy, Spain and the United Kingdom operate a variety of satellites totalling 29. It should come as no surprise, of course, that NATO relies inordinately on the United States for both core war-fighting capabilities and key enablers from the strategic to the tactical level, which has been clear from Bosnia to Afghanistan to Ukraine.[15] Given the United States' strategic rebalancing to the Indo-Pacific and the Trump administration's hostility towards Europe, however, this state of affairs leaves European NATO in a precarious position.

Space and US–China conflict

If war breaks out between China and the United States, NATO's reliance on US space capabilities presents a substantial danger. Because of the United States' strong operational reliance on space, a high-intensity conflict in Asia will likely extend to the space domain. In the worst case, a war could significantly degrade US space-based assets. Since the Space Force was established during Trump's first term, the US military has largely consolidated its space capabilities.[16] Its efforts to develop a joint command-and-control architecture point towards its own increasing reliance – approaching dependency – on the space domain. Under the heading of Combined Joint All-Domain Command and Control (CJADC2), the US joint force is seeking to integrate a diverse set of platforms and enhance the speed and precision of their effects.[17] New satellites are now being tested to function as hubs for transmitting vital tactical data – currently sent via line-of-sight means of limited range – between platforms.[18]

Chinese military practitioners have carefully observed these developments, particularly the US military's emphasis on data and network connectivity. The People's Liberation Army has deemed its effective theory of victory 'system destruction warfare'. The underlying idea is that contemporary warfare is no longer a contest of arms, services or weapons platforms, but rather a confrontation between war-fighting systems.[19] The key to success lies in paralysing or blinding the adversary by interrupting or destroying key nodes that enable networked, data-driven operations.[20]

China has developed a range of kinetic and non-kinetic counter-space capabilities, such as direct-ascent anti-satellite weapons, co-orbital satellites, directed-energy weapons (including high-power systems that the Pentagon assesses could be fielded within five years), cyber weapons and various electronic-warfare capabilities such as satellite jammers.[21] These counter-space capabilities allow China to target satellites in all orbits and interfere with communications between satellites and ground stations, as well as between ground stations. Although Russia's development of a nuclear anti-satellite weapon has received more public attention than kindred Chinese capabilities, US military leaders see China as the more potent threat in this area.[22]

China too is increasingly reliant on space for critical military and civilian functions, so mutual vulnerability could deter it from engaging in large-scale, kinetic counter-space attacks in a Taiwan-related conflict.[23] Furthermore, China has manifested a preference for 'soft-kill' or non-kinetic tools because they are likely to be less escalatory.[24] The Chinese also appreciate that mega-constellations such as Starlink, on which the United States will probably increasingly rely, are difficult to target owing to their high redundancy.[25]

At the same time, since the stakes in a Taiwan conflict would be very high for Chinese leaders, they could be willing to take risks. If China were less reliant on space-based assets than the United States, using terrestrially based or air-breathing alternatives for ISR or communication, they might see the pay-off of an attack on US systems – the wholesale crippling of the US war-fighting machine – as worth the risk.[26] In any event, China would at least engage in extensive non-kinetic counter-space operations, seeking to confound ISR systems, jam data transfers or disrupt satellites and their support systems.[27] It might target the Global Positioning System, alternatives to which are still limited. Other systems with higher redundancy are likely more difficult to target, particularly kinetically.[28]

If China decides to cross the threshold of using extensive kinetic anti-satellite weapons, it will likely target any system that directly or indirectly supports US operations. Contracted satellites owned by private companies such as SpaceX would be fair game, and Chinese analysts have debated how to target them.[29] In the worst case, the disruption or destruction of US space systems could harm the broader space environment and other satellites.

NATO's current and future vulnerability

Given NATO's reliance on US space assets, a war over Taiwan could have a substantial impact on the Alliance's ability to execute complex military operations. If China seeks to disrupt US satellite capabilities, NATO will lose significant enabling capability that will not be easy to replace, including access to bandwidth for data transfer and communications, and ISR capabilities that will have been re-tasked to the Indo-Pacific theatre.

NATO has previously managed degradations in capabilities due to the withdrawal of US assets for other operations. During the 1990–91 Gulf War, for example, the US redeployed 40% of army personnel and 54% of the US aircraft from the European theatre to the Middle East.[30] But NATO had agreed to this in advance at the political and strategic levels, and had time to prepare for and offset the loss of capability. By contrast, a war in the

Taiwan Strait could unfold rapidly, and would put US capabilities at much greater risk than they faced during the Gulf War. The United States itself is developing space capabilities with inbuilt redundancy and even surge capacity, but other NATO members cannot replace or backfill them. The United States would likely pull personnel and capabilities from NATO that European members could not readily replace.

A further challenge facing NATO would be Russia's counter-space capabilities should Moscow elect to exploit the distraction of a US–China conflict. Even if the Alliance's non-US space-based capabilities were sufficient for ISR, communication and other key functions, Russia possesses an array of counter-space assets.[31] These reportedly include a nuclear option that has received considerable attention. Russia tested the *Nudol* direct-ascent anti-satellite missile in November 2021, is developing technologies that can support co-orbital anti-satellite capabilities in both geostationary and low-Earth orbit, and has bolstered various non-kinetic counter-space capabilities.[32] Among non-US NATO countries, only France has declared an ambition to bolster offensive counter-space programmes, and it is likely still far behind Russia. In a conflict with Russia, space assets available to NATO would therefore be at significant risk.

Existing non-space-based enablers – in particular, air, land and sea-based surveillance platforms and legacy communications systems – may be able to assume much of the ISR load for NATO in a crisis. But the steepening trajectory of NATO's operational-concept development will increase the Alliance's dependency on the space domain. NATO force designers are developing command-and-control capabilities similar to those currently coming on stream in the United States.

NATO has undertaken a long-term transformation effort to leverage the power of new technologies and make the Alliance a data-enabled force. This includes building a digital backbone.[33] NATO's ultimate war-fighting objective is to use information to generate a 'cross-functional, holistic, accurate and timely characterisation of the operational environment'.[34] Other things being equal, NATO's dependence on future US enablers will increase. In particular, MDO will require persistent space-based ISR and ever-greater data-link capacity.

NATO's response

NATO is attempting to address its shortcomings in space. The Alliance has recently sought to bolster its capabilities through the Alliance Persistent Surveillance from Space initiative. Through this initiative, 17 member states have committed to spending over $1 billion to improve NATO's ability to forge a persistent surveillance capability and improve intelligence-gathering and dissemination throughout the Alliance.[35] This initiative does not provide NATO with a dedicated satellite capability but rather leverages existing and future Alliance and commercial satellites to create a 'virtual constellation', which it calls *Aquila*. How effective such a constellation will be with limited or no US contributions remains unclear.

Although NATO will soon include space capabilities and set targets for member states in the NATO Defence Planning Process, members other than the United States are building space capabilities aimed only at current needs.[36] NATO space-recapitalisation programmes appear to be aimed at replacing ageing platforms with updated but essentially similar ones. While some Alliance members such as Norway are introducing their own capabilities, they fall well short of those of the United States, whose *Starshield* programme will likely see the launch of hundreds of low-Earth-orbit ISR satellites and could give US commanders the ability to track moving targets from space.[37]

Non-US Alliance members also are not currently able to launch in numbers required for contemporary military operations. Europe's newest launch vehicle, *Ariane* 6, remains in the testing phase, leaving Europe heavily leveraged on US commercial and government launching capabilities.[38] In the first 11 months of 2024, the US government – or American companies – conducted 130 orbital launches, China 58, Europe two.[39]

For NATO, enhanced cooperation with the commercial sector and the European Union may hold promise. The EU has an established space programme, operating the Galileo global-navigation satellite system, for instance. In turn, NATO is investing in the IRIS² constellation, which, when finished, will provide secure satellite communications for EU government agencies. However, some EU members have political reservations about direct military cooperation with NATO during war.

NATO is incorporating commercial actors into its plans, including for ISR. As noted, commercial satellites will be part of the *Aquila* virtual constellation. In August 2024, NATO signed its first commercial contract with Planet Labs, which will provide it with high-resolution satellite data and give NATO unclassified but still useful imagery for monitoring adversary activities and capabilities. The content's unclassified status will allow it to be shared throughout the Alliance free of concerns about data security. Furthermore, commercial-satellite companies from some European NATO states are beginning to furnish military capabilities. The Finnish satellite manufacturer and operator ICEYE, in cooperation with Rheinmetall, for example, now provides Ukraine with vital intelligence, surveillance, target-acquisition and reconnaissance data using dedicated synthetic-aperture-radar satellites. ICEYE is working with the American and Finnish militaries on several projects that seek to leverage the same capabilities.[40] Despite these initiatives, European NATO's reliance on the United States in the space domain is likely to increase. Given that domain's centrality to NATO's future war-fighting concepts, that reliance will render it highly vulnerable if war breaks out in Asia.

* * *

European leaders must be aware that key Alliance war-fighting capabilities are exposed to significant degradation from conflicts outside NATO's core operational area, which would create openings for opportunistic aggression by a revanchist Russia.[41] NATO leaders are aware of their dependence on the United States, and many member states are currently working to build redundancy in multiple war-fighting areas. Space remains a crucial area that the Alliance can ill afford to ignore or underplay. Although European NATO currently has some non-space-based alternatives for critical functions like ISR and communications, the Alliance's future operational concepts will increasingly leverage space assets.

For non-US NATO members to produce a parallel set of space-based enablers would be prohibitively expensive and would likely impede efforts to improve inter-operability and achieve MDO capability. Nevertheless, options exist for them to enlist private industry and even the EU to backfill critical areas en route to controlling its own set of space-based capabilities and thereby mitigating risks stemming from over-reliance on US enablers in the space domain. There is now a fleeting window of opportunity for them to do so. Russian forces are depleted and bogged down in Ukraine, China probably is not yet ready to invade Taiwan and, prompted by Trump's spurning of Europe, European governments are boosting defence spending and awakening to the exigency of developing independent space-based enabling capabilities. It is crucial that they act before Russia rebuilds its armed forces and Chinese leaders gain confidence vis-à-vis Taiwan.

Acknowledgements

The authors thank Jonas Vidhammer Berge, Paal Sigurd Hilde and Jakob Clud Lund for their helpful comments. The research for this article was supported by the Security in Asia Programme at the Norwegian Institute for Defence Studies and funded by the Norwegian Ministry of Defence.

Notes

1 NATO, 'NATO 2022 Strategic Concept', 29 June 2022, p. 5, https://www.act.nato.int/wp-content/uploads/2023/05/290622-strategic-concept.pdf.

2 See NATO, 'Joint Press Conference by NATO Secretary General Mark Rutte and the President of Latvia, Edgars Rinkēvičs, at the Ādaži Military Base', 14 November 2024, https://www.nato.int/cps/en/natohq/opinions_230462.htm.

3 See NATO, 'Individually Tailored Partnership Programmes', 21 October 2024, https://www.nato.int/cps/en/natohq/topics_225037.htm.

4 See Jack Detsch and Robbie Gramer, 'NATO Wants to Plant Its Flag in Asia: But Not Everyone Is On Board with the Plan', *Foreign Policy*, 9 July 2024, https://foreignpolicy.com/2024/07/09/nato-asia-tokyo-office-indo-pacific-china/.

5 See Jonathan Landay, 'US Must Be Ready for Simultaneous Wars with China, Russia, Report Says', Reuters, 13 October 2023, https://www.reuters.com/world/us-must-be-ready-simultaneous-wars-with-china-russia-report-says-2023-10-12/; and Bonny Lin, 'The China–Russia Axis Takes Shape', *Foreign Policy*, 11 September 2023, https://foreignpolicy.com/2023/09/11/china-russia-alliance-cooperation-brics-sco-economy-military-war-ukraine-putin-xi/.

6 See Bleddyn E. Bowen, *Original Sin: Power, Technology and War in Outer Space* (London: C. Hurst & Co., 2022), pp. 236–8; Ivan Oelrich,

Paul van Hooft and Stephen Biddle, 'Anti-satellite Warfare, Proliferated Satellites and the Future of Space-based Military Surveillance', *Journal of Strategic Studies*, vol. 47, nos 6–7, July 2024, pp. 916–39; and Jack Watling, *The Arms of the Future: Technology and Close Combat in the Twenty-first Century* (London: Bloomsbury, 2023), p. 178.

7 Brett Tingley, 'Space Is Now "Most Essential" Domain for US Military, Pentagon Says', Space.com, 17 January 2024, https://www.space.com/space-command-conflict-in-space-deterrence-kathleen-hicks.

8 See, for example, State Council Information Office of the People's Republic of China, 'China's National Defense in the New Era', 2019; NATO, 'AJP-3.3 Allied Joint Doctrine for Air and Space Operations Edition B Version 1', April 2016, https://assets.publishing.service.gov.uk/media/5a82d7bc40f0b62305b94a32/doctrine_nato_air_space_ops_ajp_3_3.pdf; Juliana Suess, 'Space and the Future of War According to Russia', RUSI Commentary, 26 November 2021, https://www.rusi.org/explore-our-research/publications/commentary/space-and-future-war-according-russia; and United States Space Force, 'Sustainment Doctrine for Space Forces', Space Doctrine Publication 4-0, December 2022, https://www.starcom.spaceforce.mil/Portals/2/SDP%20 4-0%20Sustainment%20(Signed).pdf?ver=jFc_4BiAkDjJdc49LmESgg%3D%3D.

9 See Bleddyn E. Bowen, *War in Space: Strategy, Spacepower, Geopolitics* (Edinburgh: Edinburgh University Press, 2020); and Theodora Ogden et al., 'The Role of the Space Domain in the Russia–Ukraine War: The Impact of Converging Space and AI Technologies', Centre for Emerging Technology and Security, Expert Analysis, 23 February 2024, https://cetas.turing.ac.uk/publications/role-space-domain-russia-ukraine-war.

10 See Todd Harrison, 'Battle Networks and the Future Force – Part 1: A Framework for Debate', CSIS Briefs, 5 August 2021, https://www.csis.org/analysis/battle-networks-and-future-force.

11 See Lorne Cook, 'NATO Says Attack in Space Could Trigger Mutual Defense Clause', *Defense News*, 14 June 2021, https://www.defensenews.com/smr/nato-priorities/2021/06/14/nato-says-attack-in-space-could-trigger-mutual-defense-clause/.

12 See C. Todd Lopez, 'Two New Nations Join Program to Provide SATCOM Support to NATO', US Department of Defense, 27 June 2024, https://www.defense.gov/News/News-Stories/Article/Article/3819541/two-new-nations-join-program-to-provide-satcom-support-to-nato/.

13 See Jonas Vidhammer Berge and Liselotte Odgaard, 'NATO in the Global Commons: Defending Outer Space Against Threats from China', *International Journal*, vol. 78, no. 4, December 2023, pp. 634–42.

14 Satellite numbers are from International Institute for Strategic Studies (IISS), Military Balance+ database, Equipment Capability Data, accessed 12 December 2024, https://www.iiss.org/the-military-balance-plus/.

15 See Ben Barry et al., 'Defending Europe: Scenario-based Capability

Requirements for NATO's European Members', IISS Research Paper, 19 May 2019, https://www.iiss.org/research-paper/2019/05/defending-europe/; Henrik Larsen, 'Adapting NATO to Great-power Competition', *Washington Quarterly*, vol. 45, no. 4, Winter 2023, pp. 7–26; and Hugo Meijer and Stephen G. Brooks, 'Illusions of Autonomy: Why Europe Cannot Provide for Its Security if the United States Pulled Back', *International Security*, vol. 45, no. 4, 2021, pp. 7–43.

16 See Stew Magnuson, 'Reaching Pentagon's CJADC2 Goals to Require "Bridging Solutions"', *National Defense*, 2 February 2024, https://www.nationaldefensemagazine.org/articles/2024/2/2/reaching-pentagons-cjadc2-goals-to-require-bridging-solutions; and Thomas A. Walsh and Alexandra L. Huber, 'A Symphony of Capabilities: How the Joint Warfighting Concept Guides Service Force Design and Development', *Joint Force Quarterly*, no. 111, 4th quarter 2023, pp. 4–15, https://ndupress.ndu.edu/Portals/68/Documents/jfq/jfq-111/jfq-111_4-15_Walsh-Huber.pdf?ver=TwePyLVymtN8924udhzIxQ%3d%3d.

17 See United States Space Force, 'Space Force Integration Critical to CJADC2 Success', 4 March 2021, https://www.spaceforce.mil/News/Article/2524141/space-force-integration-critical-to-cjadc2-success/.

18 See Josh Luckenbaugh, 'Lockheed Martin Launches CJADC2 Demo Satellites', *National Defense*, 6 May 2024, https://www.nationaldefensemagazine.org/articles/2024/5/6/lockheed-martin-launches-cjadc2-demo-satellites; and Jordan McDonald, 'Tactical Data Link Satellites Will Soon Begin Testing over NATO Territory', GovCIO, 10 April 2024, https://govciomedia.com/tactical-data-link-satellites-will-soon-begin-testing-over-nato-territory/.

19 See Jeffrey Engstrom, *Systems Confrontation and System Destruction Warfare: How the Chinese People's Liberation Army Seeks to Wage Modern Warfare* (Santa Monica, CA: RAND Corporation, 2018), p. 12.

20 See Mark Cozad et al., *Gaining Victory in Systems Warfare: China's Perspective on the U.S.–China Military Balance* (Santa Monica, CA: RAND Corporation, 2023), p. 79; Li Haibin and Huo Yunchao, 'Cong zhisheng jili yanbian kan zuizhan zhidao zhi "bian"' ['Change' in operational guidance seen from the evolution of victory mechanism], *People's Liberation Army Daily*, 2 February 2023, http://www.81.cn/jfjbmap/content/1/2023-02/02/07/2023020207_pdf; Xiao Tianliang (ed.), *Zhanlue Xue* [Science of military strategy] (Beijing: Military Sciences Press, 2020), p. 283; and US Department of Defense, 'Military and Security Developments Involving the People's Republic of China 2024', Annual Report to Congress, pp. 35–6, https://media.defense.gov/2024/Dec/18/2003615520/-1/-1/0/MILITARY-AND-SECURITY-DEVELOPMENTS-INVOLVING-THE-PEOPLES-REPUBLIC-OF-CHINA-2024.PDF.

21 US Department of Defense, 'Military and Security Developments Involving the People's Republic of China 2024', pp. 86, 100–1.

22 See Joshua Posaner, 'China's "Mind-boggling" Space Capabilities Worry

US, Says Space Force Chief', *Politico*, 31 October 2024, https://www.politico.eu/article/china-mind-boggling-space-capabilities-worry-us-says-space-force-chief-b-chance-saltzman-russia-nasa/.

23 See Jonas Vidhammer Berge and Henrik Stålhane Hiim, 'Killing Them Softly: China's Counterspace Developments and Force Posture in Space', *Journal of Strategic Studies*, vol. 47, nos 6–7, August 2024, pp. 940–63. See also Mark F. Cancian, Matthew Cancian and Eric Heginbotham, 'The First Battle of the Next War: Wargaming a Chinese Invasion of Taiwan', Center for Strategic and International Studies, January 2023, https://csis-website-prod.s3.amazonaws.com/s3fs-public/publication/230109_Cancian_FirstBattle_NextWar.pdf?VersionId=XlDrfCUHet8OZSOYW_9PWx3xtcoScGHn. In this war game, players refrained from employing direct-ascent weapons, fearing to lose their satellites.

24 See Han Hongtao and Wang Youli, 'Guowai kongjian gongfang nengli xianzhuang yu qushi fenxi' [Analysis of the current status and trends of foreign offensive and defensive space capabilities], *Zhongguo Hangtian*, no. 9, 2015, p. 25; and Huang Zhicheng, 'Cong Wukelan zhancheng kan shangye hangtian junshi jiazhi' [Looking at the military value of commercial aerospace from the Ukrainian battlefield], *Guoji Taikong*, no. 4, 2023.

25 See Ren Yuanzhen et al., 'Xinglian jihua fazhan xianzhuang yu duikang sikao' [The development status of the Starlink project and a consideration of countermeasures], *Xiandai Fangyu Jishu*, no. 5, 2022, p. 16.

26 See Eric Heginbotham et al., *The U.S.–China Military Scorecard: Forces, Geography, and the Evolving Balance of Power, 1996–2017* (Santa Monica, CA: RAND Corporation, 2015), p. 241.

27 See Oelrich, van Hooft and Biddle, 'Anti-satellite Warfare, Proliferated Satellites and the Future of Space-based Military Surveillance'.

28 See Berge and Hiim, 'Killing Them Softly'.

29 See Ren Yuanzhen et al., 'Xinglian jihua fazhan xianzhuang yu duikang sikao' [The development status of the Starlink project and a consideration of countermeasures], *Xiandai Fangyu Jishu*, 2022, pp. 11–17.

30 William Butler, 'Desert Storm: USEUMCOM Contribution to Victory', United States European Command, August 2022, https://www.eucom.mil/about-the-command/history-of-useucom/desert-storm-useucom-contribution-to-victory.

31 See Barry et al., 'Defending Europe', p. 29.

32 See Brian Weeden and Victoria Samson, 'Global Counterspace Capabilities: An Open Source Assessment', Secure World Foundation, April 2024, https://swfound.org/media/207826/swf_global_counterspace_capabilities_2024.pdf.

33 See NATO Allied Command Transformation, 'Empowering NATO's Multi-domain Operations Through Digital Transformation', 16 October 2023, https://www.act.nato.int/article/empowering-nato-mdo-through-digital-transformation/.

34 See NATO, 'AJP-01, Allied Joint Doctrine Edition F Version 1', December 2022, p. 159, https://www.

coemed.org/files/stanags/01_AJP/AJP-01_EDF_V1_E_(1)_2437.pdf.

35 Benjamin Jensen and Erica Lonergan, 'Collective Defense in Space', Center for Strategic and International Studies, 8 July 2024, https://www.csis.org/analysis/collective-defense-space.

36 See Frank Wolfe, 'NATO Surveys the Space Capabilities of Member States', *Via Satellite*, 10 October 2024, https://www.satellitetoday.com/government-military/2024/10/10/nato-surveys-the-space-capabilities-of-member-nations/.

37 See Norwegian Defence Research Establishment, 'Norway to Develop Nanosatellite for Military Tactical Communication in the Arctic', https://www.ffi.no/en/news/norway-to-develop-nanosatellite-for-military-tactical-communication-in-the-arctic; and Joesph Trevithick and Tyler Rogoway, 'If SpaceX's Secret Constellation Is What We Think It Is, It's Game Changing', TWZ, 20 March 2024, https://www.twz.com/space/if-spacexs-secret-constellation-is-what-we-think-it-is-its-game-changing.

38 See Robert Wall, 'ArianeGroup See Ariane 64 Progress After Ariane 62 Delay', *Aviation Week Network*, 13 November 2024, https://aviationweek.com/space/launch-vehicles-propulsion/arianegroup-sees-ariane-64-progress-after-ariane-62-delay.

39 'Orbital Launches of 2024', Gunter's Space Page, https://space.skyrocket.de/doc_chr/lau2024.htm.

40 See Rachel Jewett, 'Iceye to Lead Industry Consortium for Finnish MoD F-35 Program', *Via Satellite*, 20 November 2024, https://www.satellitetoday.com/government-military/2024/11/20/iceye-to-lead-industry-consortium-for-finnish-mod-f-35-program/; and ICEYE, 'ICEYE and U.S. Army to Pursue Collaborative Research and Development', 18 November 2021, https://www.iceye.com/press/press-releases/iceye-and-us-army-to-pursue-collaborative-research-and-development.

41 Other US allies face analogous risks. South Korea and Japan are reliant on the United States for key C4ISR capabilities. Although North Korea is a less formidable challenge than Russia, the prospect of losing such capabilities is an obvious concern for South Korean and Japanese defence planners.

Copyright © 2025 The International Institute for Strategic Studies

Europe Needs *Less* Defence Cooperation

Bence Nemeth

During Donald Trump's 2024 campaign for the US presidency, he repeatedly questioned Europe's strategic relevance and the necessity of maintaining US security commitments to NATO allies.[1] After he secured his second term, European politicians and analysts renewed their calls for deeper defence cooperation among European countries. Their rationale was straightforward: if Washington's security guarantees could no longer be assumed as strong as before, Europe by itself would need to present a more credible deterrent against Russia. Since Trump's inauguration, his administration has only reinforced perceptions of American disaffection with the traditional transatlantic security bond and hostility towards Europe's political mainstream, consistently supporting Russia's position in the Russo-Ukrainian war, belittling Ukrainian President Volodymyr Zelenskyy, embracing far-right European parties sympathetic with Russia, and calling for higher European defence spending even though that of most European NATO members now exceeds the 2% of GDP benchmark.[2]

Since the end of the Cold War, Europe's default response to new security challenges has been to call for more cooperation, whether under NATO, the European Union or smaller, minilateral arrangements. Actual results have often fallen short of ambitious goals.[3] Despite such limitations, Europe has

Bence Nemeth is a senior lecturer at the Defence Studies Department of King's College London, where he primarily teaches British and international military officers at the UK Defence Academy, and author of *How to Achieve Defence Cooperation in Europe? The Subregional Approach* (Bristol University Press, 2022). He is the co-founder of the King's Centre for Defence Economics and Management, and will serve as its first executive director.

Survival | vol. 67 no. 3 | June–July 2025 | pp. 109–124 https://doi.org/10.1080/00396338.2025.2508090

long benefited from collaborative approaches to defence. After the Cold War ended, individual European governments underfunded their militaries, so pooling resources for military operations and jointly developing capabilities helped many European nations afford and maintain modern armed forces. European armed forces are now far more integrated, inter-operable and accustomed to working together than they were in the 1990s. But these financial and military advantages come with significant downsides. Political and bureaucratic complexity have slowed decision-making and increased interdependence. In effect, European militaries have traded speed and autonomy in operations and capability development for cost savings.[4]

Until recently, this trade-off was manageable mainly because funding was the scarcest resource. But the Russian invasion of Ukraine and the Trump administration's pressure on European defence have made time the more urgent constraint. European militaries must now boost their capabilities rapidly to bolster deterrence in a more volatile environment. Deeper cooperation, however beneficial in theory, often prolongs procurement and development processes. Europe's front-line states should focus on accelerating national-level preparations first, and then integrate or synchronise those efforts at higher NATO or EU levels. Such an approach balances the immediate need for speed with the longer-term benefits of collective defence and strategic alignment.

Multinational defence cooperation in Europe

States engage in military cooperation for two principal reasons. Firstly, they might lack sufficient resources to develop a given capability on their own. It was for that reason that Britain, Germany, Italy and Spain jointly developed the Eurofighter *Typhoon* in the 1980s and 1990s. Secondly, they could be seeking broader political legitimacy, as the United States, though capable of operating alone, did in enlisting allies to join it in prosecuting the Korean War, the Gulf War and the Iraq and Afghanistan wars, as well as, with less success, the Vietnam War.

Defence cooperation takes multiple forms, including joint procurement, multinational formations, integrated training exercises and doctrinal alignment. While some defence collaboration in Europe arose during the

Cold War, most NATO forces remained nationally organised under broader NATO command structures, with individual corps committed to NATO Army Group headquarters.[5] After the Cold War, when national defence budgets shrank, NATO planners feared that the Alliance's force structure would collapse.[6] Encouraging the creation of multinational units and emphasising military integration thus became politically acceptable methods for maintaining capabilities within tighter budgets. This meant establishing several multinational corps. By the 2000s, even battalion-level units could include troops from multiple countries. Today, NATO features highly integrated but fragmented multinational formations, such as its Forward Land Forces battlegroups, in which units of 1,000 to 4,000 troops, untested in high-intensity warfare, may contain soldiers from half a dozen nations.[7]

Multinational projects did help to integrate new NATO and EU members into institutional frameworks and encouraged increased interactions between European armed forces. But their military benefits remain questionable. Establishing multinational units is inherently more complex and time-consuming than forming national ones, mainly because these units are often virtual, with supporting elements based in home countries and coalescing only during exercises or operations. Although NATO standards significantly enhance inter-operability, differences in operational doctrines, problem-solving approaches, weapons systems and languages can impede seamless coordination.[8] Consequently, initiatives such as the NATO Response Force and the EU battlegroups have struggled to meet their military objectives and fill critical capability gaps.[9] Only a few bilateral and minilateral formations, such as the German–Dutch formations and the United Kingdom-led Joint Expeditionary Force (JEF), stand out as genuine success stories.

The integration of German and Dutch army units began in 1991 with the establishment of the 1 German–Netherlands Corps. This cooperation has since deepened, with three Dutch brigades now integrated into German divisions and one German battalion operating under a Dutch brigade.[10] Decades of joint experimentation between these two culturally distinct armies have streamlined division-level coordination and synchronised weapons procurement, greatly enhancing their inter-operability. Established in 2012, the

JEF's success is built on decades of close cooperation among member states through Nordic, Baltic and bilateral formats. Long-standing ties with the UK, JEF's framework nation, have further supported clear leadership and effective coordination. A shared perception of Russia's strategic threat has also reinforced political alignment and operational cohesion.[11] These cases demonstrate that successful multinational defence cooperation is possible, but they remain exceptions, requiring sustained political commitment, strategic alignment and consistent effort over long periods.

To be sure, large-scale European joint defence-industrial projects have created jobs, preserved critical European technical expertise, sustained the continent's defence-industrial base and generated financial returns through export agreements. They are also exceptional – they tend to be efforts that would likely be impossible to undertake nationally, such as a sixth-generation fighter programme – and have been plagued by delays and cost overruns. While nationally managed defence projects can also face these problems, they are generally less severe. Defence economists often apply the square-root rule to estimate the development costs of multinational projects. For example, a project involving four countries may cost twice as much overall in the development phase than a national project, though each country bears only half the financial burden it would if pursuing it independently. For development timelines, the cube-root rule is used, suggesting that a two-country collaboration could take approximately 26% longer, while a four-country effort might extend the development timeline by up to 60% relative to a comparable nationally managed project.[12]

Bastian Giegerich has aptly observed that 'collaborative programmes move at the speed of the slowest participant'.[13] Delays often stem from domestic political considerations, financial constraints or diverging national-capability requirements. The Eurofighter programme, for instance, was hampered by persistent disagreements among participating nations over design requirements, production shares and costs, leading to prolonged development timelines and inflated expenses. The A400M transport-aircraft project faced severe setbacks, arriving years behind schedule and requiring €1.4 billion in compensation to customers due to delays.[14] The NH90 military-transport helicopter encountered substantial difficulties during its development and testing phases, prompting disputes with several buyers, with Norway cancelling its contract after repeated delivery failures and maintenance issues.[15]

Bureaucratic inertia, competing national interests and inconsistent political commitment have often undermined NATO and EU mechanisms for streamlining defence planning and resource allocation. The NATO Defence Planning Process was designed to enhance coherence by aligning member states' military capabilities with Alliance-wide priorities. While it has improved transparency and encouraged burden-sharing discussions, it remains a voluntary arrangement, meaning that nations can still prioritise domestic considerations over collective goals. NATO's Smart Defence initiative sought to mitigate the effects of the 2008 financial crisis by promoting cost-effective multinational capability development, but it did not produce high-profile success.[16] At the same time, some of the NATO projects have yielded impressive operational dividends. For instance, the Strategic Airlift Capability programme provides participating NATO members with guaranteed access to three C-17 *Globemaster* III transport aircraft based in Hungary without requiring each country to maintain its own costly fleet of these assets and enabling rapid deployment of troops, humanitarian aid and military equipment.[17] For the most part, though, member states have been loath to relinquish national control over critical defence assets.

NATO's Smart Defence initiative did not produce high-profile success

Budget constraints, slow decision-making and diverging national priorities have likewise constrained EU mechanisms for facilitating joint capability development, including the European Defence Agency, created in 2004, and, more recently, Permanent Structured Cooperation (PESCO) and the European Defence Fund.[18] While the European Defence Fund provides crucial funding, these initiatives have yet to deliver significant, deployable capabilities. The Military Planning and Conduct Capability, established to enhance EU military command structures, remains under-resourced and has not achieved its goals.[19]

Smaller groups of like-minded countries have demonstrated that focused bilateral or regional cooperation can be more effective. The Nordic Defence Cooperation, comprising Denmark, Finland, Iceland, Norway and Sweden, has made notable progress in joint exercises, logistics and capability coordination.[20] The Lancaster House treaties between the UK and France have led to deeper operational collaboration, particularly with respect to expeditionary forces and nuclear deterrence.[21] But such arrangements face longer-term limitations imposed by political change (in particular, Brexit), economic turmoil and competing national-defence priorities.

Changing dynamics

Discounting shared transatlantic values and historical ties, the Trump administration is preparing to scale back its security commitments, including deployed personnel, to NATO.[22] Trump has suggested that the United States would not come to the defence of NATO allies who did not meet the Alliance's defence-spending target. In his view, with China now America's primary geopolitical concern, Europe does not matter enough or bring enough to the table to merit wholesale American protection. Intensifying this signal is the alarming pace at which Russia is rebuilding its military capabilities. Despite suffering catastrophic losses in Ukraine, Russia has been able to reconstitute its forces far more quickly than intelligence assessments initially predicted.[23] This has led Denmark, Estonia, Germany and Poland to issue independent warnings that Russia could directly challenge NATO militarily within five to eight years.[24] NATO's ability to deter and defend against a Russian military incursion may well depend largely on European capabilities. At present, most European nations are unprepared to meet this challenge at the necessary scale or speed.

Among European countries, only France, Germany and the UK have the military capacity to respond meaningfully to a major conflict on NATO's eastern and northern flanks, where allies – Bulgaria, Denmark, Estonia, Finland, Latvia, Lithuania, Norway, Poland, Romania and Sweden – are exposed to the Russian threat. Even these three European military powers face severe limitations. Under optimal conditions, they would need months to deploy a division (15–25,000 troops) – potentially too late to make a decisive difference.[25] Political paralysis in Berlin and Paris further complicates efforts to bolster military investments. The UK, however, has announced that it will increase defence spending to 2.5% of GDP by 2027.[26]

Front-line countries would expect support from allies to defend their own borders. NATO members with close ties to Russia, such as Hungary and Slovakia, would probably be reluctant to confront Moscow. Smaller members, including those in the Balkans, Luxembourg and Iceland, lack the military capabilities to offer meaningful support. Meanwhile, southern-flank countries like Greece and Turkiye face other pressing security concerns, while Italy, and Portugal and Spain allocate among the lowest proportions of their budgets to defence within NATO, and therefore would be less able to assist an ally under Russian attack.[27] This leaves only a handful of countries with extra capacity to help others, but they also have significant capability gaps. Although France and the UK possess nuclear arsenals, it is unclear whether and how these could be extended to front-line states.[28]

Less cooperation is more

Analysts and politicians have often illuminated European defence-procurement inefficiency by observing that European countries use five times as many weapons systems as the United States.[29] Kaja Kallas, the High Representative of the European Union for Foreign Affairs and Security Policy, has argued that Europeans therefore need 'to consolidate their defence industry and develop common weapons systems' and 'then use the same military systems' to help member states 'become more interoperable'.[30] Max Bergmann of the Center for Strategic and International Studies in Washington argues that the United States, in turn, needs to develop a structured plan to transition European security responsibilities to Europeans, which ideally should 'take place gradually and over decades', and that the Trump administration should pressure the EU to 'break up and integrate national defense industrial complexes, and harmonize regulations as well as reduce barriers to production'.[31]

These approaches overlook two critical factors. Firstly, lengthy integration processes for defence enhancements are a luxury that some European countries – especially on NATO's northern and eastern flanks – cannot afford. Secondly, the implicit assumption that inefficiencies are mere system flaws that can be overcome through regulation is simplistic. Redundancies are inevitable when sovereign states with differing strategic priorities, threat perceptions and industrial policies, rather than NATO or the EU as a unit, remain the primary actors in military procurement and force development.

European countries farther from Russia are likely to perceive its threat as less urgent and, consequently, spend less on defence than those closer by. While the Russian military remains formidable, it is not as powerful as the Red Army was during the Cold War, and does not pose a direct military threat to most EU and NATO members. The upshot is that NATO members on the eastern and northern flanks cannot afford to wait for consensus among their partners and allies, and must take the initiative and prioritise national-defence preparations.

Not all of them have taken this reality on board. Gotland, the strategically vital Swedish island in the Baltic Sea, now hosts only 370 Swedish troops compared to 25,000 during the Cold War.[32] When Swedish Foreign Minister Tobias Billström was asked whether it would see a military build-up, he responded merely that Sweden would participate in NATO committees handling the issue and await recommendations from the Supreme Allied Commander Europe before making any decisions.[33] This approach does not suit the new circumstances. A European country's primary responsibility is still to protect its own territory, proactively informing NATO (and the EU) of its defence plans rather than passively waiting for instructions. NATO's (and the EU's) regional defence plans should adapt to the needs of its front-line members – not the other way around.

South Korea provides an illustrative example of how a nation can develop a highly capable and efficient military without relying excessively on slow-moving multinational defence cooperation. Despite a defence budget that is approximately 60% of the UK's, South Korea maintains conventional forces comparable in size and quality to those of France, Germany and the UK combined, with higher ground-force readiness and war-stock levels, underlining the fact that military effectiveness depends on strategic focus and efficiency as much as spending.[34] It is true that South Korean forces are deeply integrated with US ones, operating under the

Combined Forces Command framework whereby war plans are jointly developed with the US, and an American general has wartime operational control over US and South Korean forces. But South Korea retains full control over its defence procurement.

Seoul has prioritised rapid indigenous arms development over lengthy multinational projects, accelerating domestic production of advanced weapons systems. This allows South Korea to domestically manufacture about 80% of its armaments, which are now highly competitive on the global defence market.[35] Nevertheless, South Korea still pursues selective foreign purchases and collaborations in areas where capability gaps remain. It bought F-35A fighters off the shelf from the United States and is cooperating on the development of the 4.5-generation KF-21 fighter jet with Indonesia. However, the KF-21 programme has been hampered by prolonged disputes over funding and technology transfer, reinforcing Seoul's wariness about large multinational defence projects.[36]

Circumstances compel NATO's front-line states to lead by example

Present circumstances compel NATO's front-line states to lead by example in rapidly expanding their forces, immediately procuring weapons and prioritising both domestic arms manufacturing and off-the-shelf solutions rather than relying on slow EU-wide initiatives. They will need to allocate to defence significantly more resources, probably 4–5% of GDP, than other European nations, which might spend around 2–3.5%. Many of them are already on the right track. Instead of waiting for multinational solutions or the slow delivery of European manufacturers, Poland has swiftly procured cutting-edge weapons systems from the United States and South Korea, inter-operable within NATO standards. Poland already spends over 4% of its GDP on defence – the highest proportion in NATO – and will reach 5% soon. This will allow it to undertake the Alliance's most ambitious military build-up and potentially make the Polish army the strongest in European NATO.[37]

In 2025, Denmark approved a significant increase in its defence budget, raising it to 3.2% of GDP within the same year, with the additional funds primarily earmarked for equipment procurement. At a press conference, Prime Minister Mette Frederiksen emphasised the urgency of the situation, stating: 'There is one message for the chief of defence: Buy, buy, buy ... If we can't get the best equipment, buy the next best. There's only one thing that counts now and that is speed.' Referring to the rising threat from Russia, she confirmed that procurement would bypass Denmark's usual lengthy tender processes to accelerate delivery.[38]

Finland too is moving in a promising direction. Having retained conscription, it maintains a large, well-trained reserve with the theoretical ability to mobilise 280,000 troops rapidly, and has acquired F-35 jets, *Leopard* 2A6 tanks and K9 howitzers. Doctrinally, the Finnish armed forces stress a self-reliant defence resonant of the South Korean model.[39] Granted, it has not tested its mobilisation capability at scale and still fields a substantial amount of Cold War-era equipment, which indexes its acknowledged need to enhance NATO-level regional cooperation and coordination.

Lithuania and Estonia too have pledged to raise defence spending to 5% of GDP.[40] Even with such increases, though, front-line states like the Baltics, with smaller populations and more limited resources, cannot field forces large enough to withstand a full-scale Russian assault alone. Despite firm commitments to building up their militaries, they will require external support to maintain a credible deterrent. Forward-stationed NATO forces – particularly from France, Germany and the UK – are essential for plugging capability gaps and reinforcing the Baltics. It follows that NATO's strongest and wealthiest European nations must continue to grow their national militaries with an eye to maintaining permanent, well-equipped forward deployments.[41]

Focusing on national-defence capabilities first, though, should not involve a disregard for Alliance cohesion or inter-operability. On the contrary, front-line states should align their capability development with NATO standards and doctrines, while continuing to inform both NATO and the EU of their plans via existing coordination mechanisms. This transparency ensures compatibility and helps avoid duplication. Furthermore, countries most likely to fight together, such as members of the JEF, must maintain close consultation as well. This approach enables the rapid development of national capabilities while preserving inter-operability from the outset, thereby strengthening NATO and EU military capacity, reinforcing Alliance cohesion and laying the foundation for deeper multinational integration over time.

* * *

The new strategic reality, with the US playing a substantially reduced role in European security, demands an urgent shift in priorities. Time, rather than funding, has become the most critical resource. Less cooperation, of course, does not mean no cooperation. Rather, it means front-loading national-defence preparations so that Europe can respond faster to threats before layering in multinational frameworks that refine and coordinate them. This strategy is particularly critical for European nations bordering Russia. Their need to boost military capabilities is more urgent than that of countries farther away, many of which do not view Russia as an immediate threat. They are compelled to rely less on substantial American support or, in the short term, allied European support, and to build national military capabilities that emphasise speed and efficiency. Increasing self-reliance should become the guiding principle for their cooperation with other European countries. A 'national capabilities first, then integrate' mindset leaves room for strategic alignment at the NATO and EU levels, but ensures that vital capabilities are not delayed by slower-moving coalitions.

Notes

1 See, for example, Varg Folkman, 'Trump's NATO Threat Denounced Across Europe', *Politico*, 11 February 2024, https://www.politico.eu/article/donald-trump-nato-threat-denounced-across-europe/.

2 See, for example, Dana H. Allin and Jonathan Stevenson, 'America and Russia Are On the Same Side Now', *New York Times*, 25 February 2025, https://www.nytimes.com/2025/02/25/opinion/russia-europe-trump-vance.html; and Sophia Besch and Tara Varma, 'Alliance of Revisionists: A New Era for the Transatlantic Relationship', *Survival*, vol. 67, no. 2, April–May 2025, pp. 7–38.

3 See Vesa Kanniainen and Juha-Matti Lehtonen, 'Cooperative Procurement in Building National Defence: Why

Are There So Few?', *Defence and Peace Economics*, vol. 31, no. 2, March 2020, pp. 201–19; and Sean Monaghan, 'Solving Europe's Defence Dilemma: Overcoming the Challenges to European Defense Cooperation', CSIS Brief, Center for Strategic and International Studies, 1 March 2023, https://www.csis.org/analysis/solving-europes-defense-dilemma-overcoming-challenges-european-defense-cooperation.

4 See Bence Nemeth, 'Military Innovation and Capability Development in a Multinational Context: The Costs and Benefits of Multinational Cooperation', *Air Power Journal*, Fall 2022, pp. 1–12.

5 See Anthony King, *The Transformation of Europe's Armed Forces: From the Rhine to Afghanistan* (Cambridge: Cambridge University Press, 2011), pp. 40–4; and Bence Nemeth, *How to Achieve Defence Cooperation in Europe? The Subregional Approach* (Bristol: Bristol University Press, 2022), pp. 24–34.

6 See Martin A. Smith, *NATO in the First Decade After the Cold War* (Dordrecht: Kluwer Academic Publishers, 2000), pp. 66–8.

7 See Sean Monaghan, Pierre Morcos and Andrew Lohsen, 'Designing New Battlegroups: Advice for NATO Planners', Center for Strategic and International Studies, 15 April 2022, https://www.csis.org/analysis/designing-new-battlegroups-advice-nato-planners.

8 See Michael Alexander and Timothy Garden, 'The Arithmetic of Defence Policy', *International Affairs*, vol. 77, no. 3, July 2001, pp. 509–29.

9 See Yf Reykers, 'EU Battlegroups: High Costs, No Benefits', *Contemporary Security Policy*, vol. 38, no. 3, July 2017, pp. 457–70; and Jens Ringsmose and Sten Rynning, 'The NATO Response Force: A Qualified Failure No More?', *Contemporary Security Policy*, vol. 38, no. 3, July 2017, pp. 443–56.

10 See Dick Zandee and Davis Ellison, 'Germany's Zeitenwende and the Consequences for German–Dutch Defence Cooperation', Clingendael Report, January 2024, https://www.clingendael.org/sites/default/files/2024-01/Report_Germany_Zeitenwende_consequences_German_Dutch_defence_cooperation.pdf.

11 See Ed Arnold, 'The Joint Expeditionary Force and Its Contribution to European Security', RUSI Occasional Paper, December 2024, https://static.rusi.org/the-joint-expeditionary-force-and-its-contribution-to-european-security.pdf.

12 See Keith Hartley, *The Economics of Defence Policy: A New Perspective* (Abingdon: Routledge, 2011), p. 175.

13 Bastian Giegerich, 'Budget Crunch: Implications for European Defence', *Survival*, vol. 52, no. 4, August–September 2010, p. 94.

14 See 'Airbus Group Hit by €1.4 Billion in Charges in the Second Quarter', CNBC, 27 July 2016, https://www.cnbc.com/2016/07/27/airbus-group-hit-by-14-billion-euros-in-charges-in-the-second-quarter.html.

15 See 'Norwegian MoD Cancelled Helicopter Contract with NHI', *Naval Technology*, June 2022, https://www.naval-technology.com/analyst-comment/norwegian-mod-cancelled-helicopter-contract-with-nhi/.

16 See Bastian Giegerich, 'NATO's Smart Defence: Who's Buying?', *Survival*, vol. 54, no. 3, June–July 2012, pp. 69–77.

17 See Nemeth, 'Military Innovation and Capability Development in a Multinational Context'.

18 See Sven Biscop, 'European Defence and PESCO: Don't Waste the Chance', EU IDEA Policy Papers No. 1, 5 May 2020, https://www.iai.it/en/pubblicazioni/c12/european-defence-and-pesco-dont-waste-chance; and Pierre Haroche, 'Supranationalism Strikes Back: A Neofunctionalist Account of the European Defence Fund', *Journal of European Public Policy*, vol. 27, no. 6, April 2019, pp. 853–72.

19 See Yf Reykers, 'A Permanent Headquarters Under Construction? The Military Planning and Conduct Capability as a Proximate Principal', *Journal of European Integration*, vol. 41, no. 6, April 2019, pp. 783–99.

20 See Håkon Lunde Saxi, 'The Rise, Fall and Resurgence of Nordic Defence Cooperation', *International Affairs*, vol. 95, no. 3, May 2019, pp. 659–80.

21 See Alice Pannier, 'The Anglo-French Defence Partnership After the "Brexit" Vote: New Incentives and New Dilemmas', *Global Affairs*, vol. 2, no. 5, February 2017, pp. 481–90.

22 See, for example, Gordon Lubold, Dan De Luce and Courtney Kube, 'Pentagon Considering Proposal to Cut Thousands of Troops from Europe, Officials Say', NBC News, 8 April 2025, https://www.nbcnews.com/politics/national-security/pentagon-considering-proposal-cut-thousands-troops-europe-officials-sa-rcna199603.

23 See Dara Massicot, 'Russian Military Reconstitution: 2030 Pathways and Prospects', Carnegie Endowment for International Peace, September 2024, https://carnegie-production-assets.s3.amazonaws.com/static/files/Massicot-Reconstitution-final_10-1.pdf; and Noah Robertson, 'Russian Military "Almost Completely Reconstituted," US Official Says', *Defense News*, 3 April 2024, https://www.defensenews.com/pentagon/2024/04/03/russian-military-almost-completely-reconstituted-us-official-says/.

24 See Bence Nemeth, 'Defending NATO Without the Americans', in Jacob Parakilas and Artur Honich (eds), *Strategic Commentaries: Essays About the UK, NATO, China, Russia, North Korea and Iran* (Santa Monica, CA: RAND Corporation, 2024), p. 31.

25 See R.D. Hooker, 'The State of NATO: An American View', *Survival*, vol. 64, no. 3, June–July 2022, pp. 103–13.

26 Stephen Castle and Mark Landler, 'U.K. Announces Increase in Military Spending Ahead of Trump Meeting', *New York Times*, 25 February 2025, https://www.nytimes.com/2025/02/25/world/europe/uk-defense-spending-starmer.html.

27 See NATO, 'Defence Expenditure of NATO Countries (2014–2024)', 17 June 2024, p. 4, https://www.nato.int/nato_static_fl2014/assets/pdf/2024/6/pdf/240617-def-exp-2024-en.pdf.

28 See Héloïse Fayet et al., 'Forum: European Nuclear Deterrence and Donald Trump', *Survival*, vol. 67, no. 1, February–March 2025, pp. 123–42; and Laura Kayali, Thorsten Jungholt and Philipp Fritz, 'Europe's Debate over US Nuclear Weapons Heats Up', *Politico*, 4

July 2024, https://www.politico.com/news/magazine/2024/07/04/europe-us-nuclear-weapons-00166070.

29 See, for example, McKinsey and Company, 'The Future of European Defence: Tackling the Productivity Challenge', 2013, p. 14, https://www.mckinsey.com/~/media/mckinsey/industries/public%20and%20social%20sector/our%20insights/enlisting%20productivity%20to%20reinforce%20european%20defense/the%20future%20of%20european%20defence.pdf.

30 European Union External Action, 'Defence: Speech by High Representative/Vice-President Kaja Kallas at the Annual Conference of the European Defence Agency', 22 January 2025, https://www.eeas.europa.eu/eeas/defence-speech-high-representativevice-president-kaja-kallas-annual-conference-european-defence_en.

31 Max Bergmann, 'Trump Needs a Plan to Get Europeans to Step Up on Defense', Center for Strategic and International Studies, 31 January 2025, https://www.csis.org/analysis/trump-needs-plan-get-europeans-step-defense.

32 Henry Foy and Richard Milne, 'Sweden Ready to Fortify Crucial Baltic Island, Says PM', *Financial Times*, 12 March 2024, https://www.ft.com/content/4d263668-87fc-44cc-846b-ff4f7c3e0414; and Alex Traub, 'Newly Alarmed Sweden Concludes Military Drill with U.S. Marines', *New York Times*, 12 June 2022, https://www.nytimes.com/2022/06/12/world/europe/us-sweden-military-drill.html.

33 'Swedish Foreign Minister: NATO Must Get Ready for a Russian Attack', DW News, 21 March 2024, https://www.youtube.com/watch?v=tvjrxQr9kB8.

34 See Bence Nemeth, 'South Korean Military Power: Lessons Europe Can Learn from Seoul on Spending Defence Budgets Efficiently', *RUSI Journal*, vol. 169, nos 1–2, June 2024, pp. 92–101.

35 See Richard A. Bitzinger, 'The Defense Industry of the Republic of Korea', in Keith Hartley and Jean Belin (eds), *The Economics of the Global Defence Industry* (Abingdon: Routledge, 2019), p. 380.

36 See Lee Keun-Pyung, 'Defense Officials Meet in Jakarta over Stalled Fighter Jet Project', *Korea JoongAng Daily*, 24 March 2025, https://koreajoongangdaily.joins.com/news/2025-03-24/national/defense/Defense-officials-meet-in-Jakarta-over-stalled-fighter-jet-project/2268705.

37 See Robert Czulda, 'Poland's Future Armed Forces Take Shape', European Security and Defence, 3 September 2024, https://euro-sd.com/2024/09/articles/40091/polands-future-armed-forces-take-shape/.

38 Quoted in Stine Jacobsen and Jacob Gronholt-Pedersen, 'Denmark Will "Buy, Buy, Buy" Military Gear, Prime Minister Says', Reuters, 19 February 2025, https://www.reuters.com/world/europe/denmark-boost-2025-26-defence-spending-by-7-bln-2025-02-19/.

39 See Heljä Ossa and Tommi Koivula, 'What Would Finland Bring to the Table for NATO?', *War on the Rocks*, 9 May 2022, https://warontherocks.com/2022/05/what-would-finland-bring-to-the-table-for-nato/.

40 Richard Milne and Marton Dunai, 'Lithuania and Estonia Pledge to Meet Donald Trump's 5% Target on Defence Spending', *Financial Times*, 27 January 2025, https://www.ft.com/content/a999f239-3104-419a-95dc-bf9c04242b2f.

41 See Nemeth, 'Defending NATO Without the Americans', pp. 32–4.

Copyright © 2025 The International Institute for Strategic Studies

Bimodal Deterrence: Sea Denial and Sea Control in US Maritime Strategy

James J. Wirtz

US Navy strategists are considering ways to deter a major conflict in the Western Pacific, which is leading towards a still-undefined bimodal maritime strategy that encompasses both sea denial and sea control.[1] The evolving maritime deterrent will be based on both deterrence by denial and deterrence by punishment. Deterrence by denial suggests that the navy is prepared to use kinetic and non-kinetic capabilities to prevent an opponent from achieving its objectives in the event of deterrence failure, while deterrence by punishment suggests that the navy is prepared to inflict costs on an opponent until it is compelled to abandon its ill-gotten gains or ongoing nefarious activities.[2] The renewed emphasis on deterrence as a strategy to preserve the peace is itself a departure in naval operations, which, though traditionally centred on deterrence, over the past few decades have involved almost continuous war fighting.[3]

A bimodal approach to maritime strategy can create a robust deterrent, encouraging an opponent to conclude that the risks and costs of undertaking overt aggression or seeking to impose a fait accompli far outweigh the potential gains. Nevertheless, no one has yet explained how deterrence by denial and deterrence by punishment are supported by a bimodal (sea-denial and sea-control) approach to maritime strategy.[4] What are the advantages

James J. Wirtz has written extensively about intelligence, nuclear deterrence and maritime strategy. He is currently co-editing the 8th edition of *Strategy in the Contemporary World* (Oxford University Press, forthcoming in 2026).

Survival | vol. 67 no. 3 | June–July 2025 | pp. 125–148 https://doi.org/10.1080/00396338.2025.2508091

of integrating bimodal capabilities into a maritime-deterrent strategy? How can deterrence by denial and deterrence by punishment work together to alter the risks and incentives perceived by an opponent, and help preserve the peace?

The strategic setting

Over the last several decades, the United States' competitors have developed anti-access and area-denial capabilities and strategies that rely on increasingly available information-age technologies to hold naval targets at risk.[5] These reconnaissance-strike complexes often outrange the force-projection capabilities of the US Navy, which are largely based on aircraft-carrier aviation. The navy can battle its way through opponents' sea-denial capabilities, but there is no telling how much time will elapse before the full force of the fleet, along with the remainder of the joint force, can be assembled, sent into harm's way and significantly attrit an opponent's forces. As currently postured, the US Navy's carrier strike groups thus constitute a deterrent threat that might appear 'contestable' to an opponent.[6] For the deterrence scenario that preoccupies today's naval officers – an amphibious assault on Taiwan by China's People's Liberation Army – the strategic balance, which is exacerbated by the tyranny of distance, suggests that the US Navy might arrive on the scene too late to prevent the occupation of the island.[7]

Because it is easier to threaten the use of force than to execute deterrent threats in the breach, a risk-accepting opponent might seek to present the United States with a fait accompli that does not inflict serious material or personnel costs on the United States.[8] The Americans might in turn conclude that the effort to force a return to the status quo ante bellum is not worth the benefits. As Elbridge Colby has put it:

> The *fait accompli* strategy works by moving or attacking in a way that forces the defender's counterpunch to have to be so costly and risky as to seem not worth the benefit of reversing it. It is most insidious when the violence needed to succeed with the *fait accompli* is less grievous, making the very great response needed to eject the attacker seem not only too perilous but also unjust.[9]

A quick victory would thus shift the onus of escalation onto Washington, which would be faced with the decision to either reach a diplomatic settlement or embark on what could possibly be a high-intensity conventional war. The United States would find itself in an inferior position when it comes to strategic bargaining because a fait accompli would squarely place the decision between peace and a potentially catastrophic war in Washington's hands, while Beijing could savour its new-found position as a champion of peace and compromise.[10]

Risk-acceptant challengers tend to believe that when deterrence fails, the victim of the setback is more likely to settle than to fight. For instance, the Japanese believed that it would be possible to reach a negotiated settlement with the United States following the attack on Pearl Harbor – after all, Nazi Germany posed a greater threat to US interests. As Roberta Wohlstetter noted, the Japanese assumed that 'the United States, with ten times the military potential and a reputation for waging war until unconditional victory, would after a short struggle simply accept annihilation of a considerable part of its air and naval forces and the whole of its power in the Far East'.[11] In the days before Iraq's seizure of Kuwait, Saddam Hussein told the US ambassador to Baghdad that while the United States possessed the military capability to eject Iraq from Kuwait, it lacked the political will to suffer 10,000 casualties per day to do so.[12] Leaders who knowingly cross deterrent 'red lines' tend to believe that their targets will experience some form of external military constraint, domestic political opposition or a fundamental change of heart when it comes to acting on its stated deterrent threats. From the challenger's perspective, the more time it takes to mount a serious response to its aggression, the more time there is to mull over the wisdom of escalating the conflict. The expectation is that the victims of the deterrence failure will eventually conclude that the game is not worth the candle.

As things turned out, Tokyo and Baghdad gambled and lost. Nevertheless, those being deterred understand that deterrence is intended to preserve the peace and to ensure that international affairs are moderated by rules-based institutions, democratic principles and diplomacy. Above all else, deterrence is intended to prevent the outbreak of hostilities; it is adopted by nations that do not want to engage in conflict as a routine instrument of foreign policy or to engage in ongoing insults to international decorum (such as hybrid warfare) to realise incremental gains or advantages, or to create chaos to undermine international or domestic stability. Risk-acceptant challengers recognise that deterrence is a 'peace-preservation strategy', and that states that adopt this strategy do so because they want to *prevent*, not engage in, war. Challengers also understand that war constitutes a failure of deterrence as a national strategy. It is not unreasonable to assume that in the aftermath of such a failure, a fundamental reassessment of national strategy and priorities will occur. History shows that challengers often expect this to lead to policies that better fit their preferences – that opponents will choose to *not* honour deterrent commitments because that would exacerbate a conflict they wanted to avoid in the first place.

It is worth noting that deterrence is not an exact science and that circumstances may still favour the side employing a deterrence strategy. Challengers may well be stymied even in the event that deterrence fails, despite the advantages they may enjoy. Still, a fait accompli strategy, including the use of strategic surprise, suggests itself as a way to alter the Taiwan issue quickly.[13]

A bimodal maritime-deterrence strategy

Although a response to a Taiwan invasion would have to involve an all-arms approach across all warfare domains, the situation in the Western Pacific highlights the specific requirements of *maritime* deterrence. Although the idea of a bimodal fleet has been around for many years, the contemporary strategic setting is pushing the US Navy towards an approach that integrates both deterrence by denial and deterrence by punishment to prevent overt aggression.[14] Sea denial provides the capability to contest an opponent's attack immediately – the fight can begin as soon as the opponent crosses red lines that exist not only in principle but also physically in situ. Sea control, by contrast, relies on the capability to support beleaguered friends and allies by keeping lines of communication open in a crisis or war, thereby increasing the credibility of deterrence by denial. Sea control also holds out the prospect of deterrence by punishment by offering a way to inflict pain on an opponent until an unwanted activity is terminated, and even to create conventional escalation dominance. In the Western Pacific, the US Navy's bimodal strategy is intended to offset a potential opponent's advantage in littoral waters that are within range of opposing reconnaissance-strike complexes.[15] It involves two different types of fleets that would present two different types of deterrent threats.

Sea denial

A sea-denial capability signals to all concerned that the United States is unwilling to cede the opening move in a nascent conflict to the opponent, or to allow it to impose a fait accompli. In other words, the US Navy's sea-denial assets, which consist of autonomous and semi-autonomous systems, crewed platforms and more exotic capabilities still under development, will always be postured to interfere with nefarious actions through a response that is geared to whatever warning (hours, days, weeks) is projected to be available. A ready sea-denial capability bolsters deterrence because it forces the opponent to deal with the immediate likelihood of active resistance to its actions and to keep up with continuously evolving sea-denial capabilities. Ongoing improvements in the sea-denial force inject doubt into the opponent's planning process – one can never be sure if some exquisite operation planned against a specific capability has accounted for the latest innovation. Sea denial deters fait accompli strategies because it eliminates the prospect of a relatively low-cost, quick grab by promising significant resistance at the point of deterrence failure. A readily available sea-denial capability reduces reliance on warning, which minimises an opponent's incentive to devise and use stratagems intended to achieve strategic surprise. Sea denial also shifts the onus of escalation back onto the opponent, because the decision to attack will result in a serious conventional conflict, especially when the authority to respond to an attack is pre-delegated by political authorities. A deterrent threat that will be executed immediately and automatically when aggression occurs is simply more credible than a threat that will take weeks or months to execute. US deterrence in the Western Pacific seems to be focused on defending the territorial integrity of Taiwan and not to involve a 'MacArthur-like' commitment to reverse Beijing's military control of the island should this be established. This strategic objective suggests that deterrence by denial and an associated sea-denial capability offer the best pathway to achieve current US objectives in the Western Pacific.

Sea denial also reduces the opponent's confidence that they can control the risk of escalation, which is the objective that can make a fait accompli strategy attractive. It is impossible to estimate with confidence what will happen once red lines are crossed and sea-denial operations commence – the attacker might suffer modest, moderate or severe equipment loss and personnel casualties, leading to the need to either back down or somehow escalate the conflict. Admittedly, deterrence by denial also creates a risk that the United States might have to choose between escalation and defeat, but at least this decision would be made in the context of preserving the status quo. A challenger might see the inherent risk of escalation as greater in a situation intended to preserve the status quo compared to its opponent's willingness to risk or to deliberately engage in escalation to reverse a fait accompli.

In any event, sea denial not only creates the prospect of immediate conflict if deterrence should fail, but it also creates an immediate risk of escalation once battle commences. This risk of escalation bolsters deterrence, because leaders who deliberately choose to cross deterrent red lines expect the ensuing conflict to be short and relatively painless.[16] By posing an inherent risk of escalation, sea denial can reduce expectations that a conflict can be controlled to produce a positive outcome quickly. This can help discourage opponents from taking a gamble on a fait accompli. A ready sea-denial capability reduces the likelihood that an opponent will believe that US officials might choose not to respond following a failure of deterrence – sea denial suggests to a potential aggressor that there is no way to sidestep active and immediate opposition and achieve limited objectives.

Sea control

The US Navy's sea-control capability – carrier strike groups, surface action groups, and the intelligence, surveillance and reconnaissance capabilities that support them – serve several important functions when it comes to deterrence by denial, deterrence by punishment, and the assurance of America's friends and allies. Firstly, sea control – meaning the ability to prevent an opponent from using regional or global ocean routes for their own commercial or military purposes – increases the credibility of the navy's deterrence-by-denial strategy by demonstrating that the United States has the wherewithal to honour its deterrent policies. It assures allies of the US commitment to their defence by signalling that, come what may, the US Navy will maintain its communications with allies and partners to prevent efforts to coerce or isolate them, and to facilitate the movement of forces and materiel to conflict regions. Deterrence by denial loses credibility if the territory to be protected can be isolated from support, becoming a lone bastion that will eventually fall to military and political pressure. Sea control suggests to opponents that sea-denial capabilities will not be short-lived, as they can be resupplied and renewed as necessary, and will eventually be supported by the entire joint force.

Secondly, sea control is denial plus the ability to use the oceans for purposes of manoeuvre, support and strike. It can enable a deterrence-by-punishment strategy by providing a way for the navy to engage in horizontal escalation to increase the cumulative costs of aggression. Indeed, this type of deterrence has been embraced by an 'offshore-control' school of US naval strategists, who suggest that in the event of hostilities, the United States should interdict China's global trade while helping the island states of the Western Pacific to protect their territorial integrity. The disruption of China's economy, accompanied by a stalemated maritime conflict around Taiwan, could help end hostilities with minimal loss of life or the destruction of economic infrastructure.[17]

Thus, sea control overcomes a limitation of deterrence by denial. By its very nature, deterrence by denial focuses on a specific location or set of adversary goals, which can encourage an opponent to perceive that it is possible to minimise the risks and costs of aggression by striking a limited target set, avoiding attacks that generate collateral damage, or not threatening or attacking third parties, actions that tend to force the burden of escalation onto others. Sea control, however, provides a way to increase the costs and risks of aggression by targeting an opponent's economic or military assets on a global scale, increasing the cost of aggression at a pace determined by the victim of deterrence failure, while securing one's own lines of communication. Sea-control forces, for example, could use prize law to seize an opponent's vessels and, with appropriate court approval, use those goods and ships.[18] Deterrence by punishment thus reduces the attractiveness of strategies that substitute time for violence to achieve their objectives – it is hard to isolate or harass an opponent indefinitely if the costs of aggression are beyond one's control and continue to accumulate with time. Most importantly, sea control provides a way to muster and move resources on a global scale to a conflict region, which adds to the credibility of both a deterrence-by-denial and a deterrence-by-punishment strategy. Sea control suggests that time is not on the side of the party that violates deterrent red lines, which reduces the attractiveness of slow-moving, 'low-cost' strategies.

Deterrence by punishment might also be used as an instrument of escalation dominance – that is, it can be used to deter escalation by the opponent. Sea control does not necessarily have to be immediately employed to compel an opponent to desist in some undesirable action; punishment can be undertaken in response to an escalatory move on the opponent's part. For instance, deterrence by punishment can be withheld as an intra-conflict deterrent to reduce the attraction of horizontal or vertical escalation. In this way, sea control also serves as a means to undertake anti-access and area denial on a global scale – it suggests that the opponent will face a non-permissive environment, limiting its military and economic options. Sea control impedes the opponent's ability to conduct a deterrence-by-punishment or compellent strategy by inflicting costs on the United States and its allies.

Thirdly, sea control assures friends and allies that the United States possesses the capability needed to execute deterrent threats if red lines are crossed. This is especially critical in a maritime setting, where governments might believe that they will have to sidestep aggression, especially if the United States finds it difficult to remain engaged in the theatre.[19] In other words, deterrence can unravel if friends and allies come to believe that US forces will not be available when needed. James H. Bergeron has described the important role sea control plays in bolstering NATO's deterrent posture:

> The maritime dimension of NATO is a spectrum and continuum; a strategic unity that links the Sea Lines of Communication (SLOCs) across

> the Atlantic, the North Atlantic and GIUK [Greenland–Iceland–United Kingdom] Gap, the Norwegian Sea, the Arctic passages to the Pole, the Mediterranean, and the Black Sea. But also, beyond that, to the global seas and oceans that feed our trade and commerce … The seas matter tactically due to the potential threat of sea-based missile attack on Allied ships or indeed land targets. It matters operationally in the ability of an adversary to disrupt SLOCs between North America and Europe and within the NATO Area of Responsibility. And it matters politically and strategically as the symbol of our essential connectedness as an Alliance.[20]

The US has global deterrent commitments, and its friends and allies have great-power neighbours that are increasingly capable and belligerent. Sea control can assure these partners that the United States will always be able to influence worldwide events.

Deterrence in practice

Although deterrence is intended to maintain the peace, it does so by focusing on efforts to prepare for war, to threaten war, to conduct war, to inflict serious costs on the opponent, and to generate risks of horizontal and vertical escalation if red lines are violated. This might surprise some naval strategists: not since the Maritime Strategy of the 1980s have naval operations sought to harness the risk of horizontal and vertical escalation, including nuclear escalation, to deter an opponent.[21] Instead, naval operations since the end of the Cold War, especially force projection against land targets, have been undertaken with an eye towards limiting collateral damage and the involvement of third parties, and thereby avoiding escalation. Since before the turn of the century, maritime power has mostly been used in measured ways to alter facts on the ground and not necessarily to deter hostilities. Using risk to bolster deterrence has not been a priority of the US Navy until recently.

Manipulating risk

Risk generation is inherent in deterrence strategies. The bimodal deterrence strategy outlined here, however, tends to force the attacker to accept the risk of immediate opposition should it violate red lines, thus moderating wishful thinking about its ability to control the costs of aggression. The threat of deterrence by punishment also can help reduce the risk of escalation because it can be held in reserve as retaliation for an opponent's decision to engage in horizontal or vertical escalation. The threat of deterrence by punishment should also be seen as a source of risk by an opponent because it reduces the ability to control the costs of aggression and the pace at which those costs are incurred.

The party that embraces a bimodal deterrence strategy also confronts a series of risks. If deterrence fails, a denial strategy will lead to war, which entails obvious risks for the party that makes good on its deterrent threats. Deterrence by punishment, which amounts to a form of compellence or coercion, is a source of risk because an opponent might decide to strike back to end the punishment, which in turn could set off further escalation. There is also a risk of horizontal escalation – the opponent could retaliate against new geographic areas (allies, the opponent's homeland) or in new domains (space, cyber, artificial intelligence), where it might enjoy an advantage. In other words, although the locations and activities envisioned by a bimodal maritime deterrent relate to a maritime setting, there is no guarantee that warfare will not deliberately or inadvertently spill into other domains.

As Thomas Schelling informed us many years ago, deterrence amounts to a competition in risk-taking. Neither side wants to start or engage in a major conflagration, but by crossing red lines and executing deterrent threats, both sides not only manipulate risk but also signal their willingness to take risks to achieve their objectives, or to deter horizontal or vertical escalation. A bimodal deterrent strategy uses a commitment to engage in a limited war to deliberately create the risk of a larger conflict. According to Schelling:

> The danger of major war is almost certainly increased by the occurrence of a limited war; it is almost certainly increased by any enlargement in the scope or violence of a limited war that has already taken place. This being so, the threat to engage in limited war has two parts. One is the threat to inflict costs directly on the other side, in casualties, expenditures, loss of territory, loss of face, or anything else. The second is the threat to expose the other party, together with oneself, to a heightened risk of a larger war.[22]

Sea control, along with its inherent threat of deterrence by punishment, heightens this perception of risk because it offers a readily observable pathway to enlarge the scope or intensity of the more limited conflict prompted by the execution of a deterrence-by-denial strategy.

The fact that deterrence must generate risk to be successful must be acknowledged *ex ante* by political authorities; a crisis in which threats might have to be executed should not be the first time these risks are thought through. This may sound simple enough, but today's naval officers have little practical experience when it comes to devising or implementing a deterrence strategy.

Commitment through pre-delegation and the role of warning

For deterrence by denial to carry the greatest credibility, authorisation to employ sea-denial capabilities would have to be pre-delegated to theatre or local commanders under certain circumstances. The decision to respond to an attack would not have to be automatic – that is, a sea-denial capability would not have to be tied to some sort of tripwire. Nevertheless, practical war-fighting requirements and plans must be honoured in the breach: responses involving the use of lethal force have to be embedded in rules of engagement and more or less communicated to an opponent before deterrence fails. If sea denial is to appear credible to an opponent, steps must be taken *ex ante* to remove opportunities to reassess strategic, operational and tactical considerations as a crisis worsens. Sea denial is most effective before the opponent reaches its objectives and begins to reinforce gains. Political discussions taking days or weeks about strategy or options can easily delay tactical and operational steps measured in hours. For sea denial to be credible, it must be constituted in such a way as to be available when the moment of crisis arrives.

The decision to adopt a bimodal maritime deterrent thus constitutes a political commitment, made in peacetime, to execute threats if deterrence fails. Admittedly, pre-delegation can conjure up images of a 'conflict spiral' reminiscent of Barbara Tuchman's analysis of the outbreak of the First World War, whereby a mobilisation race carried Europe inexorably into war.[23] This type of pre-delegation, however, is not unheard of in more recent history.

In the event of hostilities, for instance, NATO forces stationed along the inner-German border during the Cold War would have engaged in high-intensity conventional and potentially even nuclear hostilities regardless of the political deliberations under way in allied capitals.[24] Because of the time constraints involved, however, sea-denial forces must be pre-positioned, ready to go into action once an opponent approaches. According to Do Young Lee:

> The classic literature on conventional deterrence suggests that the matter of where and how to pre-position deterrent assets in peacetime is vital to deterrence robustness. Especially critical is the defense forces' physical formation, which affects the offender's judgment of the likelihood of gaining an initial breakthrough and, thus, a quick and cheap victory in the event of war … For deterrence to work, the enemy should be convinced that deterrence threats are real.[25]

Sea-denial forces must be ready at the opening moments of a conflict; their ability to influence events diminishes once the opponent begins steaming out of range or has already achieved a fait accompli.

In addition to pre-delegation, steps might also be taken to separate the ability to execute deterrence by denial from the availability of strategic or even significant tactical warning. In other words, a sea-denial force that requires weeks or months to muster could easily be overtaken by events if the opponent can stage and launch a significant operation in days or hours. At a minimum, operational expectations must be synchronised with intelligence. Sea-denial plans and capabilities that are misaligned with the availability of warning could lead to an incoherent response to aggression, or no response at all, which would undermine the credibility of the pending threat of deterrence by punishment. Ideally, a sea-denial force would represent an 'assured retaliation' capability – that is, sea denial could still be undertaken even in the absence of warning or a lacklustre response from officers and elected officials.

Pre-delegation and availability without warning are a politically, operationally and technically demanding set of requirements for a sea-denial force. These characteristics, however, reduce an opponent's incentives to resort to strategic surprise. The crossing of red lines might still be accompanied by the element of surprise, but the eruption of violence will not necessitate consultation across the military–political chain of command or leave the sea-denial force in a position in which it cannot respond. How much authority should be pre-delegated and the alert status of the sea-denial force is ultimately a political decision, based on the perceived threat posed by the opponent and the need to communicate that a response will be rapidly forthcoming in the event it takes certain steps.

Nuclear–conventional integration

Nuclear–conventional integration in a maritime setting is becoming a higher priority for the United States. During the Cold War, tactical and theatre nuclear forces were deployed on conventionally armed warships and submarines. Responsibility for nuclear command and control, and safety and surety, was borne not by theatre commands, but by the officers in command of individual platforms. This began to change in September 1991, when president George H.W. Bush announced the Presidential Nuclear Initiatives. In a unilateral step, he removed all tactical ground-based nuclear weapons from US units and all tactical nuclear weapons from surface ships, attack submarines and naval aircraft.[26] This process, which was completed in 1992, did more than just eliminate the risks and costs of a class of weapons that were rendered obsolete by the end of the Cold War: it removed dual-use, nuclear–conventional systems from conventional units and 'centralised' nuclear forces under the command and control of the newly created US Strategic Command.[27] The 'nuclearisation' of the US military, which began in the early 1950s as part of Dwight D. Eisenhower's 'New Look' policy, was reversed – nuclear weapons were now treated as a strategic asset, reserved to deter existential threats.[28]

The rising threat confronting the US in the Western Pacific and, for that matter, in Central Europe has greatly increased the salience of nuclear weapons and nuclear deterrence in strategic and political deliberations. There is a growing concern in some quarters that the lack of a limited tactical or theatre nuclear capability creates a gap that could be exploited by an opponent to create escalation dominance, to 'escalate to de-escalate' an ongoing conflict, or to simply enhance its own capacity to hold area targets (large industrial facilities, airfields, bases, ports) at risk.[29] To fill this rung on the escalation ladder, the first Trump administration's 2018 Nuclear Posture Review highlighted the desirability of acquiring a nuclear-armed sea-launched cruise missile (SLCM-N) for deployment on the US Navy's nuclear-powered attack submarines.[30] The Biden administration initially cancelled the development of the SLCM-N, but Congress voiced its concern about the future of the missile in the 2023 Strategic Posture Review, leading the House and Senate Armed Services committees to authorise funding for an SLCM-N programme in the FY24 National Defense Authorization Act.[31]

Nuclear–conventional integration, which will initially be reflected by the deployment of the SLCM-N, poses a significant challenge for the US Navy. Nevertheless, it does support a conventional bimodal deterrent strategy. As the United States' chief of naval operations told the Senate: 'SLCM-N is a tailored option the president should have.'[32] It offers a way to create theatre-level escalation dominance by creating a risk of nuclear deterrence by punishment. This should reduce an opponent's incentive to use tactical nuclear weapons to overturn sea denial or to use nuclear weapons to compel the US Navy to stand down in an ongoing conflict. Officials in the Biden administration acknowledged the deterrence and assurance objectives behind nuclear–conventional integration in 2023:

> The purpose of SLCM-N is not to hold an additional specific target set at risk, but rather to raise the level of risk to the Russian, Chinese, and North Koreans should they contemplate initial nuclear use in their respective regions to improve their military situation in a crisis or conflict or to coerce the United State to back down. For this purpose, the SLCM-N provides a tangible demonstration of US resolve to respond to any adversary's nuclear use.[33]

The SLCM-N does not have to be integrated into deterrence-by-denial operations, but can instead be held in reserve to control the risk of escalation or, in extreme circumstances, to deliberately enhance deterrence by punishment without relying on central (strategic) nuclear forces.

Adapting to a bimodal strategy

There is a significant list of well-known and emerging operational, strategic and institutional considerations that will have to be addressed by officers and elected officials as the US Navy seeks to implement a bimodal deterrence strategy. Doing so will involve significant changes that could easily undermine existing professional preferences, organisational practices and operations.

The battle of the opening salvo

The fact that deterrent threats are commonly executed after red lines are crossed suggests that both sea-denial and sea-control forces will not necessarily have the luxury of firing first against a maritime opponent. Nevertheless, firing first provides significant tactical and operational advantages in naval combat.[34] To overcome this disadvantage, options for pre-emption might be incorporated into deterrence by denial under limited circumstances. Reliance on pre-emption, however, shifts the onus for escalation back onto the side practising deterrence and creates political perceptions that can undermine the effort to deter, regardless of the tactical or operational success enjoyed in battle. Pre-emption also adds insult to injury – it can force the side attempting to preserve the peace to start the war it hoped to avoid in the first place. It is thus imperative that a bimodal deterrence strategy incorporate efforts to misdirect, mitigate or defeat an opponent's opening salvo. The perception of vulnerability, either in peacetime or during a crisis, can invite an opponent to believe it can cripple a maritime opponent with its first shot.

Multiple threats in multiple domains

While this article focuses on maritime threats in the Western Pacific and describes escalation in terms of geography (horizontal) and intensity of violence (vertical), conflict can occur within multiple domains of warfare. Horizontal and vertical escalation can follow the eruption and intensification of activity in domains such as cyberspace, outer space, artificial intelligence, chemical, biological and nuclear weapons, and so on. Interaction with these different domains needs to be factored into strategic assessments, as reflected in the notion of integrated deterrence – the effort to synchronise activity in different warfare domains to bolster deterrence. Integration efforts have not made much progress, however.[35] They should not be overlooked in any assessment of how to execute sea denial and sea control in the breach.

Does one size fit all?

This article focuses on the cross-strait amphibious threat to Taiwan, and therefore does not consider other stratagems, operations or scenarios that might characterise conflict in the Western Pacific.[36] While it does not ignore the issue of strategic surprise, it does posit that efforts will be made to guarantee that sea-denial and sea-control forces are in position to undertake their deterrence missions if necessary. What constitutes adequate preparation, however, can vary in an infinite number of ways. Hostilities might emerge, for instance, following an operational accident or during 'grey zone' activities in the South China Sea. Aggressive activities could take a variety of forms, from harassment at sea or in the air to a blockade of Taiwan or US friends and allies in the region, to a cross-strait invasion, to attacks against multiple strategic targets across the Pacific to 'reset' international affairs to suit Beijing's preferences. The capabilities provided by a bimodal maritime deterrent would have to be assessed against a host of potential contingencies. An effort to identify stratagems that might delay the execution of a sea-denial threat in various contingencies is needed.

Aspiration vs reality

In terms of force requirements, the US Navy is working to increase capabilities required to operationalise bimodal deterrence. Its sea-control fleet – comprising carrier strike groups, attack submarines, surface warships and marines embarked on amphibious ready groups – provides a global maritime force second to none that competitors will probably be unable to challenge in the foreseeable future. Steps also have been taken and are accelerating to deploy sea-denial capabilities along the First Island Chain, especially around Taiwan.[37] In light of the increasing frequency and scale of

Chinese short- or no-notice exercises that look more and more like rehearsals, Admiral Samuel Paparo, commander of US Indo-Pacific Command, has described a layered 'hellscape' defence of autonomous weapons that are already on station or can be brought on station to engage an amphibious assault if the need arises.[38]

While the numbers and capabilities of the systems involved in this layered defence remain classified, the navy's sea-control capabilities are robust, and its autonomous sea-denial capabilities appear to be increasing.[39] For example, in April 2025, the Pentagon requested proposals for a Combat Autonomous Maritime Platform (CAMP) with a range of over 1,600 kilometres and capable of operating underwater in contested environments without the aid of GPS. Among other missions, CAMP would be tasked with depositing various payloads on the sea floor.[40]

What is missing from this picture of an emerging bimodal deterrent is a strategy itself. The push to acquire an autonomous sea-denial capability is largely Admiral Paparo's initiative. 'Big Navy' back in Washington seems to be struggling with various decisions about what to buy and what to do with it. No one in the Pentagon appears interested in focusing on deterrence as the animating idea behind acquisition and operational decisions, or to appreciate that the emergent 'hybrid fleet' of crewed and non-crewed vessels can work together to produce a capability better able to discourage aggression. Autonomy, in other words, is treated as a tactical rather than a strategic issue. To fully realise the deterrence synergies produced by autonomous sea-denial and traditional sea-control forces, navy leaders need to incorporate a bimodal concept into the joint force and joint strategy, and consult allies and partners about the roles they can play in strengthening deterrence.

Integration of land and maritime forces

Both the US Marine Corps and the US Army have plans to bolster the maritime-deterrent posture in the Western Pacific, creating a need to reassess and synchronise the activities of land and naval forces in the First Island Chain.[41] The Marine Corps is developing Expeditionary Advanced Base Operations, which is a 'form of expeditionary warfare that involves the employment of mobile, low signature, persistent, and relatively easy to maintain and sustain naval expeditionary forces from a series of austere, temporary locations ashore or inshore with a contested or potentially contested maritime area to conduct sea denial, support sea control, or enable fleet sustainment'.[42] Similarly, the army is working on concepts to support the joint force in the Western Pacific, including the use of its existing long-range precision-strike weapons, and long- and mid-range hypersonic weapons under development.[43]

In a sense, both the Marine Corps and the army are preparing to play a major part in any sea-denial effort in the Western Pacific. This approach is consistent with Thomas Mahnken's recent argument that 'a maritime strategy should seek to turn geography to the United States' advantage by using the geography of the western Pacific to constrain China's access to the open oceans in crisis or war'.[44] Nevertheless, the need to coordinate land forces' operational concepts, joint fires and deterrence strategies with maritime operations is only now beginning to attract attention. The level of coordination between land- and sea-based forces has been episodic since the eighteenth century, and is much easier endorsed than accomplished.

The role of friends and allies

America's friends and allies across the Indo-Pacific can provide US forces with facilities in peacetime, at the outset of a crisis or during war, but deterrence does not depend only on securing access to facilities in other countries. According to Carlos Del Toro, formerly the US secretary of the navy, the maritime services aim to 'operationally integrate our allies and partners into strategic concepts and warfighting concepts to deter' adversaries.[45] The United States needs to work together with friends and allies in peacetime to make sure they work together in times of crisis to bolster deterrence.

Although US maritime strategy increasingly envisions direct and indirect roles for allies and partners, Washington cannot guarantee that its friends will embrace these roles, especially in a crisis when deterrence is being tested. Many countries in the region have increased their defence capabilities, granted access to US forces and enhanced the inter-operability of their militaries with that of the United States, as documented in the Indo-Pacific Strategy Report published by the US Department of Defense.[46]

Many US partners and allies have also begun to engage in cooperation among themselves, often on a bilateral basis. But the purposes of defence cooperation from their perspective are diverse, and a RAND Corporation report has noted that 'there is substantial sensitivity' about cooperation when it is 'framed as a reaction to China's growing power and assertiveness'.[47] Diplomacy must take centre stage if a bimodal maritime deterrent is to appear credible during a crisis.[48]

Institutional change

While the bimodal maritime deterrent outlined here makes maximum use of the US Navy's existing force structure, there is no denying that the balance between sea-control and sea-denial capabilities will have to shift in favour of sea denial. Resources that are today devoted to traditional forces and operations will have to be made available to new generations of autonomous and semi-autonomous capabilities that can operate in the most dangerous environments within reach of opponents' anti-access and area-denial systems. Nuclear–conventional integration also portends significant challenges for the navy. It must reinstate and, in some cases, reinvent safety and surety protocols, command-and-control procedures, and personnel-reliability programmes to support tactical and theatre nuclear systems. New skill sets, logistics and command-and-control procedures associated with autonomous technologies and systems must be integrated into the existing fleet, while education programmes and billet structures need to prepare officers to operate these new systems and synchronise maritime deterrence into an overall national strategy.

* * *

The logic and requirements of a bimodal maritime deterrent are simple enough. The sea-denial force serves as the basis of a deterrence-by-denial strategy, which shifts the onus of escalation onto the opponent while reducing opportunities to achieve a fait accompli. The sea-control force provides assurance that the US Navy will be able to honour its deterrent commitments while providing a means to sustain escalation dominance or to compel an opponent to return to the status quo ante bellum. A bimodal strategy can also accommodate new technologies and capabilities within its purview (as exemplified by nuclear–conventional integration) and can be adjusted to meet changes in the threat.

While this may be easy to describe, it will not be easy to put into practice. The operational requirements created by deterrence by denial are daunting; sea-denial capabilities must be in situ when they are needed even with no warning. Elected officials must commit to certain courses of action *ex ante*. There might not be time to fine-tune a response once an opponent has crossed a red line. Deterrence by denial and deterrence by punishment also create their largest effect by establishing the risk of escalation, which might play out globally or in the nuclear domain.

If deterrence works and peace is preserved, all of this will remain a matter of conjecture, a replay of Cold War academic and policy debates about the strengths, weaknesses and risks of various deterrence strategies. A bimodal deterrent is intended to preserve the peace; the outbreak of war would constitute a failure of the strategy. Nevertheless, bimodal maritime deterrence is not for the faint of heart. It is based on a commitment made in peacetime to engage in conflict if necessary, creating the possibility that things might get out of control. It also places the decision for war in the hands of the opponent, although it is intended to guide that decision in ways that suit US national interests.

Notes

1 See Frank Pandolfe, 'Enhance Naval Deterrence, Near and Far', *USNI Proceedings*, vol. 150, no. 4, April 2024, https://www.usni.org/magazines/proceedings/2024/april/enhance-naval-deterrence-near-and-far; and Jeffrey E. Kline, 'Revamping Fleet Design and Maritime Strategy: An Integrated Naval Campaign for Advantage', Center for International Maritime Security, 16 September 2023, https://cimsec.org/revamping-fleet-design-and-maritime-strategy-an-integrated-naval-campaign-for-advantage/.

2 See James J. Wirtz, 'Deterrence as Strategy: The Strategic Importance of Deterrence by Denial', in Alex S. Wilner and Andreas Wegner (eds), *Deterrence by Denial: Theory and Practice* (Amherst, NY: Cambria Press, 2021), pp. 123–42; and James J. Wirtz, 'How Does Nuclear Deterrence Differ from Conventional Deterrence', *Strategic Studies Quarterly*, vol. 12, no. 4, Winter

2018, https://www.airuniversity.af.edu/Portals/10/SSQ/documents/Volume-12_Issue-4/Wirtz.pdf.

3 See Robert C. Rubel, 'Command of the Sea: An Old Concept Resurfaces in a New Form', *Naval War College Review*, vol. 65, no. 4, Autumn 2012, p. 1.

4 For a brief introduction to deterrence by denial and deterrence by punishment, see Michael Mazarr, 'Understanding Deterrence', RAND Corporation, 19 April 2018, https://www.rand.org/pubs/perspectives/PE295.html.

5 Stephen Biddle and Ivan Oelrich, 'Future Warfare in the Western Pacific: Chinese Antiaccess/Area Denial, U.S. AirSea Battle, and Command of the Commons in East Asia', *International Security*, vol. 41, no. 1, Summer 2016, pp. 7–48.

6 On contestable costs, see Richard Harknett, 'State Preferences, Systemic Constraints, and the Absolute Weapon', in T.V. Paul, Richard Harknett and James J. Wirtz (eds), *The Absolute Weapon Revisited: Nuclear Arms and the Emerging International Order* (Ann Arbor, MI: University of Michigan Press, 1998), pp. 52–3.

7 For a discussion of the contemporary strategic setting in the Western Pacific, see James J. Wirtz, Jeffrey E. Kline and James A. Russell, 'A Maritime Conversation with America', *Orbis*, vol. 66, no. 2, Spring 2022, pp. 166–83.

8 See Ahmer Tarar, 'A Strategic Logic of the Military *Fait Accompli*', *International Studies Quarterly*, vol. 60, no. 4, December 2016, pp. 742–52; Dan Altman, 'By Fait Accompli, Not Coercion: How States Wrest Territory from Their Adversaries', *International Studies Quarterly*, vol. 61, no. 4, December 2017, pp. 881–91; and Dan Reiter and Paul Poast, 'The Truth About Tripwires: Why Small Force Deployments Do Not Deter Aggression', *Texas National Security Review*, vol. 4, no. 3, Summer 2021, pp. 33–53.

9 Elbridge Colby, 'Against the Great Powers: Reflections on Balancing Nuclear and Conventional Power', *Texas National Security Review*, vol. 2, no. 1, November 2018, p. 146.

10 According to Thomas Schelling, 'skillful diplomacy, in the absence of uncertainty, consists in arranging things so that it is one's opponent who is embarrassed by having the "last clear chance" to avert disaster by turning aside or abstaining from what he wanted to do'. Thomas C. Schelling, *Arms and Influence* (New Haven, CT: Yale University Press, 1966), p. 101.

11 Roberta Wohlstetter, *Pearl Harbor: Warning and Decision* (Stanford, CA: Stanford University Press, 1962), p. 355.

12 Lawrence Freedman and Efraim Karsh, *The Gulf Conflict 1990–1991: Diplomacy and War in the New World Order* (Princeton, NJ: Princeton University Press, 1993), p. 52.

13 See James J. Wirtz, 'The Balance of Power Paradox', in T.V. Paul, James J. Wirtz and Michel Fortmann (eds), *Balance of Power: Theory and Practice in the 21st Century* (Stanford, CA: Stanford University Press, 2004), pp. 127–49; and James J. Wirtz, 'Deterring the Weak: Problems and Prospects', *Proliferation Papers*, no. 43, Fall 2012.

14 See Wayne P. Hughes, 'A Bimodal Force for the National Maritime Strategy', *Naval War College Review*, vol. 60, no. 2, 2007, https://digital-

commons.usnwc.edu/nwc-review/vol60/iss2/5.

15 See Joshua R. Itzkowitz Shifrinson, 'Linkage Politics', in Jon R. Lindsay and Erik Gartzke (eds), *Cross-domain Deterrence: Strategy in an Era of Complexity* (New York: Oxford University Press, 2019), p. 292.

16 As Geoffrey Blainey suggests, anything that increases the expectation of a positive war outcome increases the likelihood of war. Geoffrey Blainey, *The Causes of War* (New York: Free Press, 1973), especially pp. 35–56.

17 See T.X. Hammes, 'Offshore Control: A Proposed Strategy for an Unlikely Conflict', *Strategic Forum*, no. 278, June 2012, https://ndupress.ndu.edu/Portals/68/Documents/stratforum/SF-278.pdf?ver=2014-08-21-140306-147; and Sean Mirski, 'Stranglehold: The Context, Conduct and Consequences of an American Blockade of China', *Journal of Strategic Studies*, vol. 36, no. 3, 2013, pp. 385–421.

18 See Ryan Ratcliffe, 'Prize Law Can Help the United States Win the War of 2026', *USNI Proceedings*, vol. 150, no. 9, September 2024, p. 34, https://www.usni.org/magazines/proceedings/2024/september/prize-law-can-help-united-states-win-war-2026.

19 See James J. Wirtz, 'The Maritime Logic of the Melian Dialogue: Deterrence in the Western Pacific', *Survival*, vol. 64, no. 6, December 2022–January 2023, pp. 43–56.

20 James H. Bergeron, 'Reflecting on One Year of War: A Transformational Year in Maritime NATO', Center for Maritime Strategy, 17 February 2023, https://centerformaritimestrategy.org/publications/reflecting-on-one-year-of-war-a-transformational-year-in-maritime-nato/.

21 See Linton F. Brooks, 'Naval Power and National Security: The Case for the Maritime Strategy', *International Security*, vol. 11, no. 2, Fall 1986, pp. 58–88.

22 Schelling, *Arms and Influence*, p. 105.

23 Barbara W. Tuchman, *The Guns of August* (Novato, CA: Presidio Press, 2004).

24 Information about how all of this might have played out is mercifully consigned to the realm of counterfactual history, but the tempo of a Warsaw Pact plan for an invasion of Western Europe in the 1960s, including the quick resort to nuclear use, guaranteed that such a situation would have quickly outpaced political deliberation, especially within NATO. See 'Taking Lyon on the Ninth Day? The 1964 Warsaw Pact Plan for a Nuclear War in Europe and Related Documents', Parallel History Project on NATO and the Warsaw Pact, May 2000, https://www.files.ethz.ch/isn/108642/warplan_dossier.pdf.

25 Do Young Lee, 'Strategies of Extended Deterrence: How States Provide the Security Umbrella', *Security Studies*, vol. 30, no. 5, December 2021, p. 769.

26 See Matthew Fuhrmann and Bryan R. Early, 'Following START: Risk Acceptance and the 1991–1992 Presidential Nuclear Initiatives', *Foreign Policy Analysis*, vol. 4, no. 1, January 2008, pp. 21–43; and Susan Koch, *The Presidential Nuclear Initiatives of 1991–92* (Washington DC: National Defense University Press, 2012).

27 Tactical weapons were removed from the surface fleet and submarine force by 1992, but one conventional system, the *Tomahawk* land-attack missile, was

retained, and its nuclear warheads were kept in warm storage until they were fully retired following president Barack Obama's 2010 Nuclear Posture Review.

28 See Lawrence Freedman and Jeffrey Michaels, *The Evolution of Nuclear Strategy*, 4th ed. (New York: Palgrave Macmillan, 2019), especially pp. 103–20.

29 For more on 'escalation to de-escalate', see Michael Kofman, Anya Fink and Jeffrey Edmonds, 'Russian Strategy for Escalation Management: Evolution of Key Concepts', Center for Naval Analysis, April 2020, https://www.cna.org/reports/2020/04/DRM-2019-U-022455-1Rev.pdf. For some examples of area targets, see United States General Accounting Office, 'Strategic Weapons: Nuclear Weapons Targeting Process', September 1991, p. 23, https://www.gao.gov/assets/nsiad-91-319fs.pdf.

30 US Office of the Secretary of Defense, 'Nuclear Posture Review', February 2018, https://media.defense.gov/2018/Feb/02/2001872886/-1/-1/1/2018-NUCLEAR-POSTURE-REVIEW-FINAL-REPORT.PDF.

31 United States Senate Committee on Armed Services, 'Fiscal Year 2024 National Defense Authorization Act: Executive Summary', June 2023, p. 29, https://www.armed-services.senate.gov/imo/media/doc/fy2024_ndaa_executive_summary.pdf.

32 Quoted in Franklin C. Miller, 'Del Toro Missed the Boat on SLCM-N and on the Submarine Force's Role', *RealClearDefense,* 10 July 2024, https://www.realcleardefense.com/articles/2024/07/10/del_toro_missed_the_boat_on_slcm-n_and_on_the_submarine_forces_role_1043438.html.

33 Robert Soofer and Walter Slocombe, 'Congress Should Fund the Nuclear Sea-launched Cruise Missile', *New Atlanticist*, 3 August 2023, https://www.atlanticcouncil.org/blogs/new-atlanticist/congress-should-fund-the-nuclear-sea-launched-cruise-missile/.

34 See Wayne P. Hughes, Jr, and Robert P. Girrier, *Fleet Tactics and Naval Operations* (Annapolis, MD: Naval Institute Press, 2018), p. 30.

35 See James J. Wirtz and Jeffrey A. Larsen, 'Wanted: A Strategy to Integrate Deterrence', *Defense and Security Analysis*, vol. 40, no. 3, July 2024, pp. 361–78.

36 See James J. Wirtz, 'Imagining Maritime Conflict in the Western Pacific: Can Analogies Substitute for Strategy?', *Defense and Security Analysis*, vol. 38, no. 3, 2022, pp. 349–68.

37 See Stacie Pettyjohn, Hannah Dennis and Molly Campbell, 'Swarms over the Strait: Drone Warfare in a Future Fight to Defend Taiwan', Center for a New American Security, June 2024, https://s3.us-east-1.amazonaws.com/files.cnas.org/documents/Indo-Pacific-Drones_DEFENSE_2024-final.pdf.

38 See John Grady, '"Hellscape" Swarms Could Be a Cost-effective Taiwan Defense, Says Report', *USNI News*, 1 July 2024, https://news.usni.org/2024/07/01/hellscape-swarms-could-be-as-cost-effective-taiwan-defense-says-report.

39 See Jared Keller, 'The Pentagon Is Planning a Drone "Hellscape" to Defend Taiwan', *Wired*, August 2024, https://www.wired.com/story/china-taiwan-pentagon-drone-hellscape/.

40 See Zita Ballinger Fletcher, 'Unmanned Undersea Vessels Eyed by Pentagon as Key Part of Navy

Growth', *Defense News*, 22 April 2025, https://www.defensenews.com/news/your-military/2025/04/22/unmanned-undersea-vessels-eyed-by-pentagon-as-key-part-of-navy-growth/.

41 The First Island Chain links Japan to Taiwan, the Philippines and the island of Borneo, which is shared by Brunei, Indonesia and Malaysia. See Donald Abenheim et al., 'American Sea Power in the Contemporary Security Environment', *Comparative Strategy*, vol. 37, no. 5, 2018, p. 400; and Wallace C. Gregson, Jr, and Jeffrey W. Hornung, 'The United States Considers Reinforcing Its "Pacific Sanctuary"', *War on the Rocks*, 12 April 2021, https://warontherocks.com/2021/04/the-united-states-considers-its-pacific-sanctuary/.

42 United States Marine Corps, 'Tentative Manual for Expeditionary Advanced Base Operations, 2nd Edition', May 2023, p. 1-2, https://www.marines.mil/Portals/1/Docs/230509-Tentative-Manual-For-Expeditionary-Advanced-Base-Operations-2nd-Edition.pdf.

43 See Abby Doll et al., 'The Backbone of U.S. Joint Operations: Army Roles in the Indo-Pacific', RAND Corporation, 5 May 2023, p. 9, https://www.rand.org/pubs/research_reports/RRA1784-1.html.

44 Thomas G. Mahnken, 'A Maritime Strategy to Deal with China', *USNI Proceedings*, vol. 148, no. 2, February 2022, https://www.usni.org/magazines/proceedings/2022/february/maritime-strategy-deal-china.

45 Carlos Del Toro, 'One Navy–Marine Corps Team: Strategic Guidance from the Secretary of the Navy', October 2021, p. 5, https://media.defense.gov/2021/Oct/07/2002870427/-1/-1/0/SECNAV%20STRATEGIC%20GUIDANCE_100721.PDF.

46 US Department of Defense, 'Indo-Pacific Strategy Report: Preparedness, Partnerships, and Promoting a Networked Region', 1 June 2019, https://media.defense.gov/2019/jul/01/2002152311/-1/-1/1/department-of-defense-indo-pacific-strategy-report-2019.pdf.

47 Scott W. Harold et al., 'The Thickening Web of Asian Security Cooperation: Deepening Defense Ties Among U.S. Allies and Partners in the Indo-Pacific', RAND Corporation, 29 August 2019, p. 349, https://www.rand.org/pubs/research_reports/RR3125.html.

48 This section is derived from Michael S. Malley and James J. Wirtz, 'Maritime Coalitions and Deterrence: Beware the Melian Choice', *Washington Quarterly*, vol. 45, no. 4, Winter 2023, pp. 99–111.

Copyright © 2025 The International Institute for Strategic Studies

The Future of Economic Warfare

Mariya Grinberg

The growth of supply chains and trade ties between states, and the way in which these have been weaponised through sanctions, have raised the profile of economic statecraft as a way of achieving national goals. Economic warfare in particular is sometimes seen as more effective and less escalatory than military action.[1] In the Russia–Ukraine war, the West has been praised for its quick, coordinated and severe 'economic warfare' to punish Russia for its revisionist behaviour.[2] Conversely, Russia has been castigated for waging economic warfare by targeting Ukraine's industrial infrastructure and manipulating gas flows to Europe.[3] Judging by the frequency with which it is invoked, economic warfare appears to be on the rise.

Undoubtedly, technological advancements have increased the potential power of economic warfare. Satellites and radar technologies make the movement of commerce more detectable.[4] Faster communication makes gathering information on shipments easier, decreasing enforcement costs. Moreover, current technologies require raw materials that are concentrated in only a few geographic locations, making more states dependent on strategic imports. Finally, supply-chain integration makes more states vulnerable to strategic disruptions. Given the fertile conditions for economic warfare, it makes sense to evaluate how it might be used.

Mariya Grinberg is an Assistant Professor of Political Science and a member of the Security Studies Program at MIT.

Survival | vol. 67 no. 3 | June–July 2025 | pp. 149–170 https://doi.org/10.1080/00396338.2025.2508083

A deeper look, however, reveals that economic warfare, properly defined and demonstrated to great effect in both world wars, is unlikely to be used today or in the foreseeable future. Defined as a policy to constrain the target's war-fighting capability by denying it the supplies it requires to continue the war effort, economic warfare necessitates a long war to produce its effects and a state willing to shoulder the escalation pressure the policy generates. The development of nuclear weapons changed the nature of war in ways that preclude the use of economic warfare. Only in conventional wars among two non-nuclear-armed states are the conditions for the use of economic warfare likely to be met. Even then, there are reasons to suspect that economic warfare will not be used. At the same time, seeking to create the conditions needed to successfully wage economic warfare – by making the war or the economic-warfare strategy less escalatory, stretching out the war, or identifying short-term tools of economic warfare – is similarly unlikely to work.

What is economic warfare?

The term 'economic warfare' has been used to refer to almost any state economic policy: economic and financial sanctions, purchases by foreign companies of domestic firms, steps to prevent foreign companies from acquiring domestic firms, boycotts, trade wars and more. Indeed, the term is frequently conflated with economic statecraft, which refers to the use of economic tools for achieving foreign-policy goals.[5] This conflation stems from some overly broad definitions of economic warfare. Some stretch the term to encompass any effect generated by economic means, or any increase in control over a market.[6] However, for the concept of economic warfare to be useful, its definition needs to capture its unique qualities, distinguishing it from other tools of economic statecraft.

This article defines economic warfare as a policy to constrain the target's war-fighting capability by denying supplies the target requires to continue its war effort. The unique quality of economic warfare is that it aims to deprive the enemy of *all* possible sources of strategic goods, which necessitates the involvement of third-party states. Unlike punitive measures such as sanctions, boycotts or resource-price manipulations, which seek to prevent the enemy from accessing a few sources of strategic goods to increase the cost of doing business, economic warfare seeks to deny the enemy almost all sources of strategic products to prevent it from doing *any* business. Such a policy necessitates imposing limits on third-party states, interfering with their normal exchange with the enemy.

This definition coheres with most conventional definitions of the term.[7] Economic warfare is expressly a wartime tool of statecraft. The war sets the political purpose, end point and content of economic warfare. As it is not an independent policy tool, the purpose of economic warfare cannot contradict the war's purpose.[8] It is designed to help the state achieve its military aims. The absolute destruction of the enemy's economy is, therefore, unlikely to be the purpose of economic warfare.[9] Even in total wars, states rarely aim at the complete annihilation of their opponents, instead seeking their unconditional surrender. Destruction is a consequence of the policy, not its goal. Likewise, capturing the enemy's overseas markets is not a feature of economic warfare. Economic warfare can separate the enemy from its overseas markets to limit its war-fighting capacity, but the question of what to do with those markets afterwards must be answered by separate processes of statecraft.

The specific supplies denied to the enemy are, likewise, determined by the war.[10] Whether a product is deemed strategic depends on its 'relative utility, substitutability, and whether or not the marginal elasticity of demand is low', according to Alan Dobson.[11] Each belligerent has its own set of strategic products.[12] Economic warfare does not need to affect the entirety of the enemy's trade – the policy could be as narrow as targeting one product.[13] Furthermore, the enemy does not need to have domestic capacity to produce the strategic product for economic warfare to be used. This differentiates economic warfare from tools like strategic bombing, which necessitates domestic production as a target for the bombs.[14] Indeed, economic warfare does not even require an existing economic relationship between the enacting state and the enemy. Provided the enemy is not fully autarkic, economic warfare can be used to deny the enemy resupply from its trading partners.

By denying the enemy as many avenues for the acquisition of strategic products as possible, economic warfare makes carrying on the war effort very difficult.[15] If the enemy lacks weapons or ammunition, or food for its soldiers, its capability to prosecute the war will be severely reduced. Enemy leaders might not be persuaded to change policies even when faced with high costs, but their willingness to fight cannot overcome a lack of capabilities on the battlefield. This further differentiates economic warfare from punitive measures, which rely on economic or reputational costs to induce a change in the target's behaviour.[16] Such policy tools seek to alter decision-makers' calculations, whereas economic warfare focuses on the enemy's capabilities.[17]

To eliminate as many avenues of enemy resupply as possible, economic warfare must sever economic exchanges between the enemy and third-party states. While drastic, this step prevents third parties from resupplying the enemy indirectly or with their own products.[18] Interference in third-party trade is the key difference between economic warfare and boycotts or sanctions, which seek to sever only direct trade with the enemy, leaving third-party trade unaffected.[19] The international organisations governing global trade, such as the World Trade Organization, recognise the right to sever direct trade with an enemy through the national-security exception.[20] States may voluntarily join collective sanctions, but the decision to do so would emerge from their own trade policies. Economic warfare, in contrast, does not depend on the choices of third parties. It is imposed on them.

Requirements of economic warfare

For economic warfare to effectively constrain the enemy's war-fighting capabilities, two necessary, though not sufficient, conditions must be met – conditions that work at cross purposes.[21] Firstly, economic warfare requires a long war. Secondly, the enacting state must be able to bear the escalatory pressures the policy generates. The longer the war, the greater the effects that economic warfare can produce, but the stronger escalatory pressures will grow.

Long war

Economic warfare cannot bring about a military victory independently.[22] War degrades military capabilities and increases demand for strategic supplies; economic warfare denies those supplies to the enemy. However, an enemy denied any new war-fighting capabilities by economic warfare still has its initial capacity, and may reasonably calculate that this will suffice to win the war, even without resupply. For example, when Italy invaded Ethiopia in 1935, it expected the League of Nations to cut off all avenues of resupply. Yet Italy still chose war, predicting that it could succeed with the available resources.[23] In the short term, the enemy might rely on national stockpiles. It might divert strategic products towards military use, sacrificing civilian production and justifying the policy as a war necessity. In anticipation of shortages, it might ration existing supplies to make them last longer.

Economic warfare relies on the war to destroy the enemy's existing capabilities.[24] The longer the policy is enforced, the greater the shortages the enemy faces, and the harder it becomes to prosecute the war.[25] But it takes time to ramp up enforcement mechanisms: interfering in trade between third-party states and the enemy requires gathering considerable information.[26] Statistics on typical pre-war levels of trade in specific products between neutrals and the enemy are needed to prevent trans-shipment. To stop third parties from supplying the enemy with strategic products, information on the content of specific shipments and their final destinations is necessary. Verifying this information, investigating deceptions and locating third parties working on the enemy's behalf require that an intelligence network be set up, a time-consuming process.

Escalation management

The effects of economic warfare are directly tied to the policy's potential for escalation.[27] The tighter the control over third-party trade, the more avenues of resupply are denied to the enemy, but also the angrier third-party states may become. Interfering with third-party trade infringes on the affected states' sovereignty. They may react in a number of ways, such as making diplomatic complaints or coercive threats, using military means to protect their commercial activities, or joining the war against the enacting state.[28] For economic warfare to achieve its goal, the enacting state has to maintain the policy despite the corresponding potential for escalation.

Escalation pressure can also stem from the enemy. If economic warfare severs the enemy's access to resupply, promising severe degradation of future military capabilities, this may incentivise escalation.[29] The enemy may seek to intensify the war in hopes of a quick victory, or to conquer neighbouring states to gain access to their strategic resources. In 1941, for example, Japanese leaders, believing that an American oil embargo might severely cripple their war effort against China, sought to eliminate the US Navy from the Pacific so that it would be easier to conquer oil-rich territories in the region.[30]

Interference with third-party states is both allowed by the rules of war and expected by third-party states. An officially declared and properly enforced blockade gives belligerents the right to stop contraband, including products sold and delivered by third parties, from reaching the enemy.[31] Yet there is no universally accepted list of products that third parties are never allowed to deliver to belligerents. Generally, belligerents prefer an extensive contraband list, while third parties prefer a limited one. Where interests conflict, escalation risks appear. Furthermore, the process of searching for contraband requires stopping shipping vehicles, inspecting them and verifying product information with a central information hub, all of which extends the transportation time and costs of third-party trade, angering third parties and generating more escalation pressures.

The shortages created by economic warfare grow over time. To damage the enemy's war-fighting capability, the enacting state needs to commit to a lengthy policy. Yet the longer economic warfare is enforced, the more third-party trade is implicated, and the more likely third parties are to interfere in the conflict to protect their commerce. Imposing economic warfare over the long term builds escalation pressures which incentivise the enacting state to end the policy. Thus, economic warfare requires long wars where the enacting state is willing to accept the escalation of the conflict. These kinds of wars are unlikely in modern times.

Economic warfare in modern wars

Perhaps the most consequential change in modern warfare has been the introduction of nuclear weapons. Wars in the nuclear age can be classified into four general categories: war between nuclear-armed opponents; proxy warfare between one nuclear-armed state and a non-nuclear opponent with a nuclear benefactor; asymmetric warfare between a conventionally stronger (and potentially nuclear-armed) state and a considerably weaker non-nuclear opponent; and conventional war between non-nuclear states. In most of these cases, either the expected length of the war or a lack of willingness to enforce an escalatory policy is likely to prevent states from relying on economic warfare. Only in conventional wars among non-nuclear opponents is there any real chance that economic warfare will be useful, yet even in these wars there are reasons to expect that states will avoid it.

Both supporters and opponents of the nuclear revolution agree that an attack threatening the survival of a nuclear-armed state is highly likely to trigger nuclear escalation.[32] If such escalation is not quickly contained, the resulting nuclear war would probably be short and disastrous for the world. There would be little reason for economic warfare.

The more plausible scenario of a war between two nuclear-armed opponents is a conventional war in which both sides work to avoid nuclear escalation. Indeed, the potential for such a confrontation between the United States and China has drawn considerable attention.[33] Yet even a direct conventional war between two nuclear-armed states is likely to end swiftly, before economic warfare could produce any noticeable effects. The two belligerents would face considerable risks of nuclear escalation.[34] The longer the war dragged on, the greater the possibility of accidents sparking nuclear catastrophe.[35] Moreover, other actors would seek to apply considerable pressure on both belligerents to end the war, to limit the potential for global destruction.[36] To date, the only example of such a war – the 1999 Kargil War between India and Pakistan – was limited in scope and lasted less than three months.

Managing escalation pressures between nuclear-armed opponents becomes considerably more difficult if economic warfare is introduced. Analysts who foresee a long conventional war between the US and China expect an attritional struggle in which both sides refrain from seeking decisive victory, specifically to avoid nuclear-escalation risks.[37] Economic warfare has no place in such a war. It is a highly escalatory policy which, when fully enforced, confronts the opponent with a future in which it will not have the capability to defend itself.[38] Destroying an enemy's war-fighting capacity is reaching for a decisive victory. Introducing economic warfare increases escalation risks to the point of shortening the war and thus preventing the policy from producing its effects. Thus, maintaining a long conventional war precludes the use of economic warfare.

Proxy warfare can extend into a protracted struggle, but in this case it is unlikely that the belligerents will wish to bear the escalation costs of an economic-warfare policy.[39] For the non-nuclear opponent in a proxy war, the nuclear patron tends to be the most important source of strategic products. Forcefully severing trade between the non-nuclear opponent and its patron greatly increases the nuclear-armed belligerent's chances of waging direct warfare with the nuclear patron. Indeed, many states interpret the targeting of their commerce, especially with military force, as an act of war.[40] For example, for Russia to use economic warfare against Ukraine in the current conflict, it would have to sever Ukraine's access to strategic supplies from the US and neighbouring NATO countries. Directly interfering with American and NATO trade with Ukraine might increase the prospect of a direct intervention on Ukraine's behalf. The benefits of possibly undermining Ukraine's war-fighting capacity through economic warfare would not be worth the addition of US and NATO war-fighting capabilities to the conflict.

The enforcement of economic warfare poses the risk of accidental escalation as well. Enforcement includes actions such as stopping and seizing third-party ships, blockading borders, shooting down deliveries by air and bombing railway transfers. Such actions can accidentally injure the patron instead of the target. Continuing with the Russia–Ukraine example, for Russia to enforce an economic-warfare policy, it would need to target deliveries of strategic products crossing Ukraine's border. This would increase the chances of accidentally striking NATO territory.[41]

On the other side of the conflict, the nuclear patron maintains a veneer of neutrality in proxy warfare. It does not have access to belligerent rights, and initiating economic warfare could easily be interpreted as a declaration of war. Given that the central benefit of using a proxy is avoiding a direct confrontation, the patron is unlikely to resort to such an escalatory policy. Neither the US, nor the various European states taking part in the sanctions regime against Russia, are engaged in economic warfare. Each state made the sovereign decision to sever aspects of its trade with Russia. The sanctions regime imposes costs, but these hardly rise to the level of denying the country access to strategic necessities. Indeed, Russia continues to resupply its military capabilities, even from Western companies.[42]

The hallmark of asymmetric conflict is that the stronger opponent has the military capabilities for a quick victory, but for political reasons keeps the war limited.[43] To increase the chances of victory, the stronger state is more likely to append its own military capabilities than to engage in economic warfare. An overwhelming influx of troops might produce a quick military victory, whereas economic warfare is necessarily a long-term policy. Moreover, a decision to increase its own military capabilities will concern only the participants of the war, while economic warfare necessarily targets third parties, which can be expected to generate ill will and potentially add more belligerents to the conflict. In the Vietnam War, for example, the relevant question for the United States was not whether it could convince its European allies to sever trade with North Vietnam, but whether it was willing to interfere with Chinese trade with Vietnam.

Economic warfare is necessarily a long-term policy

If the belligerents involved have the capacity to enforce it, a conventional war between two non-nuclear states can feature economic warfare. Conventional wars can easily last long enough for economic warfare to produce an effect, and the absence of nuclear weapons means that one of the most dangerous escalation thresholds is removed. However, even under these favourable conditions, economic warfare is likely to be used only rarely and sporadically. The belligerents would still be beholden to escalation pressures from third-party states, which are likely to be considerably more powerful than the belligerents.

In a conventional war between non-nuclear states, the use of economic warfare would likely entail interference in the trade of the world's most powerful nuclear-armed states, as they trade extensively and globally.[44] If such a state decided that its trade was being adversely affected, it would have numerous ways to retaliate, including by funding the opponent in the war, providing military equipment, training the opponent's troops or directly interfering in the conflict. Instead of limiting the military capabilities available to the opponent, economic warfare could create the counterproductive effect of providing it a new patron. Additionally, powerful states can militarily protect both their own trade and that of third parties, preventing the belligerents from enforcing economic warfare. The Tanker War, the naval component of the Iran–Iraq War in 1980–88, exemplifies this dynamic. Iraq's initial attacks on Iranian shipping were designed to provoke Iran to close the Strait of Hormuz, angering trading nations and thereby drawing the US into the war.[45] When Iran failed to oblige, both sides escalated attacks on neutral shipping to deny their opponents crucial supplies, which ultimately ended with the two superpowers (the US and the Soviet Union) providing military protection to tankers in the strait.[46]

While managing escalation pressure from third-party states is an ever-present problem for economic warfare, it is more critical in conventional wars between non-nuclear states because of the power differential between the belligerents and third-party states. In the First World War, both Britain and Germany moderated their enforcement of economic warfare to limit damage to the United States.[47] The possibility that a peer might join the conflict on the opposing side was sufficient to introduce caution and weaken the effects of economic warfare. In the modern conventional context, third parties are not military peers but substantially more powerful states, increasing the incentives to avoid economic warfare targeting their commerce.

Creating the conditions for economic warfare

States are rarely prepared to bear the escalation pressures to which economic warfare contributes, and these pressures typically incentivise states to end wars quickly, before economic warfare can produce any effects. What then might be done to restore the usefulness of economic warfare? There are four possibilities: making the war less escalatory; making economic warfare less escalatory; increasing the duration of the war; and increasing the utility of economic warfare in the short term. None of these offers the realistic prospect of making economic warfare more effective.

Making a war less escalatory requires purposefully reducing its intensity and focusing on fairly low stakes. In general, however, controlling escalation is difficult. Belligerents tend to overstate the aggression of their opponent's actions, accidents are perceived as intentional attacks, and military manoeuvres sometimes have a greater strategic effect than intended.[48]

To reduce escalation pressures, belligerents could avoid competing over high-stakes issues. Wartime policies affecting the opponent's survival or strategic interests are, therefore, likely to be off the table. Economic warfare is such a policy. When fully enforced, it slowly grinds down the enemy's ability to resupply its war-fighting capability. Not only does this affect the state's ability to wage the conflict, it also means that the state might struggle to defend itself from predation, even if it wins the war. Targeting an opponent's survival or strategic interests is in direct contradiction with the goal of lowering wartime escalation pressures.

To make economic warfare less escalatory, its effect on third parties must be limited. This is possible if all states are belligerents in a given conflict, since interference with belligerent commerce is a legitimate wartime policy. Both the League of Nations and the United Nations were designed around this idea.[49] All members of these organisations automatically become belligerents in collective defence when the international governing body designates an aggressor. This scheme failed for the League of Nations when the US declined to join, ensuring that subsequent conflicts would have a very powerful neutral state. However, the same idea succeeded under the UN, in the few cases where the Security Council designated an aggressor. The most significant triumph was perhaps the Gulf War.[50] The UN mandate lessened the escalation pressures associated with the economic-warfare policy adopted by the US and its allies, since all states were required to sever their commerce with Iraq.[51] The likelihood of a similar UN mandate in future conflicts is quite low. Much like during the Cold War, when the Soviet Union and the US prevented each other from triggering this function of the UN, today the US and China are likely to prevent the UN from taking unanimous action.[52]

Alternatively, escalation can be somewhat managed if the affected third parties are deemed to be politically, militarily and economically insignificant.

As the League of Nations exemplified, this criterion is unlikely to be met as long as a great power remains neutral.[53] Given contemporary competition between the US and China, a war involving one state will likely feature the other as a neutral, preventing the use of economic warfare. On the other hand, in a war between China and the US, Brazil, the European Union, India and Russia become salient third parties.

Purposefully stretching out a war is an awkward goal, as most states understandably prefer short, easy and inexpensive wars.[54] Moreover, the purpose of extending a war to allow for economic warfare would be to deny strategic supplies to the enemy, a policy designed to end wars. This could be justified only if the costs of prolonged warfare were offset by the benefits of economic warfare. Such a strategy has been proposed for US use in a hypothetical war against China: the US would blockade China for some time, denying it access to strategic supplies, then in a quick military engagement destroy its existing capabilities.[55] Problematically, this strategy requires the willing participation of the enemy. No state is likely to sit by knowing its potential to prevail in the long run is being destroyed.[56] Interfering in an enemy's ability to maintain the capabilities necessary for achieving conventional deterrence, its foreign-policy objectives, its desired international status or, ultimately, its self-defence touches on the enemy's vital interest. If the US attempted to economically strangle China before a military strike, an escalatory response from Chinese could be expected.[57] By attempting to stretch out a war to give economic warfare time to work, the US would provide China with every incentive to launch the war sooner rather than later.

The final question to consider is whether economic warfare can produce an effect in the short term. The main reason economic warfare takes time is because it cannot destroy existing capabilities – the enemy has to exhaust its existing capabilities and strategic reserves. Only kinetic strikes can destroy existing capabilities to the extent of quickly damaging the enemy's war-fighting capacity. In this respect, no other policy can guarantee a quick victory.

Financial tools of statecraft are sometimes proposed as a way to create havoc quickly in the targeted country.[58] These include steps to prohibit payments to the enemy, freezing its assets, denying it access to the domestic stock exchange, severing its participation in global payment systems, calling in outstanding loans and withdrawing reserves from its banks. These may well cause domestic shocks in the enemy's economy.[59] However, they are one-shot policies that cannot apply additional pressure over time.[60] After absorbing the initial impact, the enemy's economy can continue to supply the war effort.[61] Moreover, states are considerably more interdependent financially than they are commercially. Creating havoc in one economy tends to reverberate through the global financial system, potentially making the policy counterproductive.

Financial tools tend to depend on punishment to produce effects. They increase the cost of doing business in a bid to pressure decision-makers to change their policies.[62] Economic warfare, on the other hand, directly targets the capabilities of the enemy, circumventing decision-making by leaders. Enemy leaders have multiple options for dealing with financial pain. Even when denied access to foreign lending, leaders can increase domestic extraction, relying on nationalism to inspire the population to sacrifice for the war effort while possibly ensuring that the pain is felt most acutely by unfavoured groups.[63] While the enemy might be barred from making transactions in a reserve currency, it can still make payments in its own currency. If necessary, it can even resort to barter exchange. With these options available to continue the war effort, financial leverage is not a short-term bet.[64]

* * *

Economic warfare can be a powerful tool. Recent technological developments have made enforcement somewhat easier, and changes in global trade patterns can make the policy more damaging. Yet despite its awesome potential, economic warfare is unlikely to be a feature of modern wars, which are likely either to be too short for economic warfare to be useful, or to require substantial escalation management that precludes its use. Efforts to create the conditions necessary for economic warfare to succeed are unlikely to bear fruit.

This is not to suggest that wars will not have an economic dimension. If the goal is simply to impose costs on the enemy, numerous economic policies can prove fruitful in wartime. However, the success of such policies will be contingent on the enemy's will to fight. The Russian war effort today costs considerably more than it did in 2022, and is probably costing much more than Russia anticipated, thanks in large part to the numerous waves of sanctions the US and its allies have imposed on the country. Yet despite these costs, the war continues. Depending on policymakers to end a war is an uncertain strategy that relies on factors such as leaders' personalities and backgrounds, their perceptions of the conflict's stakes, their countries' domestic political stability, the consequences of ending the war unfavourably and more. This is precisely where economic warfare has the advantage – by targeting the enemy's capabilities, it avoids this uncertainty.

What does it mean, then, that future wars are unlikely to feature economic warfare? The US need not be concerned about enemies severing its access to strategic supplies. Even during wartime, the US will be able to procure products from third parties. Indeed, war tends to create additional supply as neutral states seek to profit by stepping into the breach. When direct trade between the US and China became more expensive due to the US–China trade war during Donald Trump's first presidential term, regional hubs, like Vietnam, emerged to ensure that the flow of products between the two states continued.[65] Granted, maintaining access to strategic products may come at a premium. Wartime resupply is always an expensive endeavour. If the US wants to increase potential avenues of resupply, it should encourage allies to trade more with its enemies. The more third parties China exports to, the more of them will be able to trade with the US in the event of a rupture with China.

At the same time, the US should exercise caution in its competition with China. Preventing technological transfers is very different from denying access to strategic resources required for self-defence. Prohibiting Chinese import of specific US semiconductors imposes costs on China's artificial-intelligence and supercomputing industries. Convincing, or coercing, other states to also sever their supply to China would be more escalatory, but still would not interfere with Chinese defence production given existing levels of technological advancement and indigenous innovation.[66] On the other hand, constraining Chinese access to oil, uranium or metals such as platinum – which China acquires abroad – would affect China's ability to provide for its own self-defence. This would be highly escalatory and likely lead to expansionist policies as China worked to secure protected sources of these resources.

Acknowledgements

The author thanks Kendrick Kuo, Alex Lin, Erik Lin-Greenberg and Jonathan Markowitz; workshop attendees at the Sanctions, Globalization, War and Peace Research Symposium at the University of Southern California; panel attendees at the 2022 annual meeting of the International Studies Association and the 2022 meeting of the Midwest Political Science Association; and the anonymous reviewers for their helpful comments and suggestions.

Notes

1 See Bleddyn E. Bowen, 'Neither a Silver Bullet Nor a Distraction: Economic Warfare in Sea-power Theory', in David Morgan-Owen and Louis Halewood (eds), *Economic Warfare and the Sea: Grand Strategies for Maritime Powers, 1650–1945* (Liverpool: Liverpool University Press, 2020), pp. 45–62; Nicholas A. Lambert, *Planning Armageddon* (Cambridge, MA: Harvard University Press, 2012); Tor Egil Førland, 'The History of Economic Warfare: International Law, Effectiveness, Strategies', *Journal of Peace Research*, vol. 30, no. 2, 1993, pp. 151–62, http://www.jstor.org/stable/425196; Michael Mastanduno, 'Strategies of Economic Containment: U.S. Trade Relations with the Soviet Union', *World Politics*, vol. 37, no. 4, 1985, pp. 503–31, http://www.jstor.org/stable/2010342; and Paul Knorr, *Power of Nations* (New York: Basic Books, 1975).

2 See Aaron Klein and Norman Eisen, 'Economic Warfare Is Hurting Russia. But It's Risky for the U.S., Too', *Washington Post*, 2 March 2022, https://www.washingtonpost.com/outlook/2022/03/02/swift-sanctions-russia-united-states/; Jean Pisani-Ferry, 'Will Russia or the West Win the Economic and Financial Battle?', Project Syndicate, 1 September 2022, https://www.project-syndicate.org/commentary/western-financial-sanctions-against-russia-less-effective-than-expected-by-jean-pisani-ferry-2022-08; and 'Are Sanctions on Russia Working?', *The Economist*, 5 August 2022, https://www.economist.com/leaders/2022/08/25/are-sanctions-working.

3 See Mehul Srivastava and Roman Olearchyk, 'Ukraine: The $10bn Steel Plant at the Heart of Russia's Economic Warfare', *Financial Times*, 6 August 2022; Paul Hannon, 'Russia's Economic War Hits Europe's Factories', *Wall Street Journal*, 14 September 2022, https://www.wsj.com/articles/russias-economic-war-hits-europes-factories-11663150511; Lawrence Freedman, 'Putin's Economic War on Europe Is an Act

of Desperation', *New Statesman*, 7 September 2022, https://www.newstatesman.com/world/europe/ukraine/2022/09/russia-gas-war-europe-desperation; and Jonathan Hackenbroich and Filip Medunic, 'The Kremlin's Energy Warfare', European Council on Foreign Relations, 29 April 2022, https://ecfr.eu/article/the-kremlins-energy-warfare/.

4 See Saadia M. Pekkanen, Setsuko Aoki and John Mittleman, 'Small Satellites, Big Data: Uncovering the Invisible in Maritime Security', *International Security*, vol. 47, no. 2, Fall 2022, pp. 177–216, https://doi.org/10.1162/isec_a_00445.

5 See David A. Baldwin, *Economic Statecraft* (Princeton, NJ: Princeton University Press, 1985); and Jean-Marc F. Blanchard and Norrin M. Ripsman, *Economic Statecraft and Foreign Policy: Sanctions, Incentives, and Target State Calculations* (Abingdon: Routledge, 2013).

6 Robert Loring Allen, for example, defined the term as 'the conscious attempt to increase the relative economic, military, and political position of a country through foreign economic relations'. Robert Loring Allen, *Soviet Economic Warfare* (Washington DC: Public Affairs Press, 1960), p. 28. Teoman Hagemeyer-Witzleb writes in *The International Law of Economic Warfare* (Cham: Springer, 2021), p. 4: 'Economic warfare can be understood as an act of violence to compel our opponent to fulfill our will with the addition that the violence can either be effected or directed against economic means.' Ali Laidi says in *Histoire mondiale de la guerre économique* (Paris: PERRIN, 2016), pp. 13–14: 'La guerre économique est l'utilisation de violences, de contraintes et de moyens déloyaux, ou illégaux, pour protéger ou conquérir un marché, gagner ou préserver une position dominante qui permet de contrôler abusivement un marché.'

7 See Kalevi Jaakko Holsti, *International Politics: A Framework for Analysis* (Hoboken, NJ: Prentice Hall, 1967), p. 228; Miroslav Nincic and Peter Wallensteen, 'Economic Coercion and Foreign Policy', in Miroslav Nincic and Peter Wallensteen (eds), *Dilemmas of Economic Coercion: Sanctions in World Politics* (New York: Praeger, 1983), p. 3; Michael Mastanduno, *Economic Containment: CoCom and the Politics of East–West Trade* (Ithaca, NY: Cornell University Press, 1992), p. 40; and Alan P. Dobson, *US Economic Statecraft for Survival, 1933–1991: Of Sanctions, Embargoes and Economic Warfare*, 1st ed. (New York: Routledge, 2002). This definition avoids the problem of making comparisons between countries, as when scholars have defined economic warfare as an attempt to 'reduce the economic strength, hence the war potential, of the [target] relative to our own'. Comparisons like these can lead to problematic conclusions when two belligerents are equally successful at denying the other strategic supplies and therefore fail to achieve a relative advantage, as by this definition economic warfare would be seen as having failed overall. Yuan-Li Wu, *Economic Warfare*, 1st ed. (Englewood Cliffs, NJ: Prentice-Hall, 1952), pp. 1–2. See also Knorr, *Power of Nations*, p. 138.

8 See Dobson, *US Economic Statecraft for Survival, 1933–1991*, p. 268; Førland, 'The History of Economic Warfare', p. 151; and Wu, *Economic Warfare*, p. 3.

9 For an alternative viewpoint, see Klaus Knorr, *Power and Wealth: The Political Economy of International Power* (New York: Springer, 2016 [1973]), p. 139; and David L. Gordon and Royden Dangerfield, *The Hidden Weapon: The Story of Economic Warfare* (New York: Harper and Bros., 1947), p. 1.

10 Some definitions of economic warfare specify targets such as 'raw materials' (Tor Egil Førland, '"Economic Warfare" and "Strategic Goods": A Conceptual Framework for Analyzing COCOM', *Journal of Peace Research*, vol. 28, no. 2, 1991, p. 192) and 'supply chains' (Mark Harrison, 'Economic Warfare in Twentieth-century History and Strategy', *SSRN*, 20 April 2020, p. 1, https://papers.ssrn.com/sol3/papers.cfm?abstract_id=3605458).

11 Dobson, *US Economic Statecraft for Survival, 1933–1991*, p. 275.

12 See *ibid*., p. 6; Wu, *Economic Warfare*, p. 10; and Thomas C. Schelling, *International Economics* (Boston, MA: Allyn and Bacon, 1958).

13 See Mariya Grinberg, 'Wartime Commercial Policy and Trade Between Enemies', *International Security*, vol. 46, no. 1, Summer 2021, pp. 9–52, https://doi.org/10.1162/isec_a_00412.

14 See Baldwin, *Economic Statecraft*.

15 See Tor Egil Førland, *Cold Economic Warfare: Cocom and the Forging of Strategic Export Controls* (St Louis, MO: Republic of Letters, 2009); Mastanduno, 'Strategies of Economic Containment'; and Knorr, *Power of Nations*.

16 See Gary Clyde Hufbauer et al., *Economic Sanctions Reconsidered* (New York: Columbia University Press, 2008); Etel Solingen, 'Introduction', in Etel Solingen (ed.), *Sanctions, Statecraft, and Nuclear Proliferation* (Cambridge: Cambridge University Press, 2012), pp. 3–28, https://doi.org/10.1017/CBO9780511862380; Arthur A. Stein, 'Sanctions, Inducements, and Market Power: Political Economy of International Influence', in Etel Solingen (ed.), *Sanctions, Statecraft, and Nuclear Proliferation* (Cambridge: Cambridge University Press, 2012), pp. 29–55; Julia Grauvogel, Amanda A. Licht and Christian von Soest, 'Sanctions and Signals: How International Sanction Threats Trigger Domestic Protest in Targeted Regimes', *International Studies Quarterly*, vol. 61, no. 1, March 2017, pp. 86–97, https://doi.org/10.1093/isq/sqw044; Elena V. McLean and Taehee Whang, 'Designing Foreign Policy: Voters, Special Interest Groups, and Economic Sanctions', *Journal of Peace Research*, vol. 51, no. 5, 2014, pp. 589–602, http://www.jstor.org/stable/24557443; Jean-Marc F. Blanchard and Norrin M. Ripsman, 'A Political Theory of Economic Statecraft', *Foreign Policy Analysis*, vol. 4, no. 4, 2008, pp. 371–98, http://www.jstor.org/stable/24909862; and Kim Richard Nossal, 'International Sanctions as International Punishment', *International Organization*, vol. 43, no. 2, 1989, pp. 301–22, http://www.jstor.org/stable/2706704.

17 A possible exception is comprehensive embargoes mandated by the United Nations Security Council, as these require all states to sever trade with the target.

18 See Bowen, 'Neither a Silver Bullet Nor a Distraction', p. 58; and W.N.

Medlicott, *The Economic Blockade*, vol. 1 (London: H.M. Stationery Office, 1952), p. 17.

19 See Lee Jones, *Societies Under Siege: Exploring How International Economic Sanctions (Do Not) Work* (Oxford: Oxford University Press, 2015), p. 1. If a sanctions policy is backed up by secondary sanctions targeted at all states, this would approximate economic warfare.

20 See Stephen Neff, 'Economic Warfare in Contemporary International Law', *Stanford Journal of International Law*, vol. 26, 1989, p. 70, https://www.research.ed.ac.uk/en/publications/economic-warfare-in-contemporary-international-law.

21 It is assumed that the enacting state has the capacity to enforce economic warfare.

22 See Bowen, 'Neither a Silver Bullet Nor a Distraction'; and Thomas K. Finletter, 'Foreword', in Gordon and Dangerfield, *The Hidden Weapon*, pp. vii–x.

23 Nicholas Mulder, *The Economic Weapon: The Rise of Sanctions as a Tool of Modern War* (New Haven, CT: Yale University Press, 2022).

24 The significance of war, in this context, is that battlefield destruction is occurring. Whether war is officially declared or referred to as a 'police action' or 'special military operation' is irrelevant.

25 See Harrison, 'Economic Warfare in Twentieth-century History and Strategy'; Stephen Broadberry and Mark Harrison, 'An Overview', in Stephen Broadberry and Mark Harrison (eds), *The Economics of World War I* (Cambridge: Cambridge University Press, 2005), pp. 3–40; and Knorr, *Power and Wealth*, p. 141.

26 See Peter Davies, 'Geoffrey Vickers and Lessons from the Ministry of Economic Warfare for Cold War Defence Intelligence', *Intelligence and National Security*, vol. 31, no. 6, 18 September 2016, pp. 810–28, https://doi.org/10.1080/02684527.2015.1115235; Lambert, *Planning Armageddon*; and Bruce A. Elleman and S.C.M. Paine, *Naval Blockades and Seapower: Strategies and Counter-Strategies, 1805–2005* (New York: Routledge, 2007).

27 See Bowen, 'Neither a Silver Bullet Nor a Distraction', p. 60.

28 See Hagemeyer-Witzleb, *The International Law of Economic Warfare*; Morgan-Owen and Halewood, *Economic Warfare and the Sea*; and Finletter, 'Foreword'.

29 The logic is similar to motivations for preventive war in power shifts. See Jack S. Levy, 'Preventive War: Concept and Propositions', *International Interactions*, vol. 37, no. 1, 14 March 2011, https://doi.org/10.1080/03050629.2011.546716; Dale C. Copeland, *The Origins of Major War* (Ithaca, NY: Cornell University Press, 2000); and Richard Ned Lebow, 'Windows of Opportunity: Do States Jump Through Them?', *International Security*, vol. 9, no. 1, Summer 1984, pp. 147–86, https://doi.org/10.2307/2538638.

30 See Edward S. Miller, *Bankrupting the Enemy: The U.S. Financial Siege of Japan Before Pearl Harbor* (Annapolis, MD: Naval Institute Press, 2007).

31 See Vaughan Lowe and Antonios Tzanakopoulos, 'Economic Warfare', in Rüdiger Wolfrum (ed.), *Max Planck Encyclopedia of Public International Law* (Oxford: Oxford University Press, 2012), p. 9, https://ssrn.com/abstract=1701590.

32 See Robert Jervis, *The Meaning of the Nuclear Revolution: Statecraft and the Prospect of Armageddon* (Ithaca, NY: Cornell University Press, 1989); and Keir A. Lieber and Daryl G. Press, *The Myth of the Nuclear Revolution: Power Politics in the Atomic Age* (Ithaca, NY: Cornell University Press, 2020).

33 See, for example, Graham Allison, *Destined for War: Can America and China Escape Thucydides's Trap?* (New York: Houghton Mifflin Harcourt, 2017); Adam P. Liff and G. John Ikenberry, 'Racing Toward Tragedy? China's Rise, Military Competition in the Asia Pacific, and the Security Dilemma', *International Security*, vol. 39, no. 2, Fall 2014, pp. 52–91, https://doi.org/10.1162/ISEC_a_00176; Thomas J. Christensen, 'Fostering Stability or Creating a Monster? The Rise of China and U.S. Policy Toward East Asia', *International Security*, vol. 31, no. 1, Summer 2006, pp. 81–126, https://muse.jhu.edu/journals/international_security/v031/31.1christensen.html; and John J. Mearsheimer, *The Tragedy of Great Power Politics* (W. W. Norton & Company, 2001).

34 See Barry Posen, *Inadvertent Escalation: Conventional War and Nuclear Risks* (Ithaca, NY: Cornell University Press, 1991); and Caitlin Talmadge, 'Would China Go Nuclear? Assessing the Risk of Chinese Nuclear Escalation in a Conventional War with the United States', *International Security*, vol. 41, no. 4, Spring 2017, pp. 50–92.

35 See Scott Douglas Sagan, *The Limits of Safety: Organizations, Accidents, and Nuclear Weapons* (Princeton, NJ: Princeton University Press, 2020 [1995]).

36 See Debak Das, '"The Courtroom of World Opinion": Bringing the International Audience into Nuclear Crises', *Global Studies Quarterly*, vol. 1, no. 4, 1 December 2021, pp. 1–11, https://doi.org/10.1093/isagsq/ksab028.

37 See Joshua Rovner, 'A Long War in the East: Doctrine, Diplomacy, and the Prospects for a Protracted Sino-American Conflict', *Diplomacy and Statecraft*, vol. 29, no. 1, 2 January 2018, pp. 129–42, https://doi.org/10.1080/09592296.2017.1420535.

38 See James Dobbins, 'War with China', *Survival*, vol. 65, no. 4, August–September 2023, p. 233, https://doi.org/10.1080/00396338.2023.2239074.

39 See Dominic Tierney, 'The Future of Sino-U.S. Proxy War', *Texas National Security Review*, vol. 4, no. 2, Spring 2021, pp. 49–73, http://dx.doi.org/10.26153/tsw/13198.

40 See Wu, *Economic Warfare*, p. 146.

41 See Barbie Latza Nadeau, 'Putin Begins to Target Western Weapons Deliveries', Daily Beast, 6 June 2022, https://www.thedailybeast.com/putin-begins-to-target-western-weapons-deliveries.

42 See Olena Bilousova et al., 'Challenges of Export Controls Enforcement: How Russia Continues to Import Components for Its Military Production', KSE Institute, January 2024, https://kse.ua/wp-content/uploads/2024/01/Challenges-of-Export-Controls-Enforcement.pdf?mc_cid=0f8f93389f&mc_eid=4c68c0cbf6.

43 See Ivan Arreguin-Toft, 'How the Weak Win Wars: A Theory of Asymmetric Conflict', *International Security*, vol. 26, no. 1, Summer 2001,

pp. 93–128, http://www.jstor.org/stable/3092079.

44 The five permanent members of the Security Council – China, France, Russia, the United Kingdom and the United States – are among the top-15 trading countries of the world. World Integrated Trade Solution, 'Exports to World by Country in US$ Thousand 2017–2020', https://wits.worldbank.org/.

45 See Pierre Razoux, *The Iran–Iraq War* (Cambridge, MA: Harvard University Press, 2015); and Williamson Murray and Kevin M. Woods, *The Iran–Iraq War: A Military and Strategic History* (Cambridge: Cambridge University Press, 2014).

46 See Martin S. Navias and E.R. Hooton, *Tanker Wars: Assault on Merchant Shipping During the Iran–Iraq Crisis, 1980–88* (London: I.B. Tauris, 1996).

47 See Ross Leckow, 'The Iran–Iraq Conflict in the Gulf: The Law of War Zones', *International and Comparative Law Quarterly*, vol. 37, no. 3, July 1988, p. 633, https://www.jstor.org/stable/760280.

48 See Stephen Van Evera, *Causes of War: Power and the Roots of Conflict* (Ithaca, NY: Cornell University Press, 2013 [1999]); Sagan, *The Limits of Safety*; and Posen, *Inadvertent Escalation*.

49 See Ruth Henig, *The Peace That Never Was: A History of the League of Nations* (London: Haus Publishing, 2019); and Mulder, *The Economic Weapon*.

50 See John H. McNeill, 'Neutral Rights and Maritime Sanctions: The Effects of Two Gulf Wars', *Virginia Journal of International Law*, vol. 31, no. 4, 1991, p. 641, https://heinonline.org/HOL/P?h=hein.journals/vajint31&i=643.

51 See Tim Niblock, *'Pariah States' and Sanctions in the Middle East: Iraq, Libya, Sudan* (Boulder, CO: Lynne Rienner Publishers, 2001), p. 100.

52 See Patrick M. Norton, 'Between the Ideology and the Reality: The Shadow of the Law of Neutrality', *Harvard International Law Journal*, vol. 17, no. 2, 1976, p. 252, https://heinonline.org/HOL/P?h=hein.journals/hilj17&i=259.

53 See Constantine Antonopoulos, *Non-Participation in Armed Conflict: Continuity and Modern Challenges to the Law of Neutrality* (Cambridge: Cambridge University Press, 2022).

54 See Lawrence Freedman, *The Future of War: A History* (New York: PublicAffairs, 2017).

55 See Fiona S. Cunningham, 'The Maritime Rung on the Escalation Ladder: Naval Blockades in a US–China Conflict', *Security Studies*, vol. 29, no. 4, 31 October 2020, pp. 730–68, https://doi.org/10.1080/09636412.2020.1811462; Gabriel Collins, 'A Maritime Oil Blockade Against China: Tactically Tempting but Strategically Flawed', *Naval War College Review*, vol. 71, no. 2, Spring 2018, https://digital-commons.usnwc.edu/nwc-review/vol71/iss2/6; Sean Mirski, 'Stranglehold: The Context, Conduct and Consequences of an American Naval Blockade of China', *Journal of Strategic Studies*, vol. 36, no. 3, 12 February 2013, pp. 385–421, https://doi.org/10.1080/01402390.2012.743885; T.X. Hammes, 'Offshore Control: A Proposed Strategy for an Unlikely Conflict', INSS Strategic Forum, June 2012; and Douglas C. Peifer, 'China, the German Analogy, and the New AirSea Operational Concept', *Orbis*, vol. 55, no. 1, 2011, pp. 114–31, https://doi.org/10.1016/j.orbis.2010.10.009.

56 See Erik Sand, 'Desperate Measures: The Effects of Economic Isolation on Warring Powers', *Texas National Security Review*, vol. 3, no. 2, Spring 2020, https://tnsr.org/2020/04/desperate-measures-the-effects-of-economic-isolation-on-warring-powers/.

57 See Gabriel B. Collins, Andew S. Erickson and Lyle J. Goldstein, 'Chinese Naval Analysts Consider the Energy Question', in Gabriel B. Collins et al. (eds), *China's Energy Strategy: The Impact on Beijing's Maritime Policies* (Annapolis, MD: Naval Institute Press, 2012 [2008]); and Collins, 'A Maritime Oil Blockade Against China'.

58 See Gary Clyde Hufbauer and Euijin Jung, 'Economic Sanctions in the Twenty-first Century', in Peter A.G. van Bergeijk (ed.), *Research Handbook on Economic Sanctions* (Cheltenham: Edward Elgar Publishing, 2021), pp. 26–43; Juan Zarate, *Treasury's War: The Unleashing of a New Era of Financial Warfare*, 1st ed. (New York: PublicAffairs, 2013); Ella Shagabutdinova and Jeffrey Berejikian, 'Deploying Sanctions While Protecting Human Rights: Are Humanitarian "Smart" Sanctions Effective?', *Journal of Human Rights*, vol. 6, no. 1, February 2007, pp. 59–74, https://doi.org/10.1080/14754830601098386; Paul Bracken, 'Financial Warfare', *Orbis*, vol. 51, no. 4, 2007, pp. 685–96, https://doi.org/10.1016/j.orbis.2007.08.010; Arne Tostensen and Beate Bull, 'Are Smart Sanctions Feasible?', *World Politics*, vol. 54, no. 3, 2002, p. 386, http://www.jstor.org/stable/25054192; and Jonathan Kirshner, 'The Microfoundations of Economic Sanctions', *Security Studies*, vol. 6, no. 3, 1997, p. 38, https://doi.org/10.1080/09636419708429314.

59 See Emre Hatipoglu and Dursun Peksen, 'Economic Sanctions and Banking Crises in Target Economies', *Defence and Peace Economics*, vol. 29, no. 2, 2018, pp. 171–89, https://doi.org/10.1080/10242694.2016.1245811; and Erik Gartzke, Quan Li and Charles Boehmer, 'Investing in the Peace: Economic Interdependence and International Conflict', *International Organization*, vol. 55, no. 2, Spring 2001, pp. 391–438, http://www.jstor.org/stable/3078636.

60 See Henry Farrell and Abraham L. Newman, 'Weaponized Interdependence: How Global Economic Networks Shape State Coercion', *International Security*, vol. 44, no. 1, Summer 2019, pp. 42–79, https://doi.org/10.1162/isec_a_00351.

61 Financial tools, likewise, cannot destroy the existing capabilities of the enemy. See Kirshner, 'The Microfoundations of Economic Sanctions', p. 38.

62 See Tostensen and Bull, 'Are Smart Sanctions Feasible?'.

63 See Abel Escribà-Folch, 'Authoritarian Responses to Foreign Pressure: Spending, Repression, and Sanctions', *Comparative Political Studies*, vol. 45, no. 6, 2012, pp. 683–713, https://doi.org/10.1177/0010414011427883; and Benn Steil and Robert E. Litan, *Financial Statecraft: The Role of Financial Markets in American Foreign Policy* (New Haven, CT: Yale University Press, 2008).

64 See Paul Einzig, *Economic Warfare* (London: Macmillan and Company, 1940), p. 12; and Adrian U-Jin Ang and Dursun Peksen, 'When Do Economic Sanctions Work?

Asymmetric Perceptions, Issue Salience, and Outcomes', *Political Research Quarterly*, vol. 60, no. 1, March 2007, pp. 135–45, https://doi.org/10.1177/1065912906298632.

65 See Chuin-Wei Yap, 'American Tariffs on China Are Being Blunted by Trade Cheats', *Wall Street Journal*, 26 June 2019, https://www.wsj.com/articles/american-tariffs-on-china-are-being-blunted-by-trade-cheats-11561546806.

66 See Ana Swanson, 'U.S. Tightens China's Access to Advanced Chips for Artificial Intelligence', *New York Times*, 17 October 2023, https://www.nytimes.com/2023/10/17/business/economy/ai-chips-china-restrictions.html.

Copyright © 2025 The International Institute for Strategic Studies

Review Essay

Sanctions: Failure by Other Means

Chris Clague

Chokepoints: American Power in the Age of Economic Warfare
Edward Fishman. New York: Penguin, 2025. $40.00. 560 pp.

In the penultimate chapter of *Chokepoints*, a detailed history of US efforts to use economic coercion to deter North Korea and Iran from obtaining nuclear weapons, discourage Russia from advancing in Ukraine, and prevent Chinese firms from continuing to infiltrate the world's technological infrastructure, Edward Fishman finally asks the question readers have already been asking themselves for 400 pages: '[Was] any of this worth it?' (p. 410). The answer should be 'mostly no'. Fishman's answer is more equivocal.

Much of the recent literature on economic sanctions tilts towards 'mostly no'. It is difficult to argue otherwise given the current status of the aforementioned challenges. As of January 2024, the Arms Control Association reported that North Korea possessed 50 nuclear warheads, with enough fissile material for 70–90 more.[1] Iran does not yet have nuclear weapons according to intelligence estimates, but it has resumed enriching uranium since the first Trump administration withdrew from the Joint Comprehensive Plan of Action (JCPOA) in 2018. Russia annexed Crimea in 2014 and invaded

Chris Clague is an IISS Associate Fellow.

Survival | vol. 67 no. 3 | June–July 2025 | pp. 171–178 https://doi.org/10.1080/00396338.2025.2508092

Ukraine in 2022, and is unlikely to return any territory gained. While US export controls and other sanctions on Chinese firms, especially Huawei and ZTE, did temporarily cripple those firms, Huawei has recovered, and China continues to make advances in artificial intelligence (AI) and in the semiconductors that power it.[2]

What sets *Chokepoints* apart is that it takes a narrative rather than theoretical or thematic approach to the development of sanctions regimes, tracing economic warfare through the first two decades of the twenty-first century. Fishman – who has worked in the US Department of State, the Department of the Treasury and the Pentagon – is an excellent guide. What emerges over the course of his book is that there is no single reason sanctions failed, and that for all the power the United States wields over the global financial system and economy, it is invariably subject to strategic constraints.

The new sinews of American power

Fishman spends only a few pages on North Korea, early in the book. This is mainly because, as he describes it, it was 'an economic weapons test' for the US and, specifically, for the Office of Terrorism and Financial Intelligence (TFI), a relatively new division of the Treasury established in 2004. TFI had identified a small bank in Macau, Banco Delta Asia, to which the North Korean regime was paying fees to accept large foreign-currency deposits and provide it access to the US financial system. By designating the bank a 'primary money laundering concern', the Treasury compelled banks in 'China and beyond' to stop doing business with the small Macau bank with the threat that they too could be cut off. A North Korean official is quoted as admitting afterwards, 'you Americans finally found a way to hurt us' (pp. 44–5). It's telling, however, that the official didn't say 'stop us'.

Nevertheless, sanctioning Banco Delta Asia was enough to motivate a small group of US officials to investigate ways they could expand the government's economic toolkit for future use. The foreign-policy establishment was initially sceptical. In the case of Iran, George W. Bush, then president, claimed the US 'had sanctioned itself out of leverage'. Stuart Levey, the first under secretary in charge of TFI, convinced secretary of state Condoleezza Rice that this was not the case and that the US could employ 'blocking sanctions', such as asset freezes and transactions bans, which would effectively cut Iranian banks off from the US dollar (pp. 58–63). The sanctions regime against Iran came to include a wide range of measures, including barring Iranian banks from the Society for Worldwide Interbank Financial Telecommunication (SWIFT) and secondary sanctions that involved economic penalties on foreign banks, companies and individuals doing business with Iran. Collectively, these were hurting the Iranian economy.

It wasn't enough, however. Iran was still earning significant revenue from oil exports. China, India and US allies such as Japan and South Korea were too reliant on Iranian oil to support an embargo. This highlights an important constraint on economic warfare, one that also arose with Russia and is now salient in the trade war between the US and China. Exporters of vital natural resources are difficult to sanction or threaten without serious repercussions. Few if any countries are self-sufficient in energy, metals and minerals, or food and agriculture. The mildest outcome of removing Iranian oil, Russian natural gas or wheat, or Chinese critical minerals from the global market would be a price spike. The worst is severe scarcity and economic pain affecting countries other than the target.

The US Treasury found an innovative solution to this problem. Instead of imposing an embargo, Washington allowed foreign banks to process payments for Iranian oil only if they held the funds in escrow accounts. The money in these accounts could only be used to purchase humanitarian goods such as food and medicine, and could not revert to Iran. According to Fishman, tying up the money – estimated at close to $100 billion – ultimately compelled Iran to halt its nuclear programme for six months, which led to the JCPOA negotiations (pp. 120–3).

Trump's disavowal of the JCPOA in 2018 in favour of a 'maximum pressure' policy, according to Fishman, 'achieved little of value while removing the shackles on Iran's nuclear program' (p. 418). He might be right. The larger point is that sanctions can fail on account of domestic politics. All the efforts that went into bringing Iran to the negotiating table and reaching a nuclear deal fell victim to the whims of a president who labelled it, without providing details, 'the worst deal in history' mainly to tar his predecessor and please his American supporters. Iran, of course, went back to enriching uranium.

Russia I and II

When Russia annexed Crimea in early 2014, the US sanctions apparatus faced a far more difficult task than it had with Iran, not least because Russia 'was [an economic] colossus compared with every other country America had previously sanctioned' (p. 158). Fishman points out that the technocrats at the Treasury and State departments recognised that implementing the same types of economic weapons the US had used against Iran would inevitably produce blowback in Europe and the US. 'Even at Treasury', he writes, 'there were doubts that America's sanctions arsenal could stop Putin's imperial march' (p. 159).

They tried anyway. First up were blocking sanctions, which had been so effective against banks in Iran. With Russia, however, they were blunted by the connections European banks had to American and large Russian ones. Especially given that the global financial system was just recovering from the 2008–09 global financial crisis, the risk of financial contagion was too high. There was less risk in sanctioning smaller Russian banks. Bank Rossiya, which served a number of Putin's cronies, was the first target. Other sanctions followed, but discord between the US and Europe – a recurring theme in *Chokepoints* – grew mainly over the imposition of sectoral sanctions. But Europe's reluctance to match the United States' severity disappeared when Russian forces shot down a commercial airliner bound for Amsterdam from Kuala Lumpur that was carrying 196 Dutch nationals in July 2014. In an impassioned speech, the Dutch foreign minister convinced other European governments to commit to harsher sectoral sanctions, depriving Russia of European technologies it needed for the most competitive sectors of its economy, including energy.

Now the Russian economy began a steep downward spiral. Russian firms were cut off from capital markets, oil prices fell, the rouble plummeted and the incomes of ordinary Russians shrank. Yet, as Fishman notes, 'sanctions had not changed facts on the ground in Ukraine' (p. 207) and

America and Europe declined to take harsher measures. It is impossible to know whether Putin would have relented from invading Ukraine eight years later. He had bolstered his standing with the Russian people by seizing and annexing Crimea, and decided to wait to see what the next US president – Donald Trump – would do. When Russian forces did invade Ukraine, there was little left for the US and Europe to sanction except the country's oil and gas exports. But Europe was heavily reliant on gas imports from Russia. Loath to roil global energy markets, the US Treasury chose to 'carve out energy' (p. 325).

The Biden administration identified a new source of leverage – in effect, a choke point – that could enable Russia to keep oil flowing onto world markets but deprive it of revenue: maritime insurance. Members of the London-based International Group of P&I Clubs insure over 95% of ocean-going tankers. Under a price-cap system applicable to Russian oil imposed by the European Union, the G7 and Australia, it is effectively unlawful for such entities to insure shipping firms transporting Russian oil sold above the cap.[3] The measure has caused considerable logistical inconvenience and contracted global oil supplies. On 5 December 2022, when Turkish authorities insisted that vessels provide written letters from insurers attesting to compliance with the price cap, a traffic jam formed at the mouth of the Bosphorus[4] – the physical choke point where Fishman begins the book, with the story of how Sparta seized the strait to bring down Athens. While the price cap has ended up cleaving the global oil market, it has proven difficult to enforce, strained the patience of the maritime-insurance industry and failed to change facts on the ground in Ukraine.[5]

China and Huawei

If North Korea or Iran hadn't sought nuclear weapons, or Russia hadn't annexed Crimea or invaded Ukraine, it's possible that none of these countries would have faced sanctions, at least not on the scale that they did, though Iran's support for Hamas and other terrorist organisations might have made it the exception. The reasons the US is waging economic warfare against China in general, and its technology sector in particular, are different. For years, the US allowed China to develop choke points of its own, the main one being its commanding position at the centre of many global supply chains. But it wasn't until Chinese telecom giants ZTE and especially Huawei began to overtake their Western competitors in building next-generation global telecommunications networks that the US took close notice. In 2012, the House Permanent Select Committee on Intelligence reported that the firms had strong ties to the Chinese military and the Chinese Communist Party (CCP), and was working on behalf of both.[6]

The geopolitical wake-up call for the US came when the United Kingdom approved Huawei as the vendor to build its 5G network. Fishman notes that 'if Huawei equipment formed the spine of the world's 5G networks, CCP would obtain a geopolitical asset matched only by the U.S. dollar – an economic and political kill switch of global reach' (p. 228).

In addition to encouraging its allies to ban future use of the Huawei network, or remove equipment already installed, the US targeted semiconductors, which are critical to network equipment and have extensive military and AI applications. Mere export controls proved insufficient. Most manufacturing for semiconductors and related technology was located outside the US, in countries such as Taiwan, South Korea, Japan and the Netherlands, the home of ASML, whose machines produce the most advanced semiconductors.[7] To starve Huawei and other Chinese technology firms of semiconductors, in 2020 the US devised and implemented the Foreign Direct Product Rule (FDPR), which banned companies all over the world from selling chips made using US technology to Huawei. Since virtually all important firms in the semiconductor supply chain use some form of US technology, the effect was to ban all semiconductor exports to China.

Although some companies and countries found loopholes, most adhered to the FDPR. Huawei's earnings plunged the following year. It is uncertain, however, what the long-term impact of the FDPR and more recent, even stricter restrictions imposed by the Biden administration could have. Chinese firms have since hoarded chips, and the Chinese government has been directing billions of dollars towards developing domestic manufacturing capacity. The US may have hindered China's technological development, but it is unlikely to have stopped it.

* * *

In 2011, Harvard economist Dani Rodrik judged that countries could not simultaneously advance democracy, national determination and economic globalisation.[8] Fishman concludes that the age of economic warfare may soon end for analogous reasons: 'The trade-offs facing policymakers in Washington, Beijing, Brussels and Moscow can be thought of as an impossible trinity, consisting of economic interdependence, economic security and geopolitical competition. Any two of these can coexist, but not all three' (p. 424). He concludes that, due in large part to the impossibility of the trinity, 'someday, the Age of Economic Warfare will end, but we might miss it when it's gone' (p. 425). The word 'might' is doing some heavy lifting in that sentence. It took decades for the US to accumulate the power to prosecute such warfare on the scale it did and, even so, its policy objectives went mostly unachieved.

Notes

1 Arms Control Association, 'Arms Control and Proliferation Profile: North Korea', June 2024, https://www.armscontrol.org/factsheets/arms-control-and-proliferation-profile-north-korea.

2 See Liza Lin, Stu Woo and Raffaele Huang, 'The U.S. Wanted to Knock Down Huawei. It's Only Getting Stronger', *Wall Street Journal*, 29 July 2024, https://www.wsj.com/business/telecom/huawei-china-technology-us-sanctions-76462031.

3 See, for example, Simon Johnson and Catherine Wolfram, 'Strengthening Enforcement of the Russian Oil Price Cap', Economic Studies at Brookings, May 2024, https://www.brookings.edu/wp-content/uploads/2024/05/20240528_ES_Sanctions_JohnsonWolfram_Final.pdf.

4 See, for example, 'Oil Tanker Traffic Jam Forms in Turkey After Russian Price Cap', *Middle East Eye*, 5 December 2022, https://www.middleeasteye.net/news/oil-tanker-jam-forms-turkey-after-russian-price-cap.

5 See, for example, Richard Meade, 'Insurers Tell UK Government that Oil Price Cap Is "Increasingly Unenforceable"', Lloyd's List, 29 April 2024, https://www.lloydslist.com/LL1148993/Insurers-tell-UK-government-that-oil-price-cap-is-increasingly-unenforceable.

6 See Mike Rogers and Dutch Ruppersberger, 'Investigative Report on the U.S. National Security Issues Posed by Chinese Telecommunications Companies Huawei and ZTE', US House of

Representatives, 112th Congress, 8 October 2012, https://intelligence.house.gov/sites/intelligence.house.gov/files/documents/huawei-zte%20investigative%20report%20(final).pdf.

7 See Chris Miller, *Chip War: The Fight for the World's Most Critical Technology* (New York: Scribner, 2022).

8 See Dani Rodrik, *The Globalization Paradox: Democracy and the Future of the World Economy* (New York: W. W. Norton & Co., 2011).

Copyright © 2025 The International Institute for Strategic Studies

Book Reviews

Deterrence, Arms Control and Nuclear History

Matthew Jones

Disarming Apartheid: The End of South Africa's Nuclear Weapons Programme and Accession to the Treaty on the Non-Proliferation of Nuclear Weapons, 1968–1991
Robin E. Möser. Cambridge: Cambridge University Press, 2024. £85.00. 224 pp.

Among the many remarkable stories that accompanied the final years of the apartheid system in South Africa, the dismantling of the republic's indigenous nuclear-weapons programme stands out as a singular event of the nuclear age. Initially developed as a putative means of deterring any Cuban or Soviet threat from the north, during the 1970s the programme was hidden behind domestic nuclear-power projects. South Africa is home to abundant sources of natural uranium, and was, ironically, one of the founding members of the International Atomic Energy Agency (IAEA) in June 1957. With US assistance during the 1960s, it began to develop a home-grown reactor programme and import quantities of highly enriched uranium (HEU). In 1970, the B.J. Vorster government announced it would begin producing its own HEU for peaceful purposes, and was open to negotiations leading to signature of the Nuclear Non-Proliferation Treaty (NPT) that had recently entered into force. But seeing few benefits from accession, the regime turned instead to developing a weapons programme that coincided with the collapse of white-minority rule and colonial power in southern Africa as a whole, amid the sense that apartheid was under siege. A prototype nuclear device was apparently ready for testing by August 1977, but open disapproval from the Carter administration, which was keen to advance the cause of global nuclear non-proliferation, led to the abandonment of test plans.

 https://doi.org/10.1080/00396338.2025.2508093

As Robin Möser's fascinating and well-documented study shows, from this point onwards, the government in Pretoria played a cat-and-mouse game with Washington, as US officials tried to persuade South Africa to accede to the NPT and its safeguards regime. As a reward for doing so, South Africa might have been allowed to sell its natural uranium on the international market, which was then prohibited by sanctions, and to secure external supplies of low-enriched uranium for domestic electricity production in its nuclear reactors. But the preferred course of the P.W. Botha government that took power in September 1978 was to proceed with a secret weapons programme while maintaining public ambiguity over its nuclear stance. By 1982, a first gun-type weapon had been manufactured.

Möser reveals how the preconditions disingenuously placed by the South African government on NPT accession masked a basic unwillingness to forgo its weapons programme, even though it was proving an expensive and militarily dubious undertaking. The Ministry of Foreign Affairs under Pik Botha's direction was eager to engage with Western governments, showing an interest in signing up to the NPT and international safeguards, but it encountered domestic resistance from the arms industry and the Atomic Energy Corporation.

Attitudes began to change with negotiations in 1987–88 that led to the withdrawal of Cuban troops from Angola and Namibian independence, but it was the coming to power of F.W. de Klerk in September 1989 that marked a real change in approach. By the following year, de Klerk's policy had become clear – he would prioritise domestic reform, dismantle the nuclear-weapons programme and begin seriously to discuss accession to the NPT. There was a continuing reluctance to take this final step, however, unless tangible rewards were offered by the West, in the form of a relaxation in sanctions and support for the republic's civilian nuclear activities – steps that the United States made clear could not occur until the structures of apartheid were pulled down.

As Möser tells it, de Klerk was vulnerable in 1990–91 to a challenge from the unreconstructed right, and the Conservative Party in particular, if he made concessions over the NPT for no apparent end (pp. 130, 136–7). As a result, the Ministry of Foreign Affairs hoped to see Western influence used over front-line states such as Angola, Mozambique, Tanzania, Zambia and Zimbabwe to also sign the NPT, and to push forward the idea of a nuclear-weapons-free zone in southern Africa. When these states signalled their willingness to sign, de Klerk duly announced that South Africa would accede to the NPT in June 1991. Signature of a safeguards agreement soon followed, and between November 1991 and September 1993 IAEA inspectors verified that South Africa had declared all its stocks of fissile material. The government dismantled the six nuclear weapons it had by then fabricated, simultaneously destroying as much documentary evidence as possible about its military nuclear programme. Möser shows in closely argued fashion that de Klerk's path to NPT accession, because of its very public features and the domestic political situation, was more difficult than his decision to dismantle the weapons themselves. In telling this story, and by demonstrating how the development of South Africa's military programme was intertwined with pressures to accede to the NPT, Möser has made a valuable contribution both to contemporary South African history and to our understanding of the emergence of the global nuclear non-proliferation regime.

The Big Three Allies and the European Resistance: Intelligence, Politics, and the Origins of the Cold War, 1939–1945
Tommaso Piffer. Oxford: Oxford University Press, 2024.
£35.00. 304 pp.

While there have been many studies of individual European resistance movements in the Second World War and the support they received from the Allies, the great merit of this book is to consider them collectively as part of a complex web of diplomacy that emerged as Britain, the Soviet Union and the United States manoeuvred for post-war advantage. To this end, Tommaso Piffer juxtaposes the work of the British Special Operations Executive (SOE) in countries such as France, Greece, Italy, Poland and Yugoslavia with Soviet efforts to use indigenous communist movements as tools of post-war foreign policy. He also highlights the increasingly assertive attempts of the American Office of Strategic Services to play a role in fomenting anti-Nazi resistance.

Piffer has mined some of the more recently released British SOE files to provide more telling detail on, among other matters, the discordant British attempts to turn the Balkans into a major liability for the Germans, while also trying to ensure that post-war British interests in the reduction of communist influence were maintained. The result was often incoherence: 'rather than being set on a clear long-term strategy, British policy evolved as the result of a series of crises caused by the attempts of each of the actors involved to impose its own priorities' (p. 126). The clashes between SOE Cairo and the Foreign Office over Greece are familiar terrain to scholars of British wartime policy towards Southeast Europe, but Piffer provides extra nuance by integrating British material with insights from local players on all sides, using less familiar Russian and East European sources to good effect. Indeed, the book's extensive and informative bibliography is a testament to the author's wide research and language skills.

One of Piffer's main arguments is that the British were ham-fisted in their efforts to manipulate and direct the movements they supplied, and the SOE naive in believing it could make a major contribution to victory over the Axis (by, for example, building formidable resistance armies in Poland). Partisans, particularly in the Balkans, would use British support to settle their own scores with internal opponents and position themselves to take power when liberation finally came. But Piffer also suggests that the British had more freedom to follow their preferred policies than they knew. This was especially so with regard to the Chetniks, whom Josip Broz Tito successfully branded as collaborators with the German occupiers of Yugoslavia, but whom Piffer suggests might have proved better partners than Tito's partisans.

Josef Stalin was consistent but cautious in his attempts to promote local communist parties as leading contenders to seize power, and Piffer shows how in Poland, for example, he delayed issuing instructions to the Polish communists to destroy their rivals until he was sure this would not break his relationship with Winston Churchill. Stalin showed, moreover, a lack of interest in the Greek communists, as he considered Greece to lie in the British sphere. In fact, the strangest omission in Piffer's otherwise excellent study is any mention or discussion of the 'percentages agreement' between Churchill and Stalin of October 1944, which divided the Balkans between the Western allies and the Soviet Union. In general terms, Piffer makes the interesting case that the Allies may have had 'more leverage at the negotiation table with the Soviets than they ever realized' (p. 247), having failed to fully discern Stalin's cautious approach. Overall, this is an excellent, multilayered contribution to the literature on European resistance in the Second World War – and, in particular, the role of the SOE – showing how the interaction between local movements and the members of the Grand Alliance helped to shape post-war Europe.

America's Cold Warrior: Paul Nitze and National Security from Roosevelt to Reagan
James Graham Wilson. Ithaca, NY: Cornell University Press, 2024. $32.95. 336 pp.

As this lively, readable and informative biography reminds us, Paul Nitze's name is forever associated with some of the key episodes of the Cold War. Having drafted major parts of the seminal document NSC-68 as head of the US State Department's Policy Planning Staff in 1950, compiled the Gaither report in 1957, harshly critiqued the Strategic Arms Limitation Talks (SALT) in the mid-1970s and served as an arms-control negotiator during the Intermediate-Range Nuclear Forces (INF) talks of the early 1980s, Nitze's name pops up with

Zelig-like regularity in any Cold War history. Few other Americans could boast of wielding insider influence for as long as Nitze did, having played important roles in both Democratic and Republican administrations. Yet aside from a few articles, and discounting a stolid memoir (*From Hiroshima to Glasnost*) and the reflections he wrote towards the end of his life in *Tension Between Opposites*, he never penned a major academic work setting out his fundamental beliefs and prognoses, unlike his scholar–practitioner nemesis, Henry Kissinger. Indeed, James Graham Wilson notes in *America's Cold Warrior* that Nitze's relations with the prolific Kissinger were wary and tinged with resentment after Kissinger published his influential 1957 study *Nuclear Weapons and Foreign Policy*, which Nitze believed contained some of his own ideas (pp. 97–8). Their sparring was to continue in the 1970s, when Nitze took aim at Kissinger's approach to arms control, which he argued was prejudicing US security.

Given his swashbuckling Wall Street background, Nitze saw himself as a man of action rather than a contributor to intellectual debates over defence and foreign policy. In the mid-1960s, when he held the job of secretary of the navy, he did not play a central role in Vietnam policy, and in 1965 he appears to have held back from expressing his reservations over escalation. For Nitze, 'the highest tragedy was not Vietnam but rather that the United States had failed to preserve the strategic advantages that forced the Soviets to back down in the Cuban Missile Crisis' (p. 144). Made deputy secretary of defense in July 1967, he expected to assume the top position at the Pentagon when Robert McNamara departed at the end of that same year, but in what amounted to probably the biggest disappointment of his career, he was passed over in favour of Clark Clifford. Characteristically, Nitze had expended no effort in cultivating personal favour with president Lyndon Johnson.

Even so, it was a sign of Nitze's perceived worth to an administration of a different political complexion that by the early 1970s, having successfully lobbied Congress for the deployment of the Safeguard Anti-Ballistic Missile system, he resurfaced as the secretary of defense's representative in the US delegation during the early stages of the SALT negotiations. Yet his frustration with the compromises that were necessary to reach an agreement led him to reject the process, and he eventually began to issue dire warnings that the US had surrendered its nuclear superiority and left itself vulnerable to a Soviet counterforce first strike delivered by that country's now numerous intercontinental ballistic missiles. Having played a part in spiking the SALT II Treaty, his detailed knowledge of the nuclear landscape was then put to good use by the Reagan administration in the INF talks at Geneva that began in 1981, at which he genuinely sought a compromise agreement that would preserve the unity of the Western alliance. He was dismayed when the negotiations collapsed with the Soviet walkout in late 1983 as the first cruise missiles arrived in Western Europe.

While much of this history will be familiar to afficionados of US defence policy, Wilson offers new and enlightening material on Nitze's surprising role from 1984 onwards as an arms-control advocate supported by Ronald Reagan (who saw Nitze as a link to Harry Truman's Cold War policies, which Reagan admired). Nitze played a key part in generating constructive proposals for George Shultz at the State Department as Cold War tensions finally began to dissipate. Although Nitze was often, and with some reason, characterised as a hawk, Wilson reveals a man who appreciated that negotiations with the Soviet Union were always preferable to confrontation. In this Nitze dutifully followed Reagan's own instincts, even to the extent of seeking pathways to the abolition of all nuclear weapons. The conclusion to this last part of his career was the INF Treaty of 1987, and the beginnings of what was later to become the Strategy Arms Reduction Treaty (START).

After his retirement, Nitze turned to another existential threat, climate change, delivering sage warnings on the dangers of inaction and pointing once more to the importance of attaining international agreement on reductions, mirroring what had been achieved in the nuclear realm. Packing such an eventful life into one manageable volume was never going to be easy, but Wilson, the author of an excellent account of Reagan's approach to the Soviet Union (*The Triumph of Improvisation*), has done a fine job of researching and synthesising Nitze's major contributions to US Cold War policy.

The Royal Navy in the Cold War Years, 1966–1990: Retreat and Revival
Edward Hampshire. Barnsley: Seaforth Publishing, 2024.
£35.00. 728 pp.

In this massive and encyclopaedic work, Edward Hampshire delivers an impressive survey of the Royal Navy from the painful defence reviews of the mid-1960s to the end of the Cold War. Backed by exhaustive research in numerous archives, Hampshire starts his study with the resignations of the navy minister and the first sea lord in 1966 over the Labour government's decision to cancel the contract for a new aircraft carrier. Over the next few years, as Britain drew back from several of its overseas commitments 'East of Suez', the navy retreated from a succession of bases and outposts which had once been totemic of Britain's imperial power and began to focus on its NATO role in the Eastern Atlantic and Mediterranean, though without renouncing all aspirations to maintain a global reach and presence.

One of the great merits of this heavyweight book is its presentation of the nuts and bolts of the navy's development, including the conditions experienced by service personnel; the procurement of ships, submarines and weapons systems; and the organisation of the service, from the rarified heights of the Admiralty and Ministry of Defence to the maintenance of naval dockyards. There is space for esoteric but fundamental subjects such as oceanographic research, hydrography, and the crucial and unseen technical progress made in the areas of sonar, whether towed arrays from ships or sonobuoys. Indeed, one of the greatest challenges faced by navy planners was to keep abreast of the latest technological developments, including guided missiles, advanced radar and sonar tracking systems, and torpedoes. Hampshire shows how these advances were incorporated into ship and submarine design, and how they affected the navy's personnel requirements. Some of the navy's procurement policies were more successful than others – the *Trafalgar*-class nuclear-powered attack submarines were some of the best in the world, but the Type-22 frigates were expensive. Despite some well-known deficiencies in equipment, notably in the field of air defence, the navy rose to the challenge of the Falklands War in 1982 with its customary elan and professionalism – Hampshire's coverage of the conflict is full of fresh insight and delves into the lessons learnt.

The climactic battle that never occurred, of course, was the clash between the Soviet Union's Northern Fleet based at Murmansk and the navy's surface and sub-surface units that was expected in the event of war between the Warsaw Pact and NATO. Navy chiefs fretted over the ability of British forces to intercept Soviet submarines as they tried to break through the so-called Greenland–Iceland–United Kingdom (GIUK) Gap, where they might then decimate the reinforcing convoys that would deliver the fresh troops and materiel required to keep the European Central Front adequately supplied.

Aside from the Soviet Navy, the most formidable adversary confronted by the Royal Navy during this period were Treasury officials eager to make reductions in the defence budget. Hampshire guides the reader through these extended Whitehall battles, including an account of how the navy finessed the 1974 defence review and escaped with smaller cuts than anticipated. Things had changed by the famous 1981 defence review, which placed the surface fleet in the firing line. The Falklands provided some pushback against defence secretary John Nott's ideas, but Hampshire notes how both he and Frank Cooper, the Ministry of Defence's permanent under-secretary, regarded the war as an inconvenience that might disrupt their plans. Hampshire tells the story of the Royal Navy in this era with an impressive depth of research and range of coverage, offering a cool and judicious presentation of his findings.

Latin America
Ryan C. Berg

Narcostates: Civil War, Crime, and the War on Drugs in Mexico and Central America
William L. Marcy. Boulder, CO: Lynne Rienner Publishers, 2023.
$115.00. 359 pp.

William L. Marcy's *Narcostates* is an exciting read that manages to capture some of the most important history of cartels, violence and US counter-narcotics operations in Mexico and Central America. The historian asks how Central America and Mexico became such lawless and violent corridors of drug trafficking, and why significant efforts to reorganise and aid police and military organisations failed to rein in the cartels. Beginning with the Nixon administration's *Operation Intercept* in the 1960s, Marcy tells the story mostly through primary-source documents and recently declassified materials housed in national-security archives. Deviating from the prose of a typical academic historian, Marcy writes with a narrative flair that captures the intrigue of the backroom dealings of the region's capos, informants and agents, accounts that form the bulk of his story.

Many deeply researched histories have been written on the astronomical rise of the Colombian cartels and their eventual fall at the hands of their erstwhile partners, the Mexican cartels. Figures such as Joaquín 'El Chapo' Guzmán and Pablo Escobar have captivated many writers, but Marcy's original contribution may lie in recounting the number of oft-overlooked Central American figures connected to major players in both the Mexican and Colombian cartels. In Marcy's words, Mexico was the 'trampoline for Colombian cocaine' entering via Central America (p. 101). That region, engulfed in bloody civil wars that destroyed states' capacity to resist and provided financial incentives to participate in drug trafficking as a means of financing and exporting revolutions, emerged as the key air bridge between the Colombian and Mexican cartels. This explains the persistence of a Mexican cartel presence in the region many years later, and the splintering of groups over personal rivalries and the massive sums of illicit revenue at stake.

Marcy also unpacks decades of US security assistance. After a thorough analysis of the Mérida Initiative's failure to bring greater security to Mexico, as well as the lack of improvement under the Central America Regional Security Initiative, Marcy repeats a common criticism of US security assistance, writing that it over-militarised assistance and contributed to a surge in violence. Marcy calls this the 'Colombianisation' of Mexico and Central America (p. 204), drawing on Plan Colombia, the multi-decade security-assistance programme intended to help Colombia beat back guerrilla groups. This critique, however,

 https://doi.org/10.1080/00396338.2025.2508094

ignores a recent body of work by scholars such as Paul Angelo, who has detailed the differences between Plan Colombia and the Mérida Initiative, and the many reasons for their divergent outcomes (see his 2024 book *From Peril to Partnership*).

Narcostates is especially relevant considering renewed efforts by the United States to combat criminal cartels in Mexico. Both sides have determined that the Mérida Initiative is dead, but what will follow in its wake is unclear. Readers of Marcy's book will be poised to understand the history of various past efforts, and to detect whether the Trump administration is pushing for a new paradigm in security cooperation or treading old paths.

Autocracy Rising: How Venezuela Transitioned to Authoritarianism
Javier Corrales. Washington DC: Brookings Institution Press, 2023. $32.00. 256 pp.

According to the International Monetary Fund, Venezuela has experienced the largest peacetime economic collapse in world history, losing about 70% of its gross domestic product. Yet the country's dictatorship, now led by Nicolás Maduro, has managed to retain its power, stealing election after election. In *Autocracy Rising*, Javier Corrales wrestles with this paradox.

Corrales documents the rise of *Chavismo* as a political movement (named after former president Hugo Chávez) and the dominance of the associated United Socialist Party of Venezuela (PSUV). The PSUV's initial electoral success under Chávez gave it large parliamentary majorities, which in turn lent it the clout to capture more of the state and severely fragment the opposition. Under Chávez, the Venezuelan government started to co-opt state institutions such as electoral authorities, media outlets, the courts and the armed forces – a process that was supercharged under Maduro. Corrales's book documents these developments in considerable historical depth.

Autocracy Rising makes an original contribution in analysing the institutional sources of Venezuela's slide into authoritarianism. Corrales spends time unpacking the state's capture of courts to alter rules, norms and laws in a process he describes as 'autocratic legalism'. Up to this point, Venezuela's path resembled that of other states as it wielded an inventory of conventional authoritarian tools to fend off challenges from the domestic opposition and the international community alike. However, as the Maduro regime became electorally uncompetitive and the opposition more competitive, it invented and repurposed some of these tools. Institutional graft and capture lent themselves to the hollowing out of the state. Public-sector innovation under Maduro came to mean a kind of institutional multitasking. The Venezuelan armed forces took critical slices of the economy, parallel assemblies acquired the patina of legitimacy to erase the opposition's congressional victories, local authorities became intelligence-gathering and food-distribution networks, and criminal organisations became partners in governing vast swathes of territory. Corrales terms this dynamic 'function fusion', denoting a new mode of governance that assigns multiple functions to state bureaucracies and public institutions. Similar concepts have been developed by other scholars, such as Erica de Bruin's theory of 'coup proofing', but function fusion appears critical to explaining Maduro's survival. In Corrales's telling, some aspects of the Maduro regime's behaviour that appeared improvisational were instead calculated and intentional. Simply put, to survive, Maduro felt compelled to share power – often with sinister partners – even as he simultaneously concentrated it.

Students of democracy and democratic backsliding should familiarise themselves with the dramatic example of Venezuela, a case with which few are as familiar as Corrales. Other books on Venezuela's unprecedented economic collapse and descent into authoritarianism have been written: many of these, such as William Neuman's *Things Are Never So Bad That They Can't Get Worse*, grapple with the country's meltdown from a more journalistic perspective. *Autocracy Rising* gives the subject a deep academic treatment. Given that, since its publication, yet another election has been stolen in Venezuela, the tome has become required reading for those wondering how the Maduro regime manages to hang on despite its obvious lack of legitimacy.

The Chile Project: The Story of the Chicago Boys and the Downfall of Neoliberalism
Sebastian Edwards. Princeton, NJ: Princeton University Press, 2023. £28.00/$32.00. 376 pp.

Few schools of thought from the twentieth and twenty-first centuries have been as maligned as neo-liberalism. Sebastian Edwards sets out to tell the story of neo-liberalism in Chile, where it was implemented in some of its purest forms, especially under Augusto Pinochet. In the mid-1950s, the US State Department sponsored a programme dubbed the 'Chile Project' for economists from the Pontifical Catholic University of Chile to train at the University of Chicago. At the time, the school was known for its eponymous school of economic thought that prized free-market thinking and rational expectations, and boasted future Nobel-prize-winning economists such as Milton Friedman. The 'Chicago Boys', as the school's Chilean students came to be known, achieved prominence during Pinochet's dictatorship, with many serving as his economic advisers.

Edwards traces the influence of these advisers through distinct periods of Pinochet's rule and into the democratic era. An incipient phase of neo-liberalism

(1973–82) was followed by a pragmatic phase (1983 through to the founding of democracy in 1990) and then an inclusive phase (1990–present). All three periods featured a market approach to bettering social conditions and the privatisation of many state companies.

By 2019, notwithstanding Chile's attainment of the highest health, education and life-expectancy outcomes in the region, Chilean society was experiencing a growing malaise. Mass protests broke out over a four-cent hike in Santiago's metro fare. The protests quickly grew to symbolise general societal discontent. Edwards's work demonstrates the reorientation of Chile's horizons away from Latin America. No longer content to be the wealthiest country in the region, many Chileans professed a desire for a Scandinavian-style system. Despite its successes, Chile's neo-liberal system has contributed to what Edwards calls 'horizontal inequality', which is less about income distribution and more about social interactions and the distance between commoners and elites. Yet effecting change has proven difficult.

Edwards shows that neo-liberal thought achieved widespread acceptance in Chilean society, even after Chile had transitioned to democracy. This finding differs drastically from Juan Gabriel Valdes's interpretation in his well-known book *Pinochet's Economists*. Valdes posited that neo-liberalism was a foreign imposition that trampled on Chile's unique cultural heritage. He predicted that neo-liberalism would be reversed once the country returned to democracy. While many books on neo-liberalism debate the merits of the theory on its outcomes, Edwards suggests another factor, which he calls the 'persuasion approach'. Neo-liberal thought found fertile soil not because Chile was a dictatorship, à la Valdes, but because it managed to persuade many Chileans. This explains the widespread acceptance of neo-liberal logic and programmes even well after the fall of Pinochet's dictatorship. Defying expectations, presidents in the country's democratic age, many of whom were persecuted by the murderous Pinochet regime for being socialists, left in place many of the economic policies that can be traced to his government. To be sure, social programmes expanded, but almost always through market mechanisms, as was the case under Pinochet.

Edwards published his book in 2023, in the wake of the failure of the country's first attempt to rewrite its constitution through a constituent assembly. In the book's introduction, Edwards declares confidently that

> Chile will replace the old constitution with a new one that will enshrine and guarantee many social rights that will be provided for free by the state. It is unlikely that there will be as many as in the rejected draft, but the number will be substantial … The neoliberal era will not be revived; most of the economic system built by the Chicago Boys will be replaced

> by a social democratic system like the one that prevails in European and, especially, Nordic nations. (p. 8)

Unfortunately for Edwards, nothing could be further from the truth. Although a second plebiscite held after the book's publication failed less decisively than the country's first constitutional rewrite, it was still rejected by 56% of voters. Thus, the book's subtitle could be interpreted as offering a kind of false premise: there has been no downfall of Chile's neo-liberal model, but rather a new equilibrium. The book does succeed in unearthing the roots of the so-called neo-liberal project in Chile, assessing its impact and describing its declining support among the Chilean people. This analysis has enduring value precisely because current Chilean president Gabriel Boric has not managed to extricate Chile from a neo-liberal model, despite his pledge to 'bury neo-liberalism'. With a presidential election in 2025 likely to see a centre-right candidate win, any rejection by Chile of its neo-liberal legacy may be significantly delayed.

Brazilian Politics on Trial: Corruption and Reform Under Democracy
Luciano Da Ros and Matthew M. Taylor. Boulder, CO: Lynne Rienner Publishers, 2022. $35.00. 281 pp.

When a money-laundering investigation at a petrol station in Brasilia ballooned into a sprawling, countrywide graft probe in Brazil, many thought they were witnessing a new type of anti-corruption model. The so-called Lava Jato (Car Wash) investigation held promise because it enjoyed a deep wellspring of support in society, and no politician – no matter how senior, including speakers of the house and presidents – appeared beyond its reach.

Luciano Da Ros and Matthew M. Taylor's book *Brazilian Politics on Trial* recounts the successes and explains the failures of the Lava Jato investigation. Importantly, it explores why an anti-Lava Jato political coalition arose to offer substantial pushback to the investigation. Indeed, present-day Brazil appears to have returned not to the status quo ante, but something worse. By tracing the history of Brazil's corruption scandals from the return of democracy in 1985 to the present day — many of them caused by what the authors deem a 'perilous combination' of a coalitional president and a highly fragmented party system dependent upon political favours to maintain congressional unity – Da Ros and Taylor demonstrate the uneven nature of the country's anti-corruption measures. The authors also identify the 'developmental state' (the state's considerable intervention in the economy) and weak campaign-finance laws as major sources of corruption.

Anti-corruption advocates fall into two camps: incrementalists, and 'big push' or 'big bang' theorists. Da Ros and Taylor's detailed cataloguing of anti-corruption legislation and bureaucratic rule-making shows that many of the country's anti-corruption measures have been incremental. Lava Jato, however, was unprecedented in size, scope and duration, and held the promise of forever changing the anti-corruption paradigm. It was only possible, according to the authors, precisely because of Brazil's incremental progress between 1985 and 2013. The country's political elites did not envisage that incremental changes would one day result in a spectacular graft probe targeting them.

According to Da Ros and Taylor, the early days of Lava Jato (2014–16) featured so many revelations, and so much chaos and shock, that political elites ensnared in the investigation found it difficult to fight back or forestall their own downfall. Beginning after the impeachment of former president Dilma Rousseff, however, an anti-Lava Jato coalition appeared. In 2018, Jair Bolsonaro was elected to the presidency. Slowly, political elites took aim at the accountability mechanisms that had laid the groundwork for Lava Jato, aided by bombshell revelations that, in several cases, judges and prosecutors colluded through text messages to achieve convictions against elite politicians.

The book concludes by ruminating on the difficulties of anti-corruption reform in large democracies. Few case studies exist of large countries like Brazil successfully rooting out corruption. In fact, some of the best examples are small states, and not all of them democracies. Lava Jato was an extraordinary example of a 'big push' anti-corruption effort that eventually flamed out. It failed to establish a new accountability equilibrium.

Even though the key events of the book occurred over a decade ago, the work feels relevant to present-day Brazil. Some of the main political protagonists are still with us, especially Bolsonaro and Luiz Inácio Lula da Silva. The book is worth a read by those who want to understand why anti-corruption reform is so often halting, and why Brazil appears to be hurtling toward yet another presidential election with an anti-corruption regime that appears weaker than ever.

Default: The Landmark Court Battle over Argentina's $100 Billion Debt Restructuring
Gregory Makoff. Washington DC: Georgetown University Press, 2024. $29.95. 424 pp.

Few institutions are as reviled in Argentina as the International Monetary Fund (IMF). The global lender of last resort, the IMF has established 23 programmes with Argentina, a serial defaulter. On the streets of Buenos Aires, mere mention of the IMF is usually sufficient to elicit negative comments and verbal tirades.

Gregory Makoff's *Default* is thus unusual in departing from the traditional focus on the IMF in explaining Argentina's financial woes. While the IMF still plays a prominent role in the story, the focus is on international investors and so-called 'distressed debt'.

Default traces the shift in sovereign lending from private-sector banks in the 1980s to international bond markets in the 1990s and 2000s. This shift created coordination challenges when countries such as Argentina flirted with default. Without a central point of contact – or several large, institutional banks, as in the 1980s – renegotiating bond-repayment conditions proved challenging for Argentina. It was even harder when the IMF proved reluctant to endorse Argentina's restructuring process. When the country defaulted on about $100 billion in bonds at the end of 2001, many bondholders refused to accept a 'haircut'. Instead, some firms hit the country with a wave of litigation. They tried to seize state assets, including a presidential plane, diplomatic properties, bank accounts and even satellites. The torrent of court cases was mostly unsuccessful, but holdout bondholders scored their biggest victory in 2012, when US District Judge Thomas B. Griesa issued an unprecedented injunction on Argentina's ability to pay the bondholders who had accepted a haircut until holdout creditors were paid in full. Griesa intended this ruling to be a positive step, but politicians in Argentina quickly began referring to these funds as *fondos buitres* (vulture funds). Since then, many bond papers have included 'collective action clauses', augmenting the issuer's ability to force a minority of bond holdouts to accept any restructuring that the majority of bondholders accept.

Makoff's book is well researched, relying mostly on primary sources for citations and insider knowledge of IMF meetings and strategy. As a result, it sometimes veers into highly technical matters that the economic neophyte may not fully comprehend. It also contains legal analysis bolstered by an impressive array of citations. The book can thus be enjoyed by historians, economists and lawyers, as well as by casual readers, though few will be able to match Makoff's knowledge in all these fields.

While many of the events recounted in *Default* occurred ten years ago, their consequences remain relevant to the presidency of Javier Milei, who has endeavoured to completely remake Argentina's fiscal outlook through austerity measures and government trimming approved by the IMF (and, it should be noted, by many Argentines). Notably, the country is still repairing its tense relationships with creditors.

Europe
Erik Jones

A Federalist Alternative for European Governance: The European Union in Hard Times
Sergio Fabbrini. Cambridge: Cambridge University Press, 2024.
£26.99. 272 pp.

Contemporary theories of European integration emphasise power and process. They focus on intergovernmental bargaining among the member states, policy entrepreneurship within the European Commission, or coalition politics in the European Parliament. This focus sheds important light on how the European Union passes legislation and how it responds to crises, but tells us little about where the European project can and should be headed. Scholars and policymakers can imagine how to improve procedures on the back of existing theories – for example, through greater use of qualified majority voting, more effective ring-fencing or sharing of competences, and more frequent engagement with popular representatives. They have greater difficulty imagining how to build political support around such reform measures, particularly when faced with countervailing narratives about the importance of preserving national sovereignty or cultural distinctiveness. And once member states or other affiliated governments begin to demand and receive exceptions, the resulting pattern of differentiated integration looks increasingly incoherent.

The solution, Sergio Fabbrini argues, is to stop pretending that the European project is unique or *sui generis*, and to strengthen the theoretical toolkit by comparing the EU to other systems of governance. The word 'system' is important. Fabbrini insists on the need to redirect attention from the operation of specific institutions like the European Council, Commission, Parliament or Court, to look at how these institutions work both with each other and with the member states to meet the basic requirements of governance. From that systemic perspective, the EU is a compound polity like a confederation or federation, and can be compared with other more or less similar arrangements. When doing so, the first question to consider is whether the goal of Europe is to bring together otherwise separate political entities as in Switzerland or the United States, or to decentralise political authority from an already strong centre, as in Germany or Canada.

Fabbrini identifies the EU as a coming-together kind of federalism, which implies that some areas of sovereignty remain inextricably attached to its member states. It also means that member states are more different from one another in terms of their populations or other endowments than are the constituents of compound polities designed to decentralise authority. This

 https://doi.org/10.1080/00396338.2025.2508095

combination of sovereignty and diversity places powerful constraints on the constitution of a centralised political authority that do not exist in decentralising federal arrangements. Those constraints explain why it is so difficult to reform specific institutions in the way existing theories of European integration recommend. They also point to a federalist alternative based on the constitutional features that work best in other coming-together arrangements. Fabbrini shows how we could reorder the EU as a three-tiered structure with a strong constitutional union at the centre, a community arrangement for those member states that do not want to work so closely together, and a confederacy offering even weaker association.

This federalist alternative gives a fresh and compelling perspective on how the EU can address current challenges, particularly as it confronts the need to develop new competences and take on new member states in the face of a hostile geopolitical environment. Nevertheless, Fabbrini admits that finding the political will to embrace his recommendations extends beyond the scope of his analysis (p. 210). That concession raises questions about whether the two types of federalism he offers can be taken as given. Coming-together arrangements can evolve into centralised authority as in the Netherlands; centralised authority can take on the characteristics of coming-together arrangements as in Belgium. Spain and the United Kingdom have arguably moved in both directions, first centralising and then decentralising. The political dynamics that explain such transitions also require attention. The EU is coming together, but that cannot be taken for granted. Europe needs a compelling vision of where it should be headed.

Frontiers of Empire: Max Sering, Inner Colonization, and the German East, 1871–1945
Robert L. Nelson. Cambridge: Cambridge University Press, 2024. £85.00. 320 pp.

European nation-states are anything but natural. The idea that one people, one culture and one land would somehow come together took effort both to imagine and to put into practice. Firstly, someone had to identify the language that connected different and often mutually unintelligible dialects. Then they had to sort and shift different populations to bring like-minded or culturally affinitive groups together in the same place. Finally, they had to defend the fruits of that effort – both the people and the land – from other, competing projects. This process of nation-building involves both violence and institution-building. The more successful individual nations become, the more they threaten their neighbours through their attempts at consolidation.

The inner colonisation of Europe started soon after the period of national integration in the mid- to late nineteenth century, as different nation-state building projects competed over the space between them. Everyone involved understood that national survival was at stake. Therefore, some of Europe's greatest minds focused on how to make sure this inner colonisation was successful – economically, legally, socially and politically – even if they recognised that success would come at another people's expense. What they failed to appreciate was the cost to their own societies.

Robert L. Nelson does a brilliant job using the life and work of Max Sering to reveal the clinical, scientific dimension of European nation-state building. Sering was an agricultural economist who spent the better part of 1883 travelling across the United States and Canada to study different strategies for homesteading in the Great Plains region. He focused on the complex challenges associated with creating self-sustaining agricultural communities built around family-owned farms and relatively small urban spaces. Having grown up during the German occupation of Alsace-Lorraine after the Franco-Prussian War, Sering was familiar with the issues Germans faced with intra-European colonisation. His goal was to draw lessons from the United States related to land speculation, inheritance law and trade policy for the German empire to use in settling Germans in Eastern Europe. Sering also gained insights on the differences in how Americans and Canadians treated their indigenous peoples; he preferred Canadian assimilation to the more genocidal American alternative.

Sering quickly rose to prominence for his insights on inner colonisation, agriculture, industry and trade. His work gained attention and recognition on both sides of the Atlantic. Even scholars from Poland, whose people competed with the Germans for control over much of Eastern Europe, sought Sering's advice in trying to understand how to colonise the land successfully. When Britain blockaded Germany and threatened the country with starvation during the First World War, Sering's ambition to colonise Eastern Europe became a German imperative. What Sering did not anticipate is that his life's work laid the groundwork for the more extreme approach adopted by Nazi Germany, with its violently racialised politics. He also did not recognise how the dispossession of people on the frontiers of Germany could undermine support for the rule of law across the country. Sering opposed the Nazis, and yet he inadvertently empowered them through his ideas and scholarship, both in their authoritarianism and in their atrocities.

Nelson ends his history with the ironic twist that Poland succeeded in colonising that part of Eastern Europe Sering most coveted for Germany. He also shows how interest in inner colonisation extended into the 1970s with explicit reference to Israel and Turkiye. His stated goal is to normalise this European experience: all parts of the world have gone through similar moments, Nelson argues. Accepting this comparison does not diminish the experience of Europe's external colonies. Their suffering deserves recognition, as does Europe's culpability.

Lost Fatherland: Europeans Between Empire and Nation-states, 1867–1939
Iryna Vushko. New Haven, CT: Yale University Press, 2024.
£25.00/$35.00. 352 pp.

Nationalism and extremism often seem like unstoppable, disintegrative forces. The collapse of Yugoslavia was a bloody, violent demonstration. Great Britain's exit from the European Union 20 years later was very different in character, yet still powerfully disruptive. By contrast, cosmopolitan ideas of international or federal cooperation seem ephemeral and weak. Donald Trump's administration can shake the foundations of the multilateral system that the United States created; right-wing nationalists in Europe can jam up the functioning of the EU. Meanwhile, globalist or federalist idealists struggle to offer a compelling or coherent alternative.

Then again, the debates that have dominated news cycles for the past 30 years may not be revealing of more powerful forces at work. Iryna Vushko underscores that possibility in her fascinating account of the lives and influence of key politicians at the twilight of the Habsburg Empire around the turn of the twentieth century. Her argument is that the end of the First World War in 1918 was less of a rupture than many imagine. There were strong elements of continuity before and after that watershed that reveal much about the relative influence of nationalism, communism, fascism and Nazism. Vushko's goal is not to make comparisons between that period and the present – it is to stress that the influence of cosmopolitan experiences on the history of the twentieth century is greater than we might think.

Vushko focuses her attention on politicians who came from liminal communities in the Austro-Hungarian Empire, in which nations and languages mixed freely, Jewish people had the choice to assimilate or remain separate, and the institutions of state and the rules, norms and conventions of society often operated separately. This environment was far from idyllic. The Austrians were capable of great brutality. The Poles and Ukrainians battled each other for territory and recognition. Different ideological groups – conservative, liberal, social Catholic and Marxist – competed for political influence. Meanwhile, irredentist forces sought to undermine the imperial state and to seize those territories that were owed to them by dint of historical providence. Vushko's point is only that such an environment fostered important forms of pragmatism where language and nation did not have to coincide; politicians could work easily across different ethnic communities; ideology could make space for national autonomy – even among Soviet communists; territorial autonomy could be tempered by personal rights; and coalition-building could operate freely.

Vushko claims this pragmatism played a crucial role in the development of Christian Democracy and communism in Italy through the influence of key figures from Trentino and Trieste. She shows how it influenced the development of Czechoslovak nationalism, how it created resistance to Germany's *Anschluss* designs on Austria, and how it divided families between Ukraine and Poland. These insights matter in ways that Vushko only hints at in the penultimate chapter of her book, but that warrant strong repetition in the current environment. The extremes may capture attention in the popular conversation, but that does not mean they alone are important.

Vushko also implicitly highlights the difference between those political entities that fell apart, like Austria–Hungary, and those that came together, like Italy, Germany and Poland. The coming-together entities are less pragmatic, more self-confident and ultimately more aggressive. In that sense, Vushko's book is a strong complement to Robert Nelson's study of competitive colonisation within Europe. It also offers a cautionary note on Sergio Fabbrini's ambitions for a more self-confident, coming-together form of European integration. Such self-confidence may be necessary for Europe to succeed in a more competitive environment, but it may also unleash powerful integrative forces that few European federalists would willingly embrace.

Europe Without Borders: A History
Isaac Stanley-Becker. Princeton, NJ: Princeton University Press, 2025. £30.00/$35.00. 416 pp.

The tensions between nationalism and cosmopolitanism cut across the European project. Supranational, functionalist and neo-functionalist forces are technocratic and therefore implicitly cosmopolitan. What matters is better policymaking, and whoever can deliver more effective policy should receive authority. Intergovernmental forces are nationalist and focus on the legitimacy of policymaking in a more representative, democratic sense. Such legitimation is unavailable to supranational institutions because they lack a coherent polity (or demos). The European Union is a political system, but it is not the Habsburg Empire reborn. And while the EU may be comparable with other coming-together political communities (to borrow from Sergio

Fabbrini, above), it remains dependent upon the ability of its member states to reach agreement.

Nowhere is this dependence more evident than in the free movement of peoples. The Schengen Area – which is the name given to the intergovernmental arrangement launched in the mid-1980s and since incorporated into the EU to facilitate borderless travel among countries whose governments are willing and able to participate – is a powerful illustration. As Isaac Stanley-Becker shows in this compelling history of Schengen, the right to borderless travel applies only to citizens of participating countries. Non-nationals can benefit from the lack of border controls on a temporary basis and at the cost of constant surveillance. If non-nationals have residence, they can move freely, but without relocation rights. If they lack formal papers, including temporary tourist status, they cannot move at all.

This agreement reflects a delicate balance between the economic advantages of borderless travel and the security concerns that any relaxation of border controls represents. Stanley-Becker shows how national negotiators achieved this balance, often with the assistance of European jurists. The language of the Schengen agreement characterises freedom of movement as complementary to the completion of Europe's internal market, and not an expression of human rights. The relaxation of border controls makes it easier for Europeans to do business but also – at least potentially – exposes participating countries to greater risks of crime, terrorism and abuses of social-welfare systems. The citizens of participating countries benefit from this freedom – and supranational officials hope this will help them identify with 'Europe' – but governments must earn the ability to participate through the collection and sharing of information on the movements of non-nationals, the harmonisation of policing practices, and the acceptance of transnational arrangements associated with processing asylum cases, extradition requests and hot pursuits. Such security matters make up more than half the text of the implementing agreement.

Governments accepted these conditions only reluctantly, and with the reassurance that they could reintroduce border controls in case of need. Sharing information, amending asylum rules and fostering cross-border cooperation in policing touch deeply on core state competences and hence national sovereignty. In turn, such arrangements expose politicians in all countries to right-wing accusations that they are putting their own people at risk and watering down national identity. Politicians also face complaints from the left that the arrangement gives more freedom to goods, capital and labour – as an economic activity – than to human beings. The fall of the Berlin Wall magnified such debates, as West European governments suddenly faced the liberalisation of formerly communist, and hence 'undesirable' (p. 125), countries to the east. The more recent increase in migration from conflict-stricken former European colonies in Sub-Saharan Africa and the Middle East created similar pressures. Stanley-Becker does an excellent job puncturing the myths that Schengen is either a 'laboratory of freedom' or an expression of 'fortress Europe' (p. 272). Neither of these visions for Europe would have been possible without the other, and both are necessary for the Schengen Area to exist.

Embedded Autocracy: Hungary in the European Union
András Bozóki and Zoltán Fleck. Lanham, MD: Lexington Books, 2024. £104.00/$135.00. 382 pp.

The tensions between nationalism and cosmopolitanism are not always constructive for the European Union. At times, they chip away at the functioning of the European project. The love–hate relationship between Viktor Orbán's regime and the European People's Party (EPP) is a good illustration. Although Orbán's Fidesz party is no longer part of the EPP, it benefited for many years from the support and cover of that transnational political family to secure funding and escape sanction. In turn, Orbán used the time and resources the EPP made available to capture the Hungarian state and to embed Fidesz's control across state institutions and Hungarian civil society. Now that Fidesz is outside the EPP, European institutions may have a freer hand to deal with Orbán's government, but they have little power to reverse the damage it has done.

András Bozóki and Zoltán Fleck paint this bleak picture in their must-read book, *Embedded Autocracy*. Autocracy is embedded in Hungary, in the sense that Orbán and his supporters have recoded the norms and values that surround Hungarian political institutions. Hungarian autocracy is embedded in the EU by dint of the country's formal membership. Orbán and his party are sceptical of the EU, reject cosmopolitan values and programmes, and are committed to defend the interests of the Hungarian nation, but they are also pragmatic. If the EU can provide resources that will support their efforts and enrich their cronies, they will not seek to leave. This argument raises questions about how Hungary got into the EU, and why its democracy collapsed thereafter.

The second question, about the collapse of Hungarian democracy, is a focus for Bozóki and Fleck. They argue that the transition from communism to capitalist liberal democracy resulted in a change of institutions, but not a change in political culture. Hungarians could participate in free elections and enjoy the rule of law, but that new institutional context said little about popular attitudes toward politics. On the contrary, most Hungarians were less interested in liberal democracy than in the putative advantages of capitalist economics. When those advantages did not materialise, they grew frustrated, turning against incumbents and cycling through opposition parties. Meanwhile, Orbán took control of Fidesz and positioned himself to govern from the political right with an appeal to Christian nationalism and rural values. His turn at the wheel started after elections in 1998.

What Orbán delivered in his first government was a mixture of polarised discourse and centralised power. He also showed a capacity to use law and procedure against checks and balances, and other forms of institutional constraint. His control was not absolute, and his influence was not overpowering, but it was enough to convince opposition parties that they would have to work together to push him out. It was also enough to convince Orbán that he could never achieve his goals within a liberal constitution. The 2002 election crystallised that division. Orbán lost control over the government, but he consolidated his hold over the political right and extended his reach into business and civil society. Voters may have tired of Orbán's combative style of politics, but they did not suddenly embrace liberal values or democratic enthusiasm. They kept Orbán out of power in 2006, but brought him back in 2010 during the economic and financial crisis. Very quickly, Orbán learned to use 'crisis' to justify dispensing with liberal-democratic institutions.

The rest of the story explains how Orbán embedded his autocracy in Hungarian law and society. What it does not explain is how we can recognise when countries are susceptible to that kind of state capture. A survey of Hungarian political institutions of the kind used by the EU to assess the country's suitability for membership was insufficient. Bozóki and Fleck show how easily politicians like Orbán enlist support from intellectuals and jurists to rewrite the norms and rules for politics. The challenge is to imagine how to recognise and stop such efforts before they get going.

Politics and International Relations

Chester A. Crocker

Political Rumors: Why We Accept Misinformation and How to Fight It
Adam J. Berinsky. Princeton, NJ: Princeton University Press, 2023. £25.00/$29.95. 240 pp.

Adam Berinsky, a professor of political science at MIT, specialises in public-opinion research and political behaviour. He tells us that *Political Rumors* was ten years in the making, inspired by his reaction to the growth of unsubstantiated partisan rumours around Barack Obama's presidency. Starting in 2010, the author engaged in extensive opinion research to grasp the 'prevalence of rumor beliefs among the American mass public' (p. 5). Citing the work of many other specialists, Berinsky drives home several core messages: fake political rumours targeting the left are more than twice as common as those targeting the right; belief in political rumours is widespread (more than 70% of survey respondents expressed support for at least one of the seven rumours used in his surveys); and the root of such belief lies in the combination of conspiratorial thinking and partisan attachments within the American political ecosystem (pp. 7–9). Turning to the question of what to do about the prevalence of weaponised falsehood (my term, not his) in American political life, Berinsky argues that special attention should be given to the 'uncertain' respondents group which, by not rejecting false claims, ends up helping the believers (p. 15).

This short book begins by exploring the phenomenon of political rumours and misinformation, and how they take hold in mass opinion. This is followed by a heavy dose of empirical data drawn from ten surveys conducted between 2010 and 2016, in which Berinsky notes once again that partisanship shapes support for rumours in asymmetrical ways. The author discusses the question of who is best placed to discredit and defeat rumours, and finds that the best messenger is often a person from the same political camp as believers, who can 'turn the power of partisanship on its head' by rejecting a rumour that attacks the other side (p. 18).

After some definitional clarifications and a reminder that political rumours are not new in American life, Berinsky introduces a 'pebble in the pond' analogy describing four social types: creators, believers, uncertains and disbelievers. The uncertain cohort comprises the disengaged, the sceptical ('not sure') and the truly unsure. Using examples such as 'birthers' (who believed Obama was not a US citizen) and the QAnon claim that Democrats operate child sex-trafficking rings, the author describes how rumours spread from creators to believers (typically a narrow group). Internet-based hubs of 'rumor diffusion' build 'self-reinforcing bubbles' which then broadcast rumours and conspiracy theories

 https://doi.org/10.1080/00396338.2025.2508096

into the broader information environment (pp. 32–5). Most individuals are not direct consumers of fringe websites, but the combination of low knowledge and high reliance on social media enables rumours to reach broader portions of society through selective or incidental exposure (p. 40).

Chapter 3 presents elaborate statistical evidence from opinion polls to show that the 'generalized propensity of a person to adopt a conspiratorial orientation', further shaped by partisan beliefs, determines whether a rumour is accepted or rejected, a finding affecting both Democrats and Republicans (p. 56). Chapter 4 asks if rumours can be corrected and rejected by the public. The results are discouraging. Exhaustive statistical experiments focus on the false rumour that Obama's signature Affordable Care Act included 'death panel' interviews that urged seniors to consider euthanasia. The rumour was checked not by scientific experts or official denials, but by Republican debunking, turning partisanship into a 'double-edged sword' (p. 75). It appears that 'costly signals' work better than 'cheap talk' (p. 78). The problem, however, is that the lifespan of such correctives may not be sufficient as falsehoods are repeated over and over again.

Experiments discussed in Chapter 5 test the impact of fact-checking by independent outfits such as NewsGuard (discussed in more detail in my review of Stephen Brill's *The Death of Truth* below) and find that their impact depends more on levels of trust in the source than on the expertise of the source (p. 115). Experiments comparing the impact of fact-checking on supporters of Donald Trump and Democratic Senator Bernie Sanders arrive at the encouraging conclusion that 'individuals of all partisan stripes seemed amenable to belief change in response to fact-checking information' (p. 116). But the good news ends there: correcting falsehoods appears to have 'no meaningful impact' on participants' support for a political figure; politicians who spew misinformation face 'few political ramifications' (p. 121). In Chapter 6, Berinsky finds that Republican elites spread more rumours than Democrats and, when the former challenge rumours, they typically issue 'softer' corrections (p. 129). Moreover, Republicans are more actively linked to untrustworthy news outlets (pp. 139–43).

The Death of Truth: How Social Media and the Internet Gave Snake Oil Salesmen and Demagogues the Weapons They Needed to Destroy Trust and Polarize the World – and What We Can Do About It
Steven Brill. New York: Alfred A. Knopf, 2024. $30.00. 336 pp.

Steven Brill has penned an accessible and compelling account of the technological, financial and political roots of democratic decay. He dissects this highly technical story with rare clarity, pinpointing the sources of the crisis and outlining what must change to rescue us from a surging sea of disinformation and misinformation.

A best-selling author (*Tailspin*, 2018), Brill is the co-founder and co-CEO of NewsGuard, a non-governmental organisation that monitors and rates the accuracy of news and information websites. He begins his story by unpacking how and why the United States' 1996 Telecommunications Act included a little-known Section 230 that basically absolved internet platforms from responsibility for their content. This legislation had strong bipartisan support, passing the House of Representatives by a vote of 420–4. At the time, says Brill, 'Section 230's grant of immunity made sense' (p. 18). No one foresaw that tech entrepreneurs such as Mark Zuckerberg (then barely 12 years old) and Elon Musk would one day be the beneficiaries of this 'Good Samaritan' protection.

Twenty year later, the rise of social media has given everyone the ability to publish their opinions on platforms whose recommendation algorithms and dependence on advertising revenue favour anger, divisiveness and extreme reactions. The result has been a great wave of conspiratorial, anti-expert and anti-scientific theorising about everything from vaccines to elections (p. 26). Brill writes that 'technology platforms had been given the freedom to sell the first consumer product ever that was absolutely immune from age-old common-law or modern regulatory oversight' (p. 32).

Brill describes how NewsGuard failed to persuade platforms such as Facebook and YouTube to embrace its fact-checking services so that they might actually behave like Good Samaritans. While the European Union in 2018 published a Code of Practice on Disinformation, NewsGuard found it was unable to make common cause with leading 'tech bros' in the United States. According to Brill, NewsGuard's founders 'did not understand … that misinformation and disinformation *was* their business' and that they had 'no intention' of trying to solve the problem (p. 56, emphasis in original).

Brill devotes several chapters to explaining how a second set of algorithms developed by ad-tech companies using 'programmatic advertising' compounds the assault on truth and standards. Described as 'opaque, unaccountable, and massively lucrative for those who operate them', these algorithms essentially break the link between blue-chip advertisers and websites carrying the sort of scurrilous content that would embarrass them if they (or their shareholders) knew about it. They don't (pp. 64–5). The ad-tech industry and its clients have 'provided [unwitting] financial support' for misinformation and disinformation 'because the system is auctioning off access' to target audiences with no regard for the accompanying content (p. 82). While much of the faux content comes from the right, progressives also engage in malign influence operations described as 'pink slime' (pp. 94–7). In the process, the trust people have in traditional sources – 'referees' such as doctors, teachers, police officers, judges, librarians, poll workers – is undermined and replaced by endlessly repeated content often coming from 'Russian disinformation, conspiracy theorists, a crazy uncle, or Trump' (p. 113). A chapter describing the raging falsehoods around COVID-19 concludes that the debates were not about policy, but were part of an 'us versus them' media ecosystem that lures people into believing 'there is no knowable truth' (p. 124). A scary chapter on the role played by social-media platforms in the 6 January 2021 attack on the US capitol points to a complete abdication of responsibility for content moderation (pp. 150–3). While generative AI does not enjoy the immunity offered by Section 230, this will not stop malign actors such as Russia from exploiting this powerful technology.

In the final chapter, Brill spells out a sweeping set of potential reforms that can be divided into three broad categories: 'fixing the platforms' by requiring them to live up to their publicly listed – but seldom enforced – terms of service respecting 'community standards'; tweaking Section 230, ending online anonymity and promoting online-literacy programmes; taming the 'programmatic advertising monster' (p. 230) by making shareholders aware of how their dollars support disreputable news websites; and tackling polarisation head-on through a range of ballot initiatives and referendums.

Adventures in Democracy: The Turbulent World of People Power
Erica Benner. London: Allen Lane, 2024. £25.00. 224 pp.

Written by a political philosopher and intellectual historian, *Adventures in Democracy* is an unusually accessible gut punch of a book. Comprising 20 chapters of roughly five to eight pages each, Erica Benner takes readers on a journey across the ages, visiting ancient Greece and Rome, Florence under the Medicis, and France, Hungary, the Philippines, Poland, the United Kingdom and the United States in more recent times to explore what happens when the core ideas of democracy are subverted by demagogues and self-absorbed citizens.

Paralleling Moisés Naim's *The Revenge of Power* (reviewed in these pages in the June–July 2023 issue), Benner offers a conclusive checklist detailing 'how to turn democracy into despotism without people noticing' (p. 182). It is a chilling summary of tactics that would have been all too familiar to the likes of Adolf Hitler and the Medicis.

The central theme, as suggested by the book's subtitle, is the role of 'people power' – a term Benner uses to argue that we must look beyond leaders and institutions, and focus on the role of citizens in creating or undermining democracy.

The analysis begins with brief chapters whose titles convey her point, such as 'Are Democracy and Tyranny Opposites?', which explores Theseus' behaviour in the founding of Athens. Unless we look behind our ancestors' 'myths of origin', writes Benner, 'we'll never get a clear picture of what makes our own democracies fragile' (pp. 16–17). After presenting evidence of an inherent human desire for mastery over others, Benner explores 'why power struggles never end' in a chapter that looks at the fear of losing power, a fear that is not easily assuaged by 'checking-and-balancing' institutions. 'In the end it's up to us', she writes (p. 72). 'Struggles to keep all sorts of monopolistic urges under control take up a large part of democracies' lives' (p. 77). Underscoring the point in a chapter on 'How to Pick a Leader', she reminds readers that 'you are democracy's guardians, and … no leader can usurp that job of yours' (p. 86).

Benner offers a challenging chapter on 'free and offending speech', arguing that speech is not a 'mere instrument', but how we 'influence, motivate, lead, mislead, and intimidate', and part of 'democracy's endless battles against unequal freedom'. Thus, free-speech arguments are not only about freedom; they are about power (p. 115). The author urges us to distinguish between respectful, self-disciplined freedom and licentious speech that can 'play havoc with any decent social order' and become 'one of democracy's most lethal poisons' (pp. 118–21).

Drawing on the down-to-earth wisdom of the Athenian statesman Solon, Benner recommends that democracies strive to make life 'safer, fairer and freer than it would be under non-democratic government' (p. 143). This should take precedence over any utopian efforts to achieve human perfection, because 'it takes a lot of tiny acts of self-entitled hubris to topple a democracy' – acts that we may not even notice (p. 144). She warns that 'significant inequalities pose one of the deepest threats to democratic freedom' (p. 155), and argues that an 'element of restraint' (p. 163) is healthier than an atmosphere of hyper-competition. This is an enjoyable dive into political philosophy.

Post-imperial Possibilities: Eurasia, Eurafrica, Afroasia
Jane Burbank and Frederick Cooper. Princeton, NJ: Princeton University Press, 2023. £30.00/$35.00. 320 pp.

Jane Burbank, professor emerita of history, Russian and Slavic studies at New York University, and her husband Frederick Cooper, professor emeritus of history, have developed the field of global history focusing on imperial and colonial history, decolonisation and post-colonial political structures. In *Post-imperial Possibilities*, they offer an engrossing overview of how and why empires gradually devolved into scores of separate territorial entities through the history of three post-imperial visions: Afroasia, Eurafrica and Eurasia.

A central theme that unites the cases is that the advocates for these visions 'had experienced the layered dimensions of imperial formations and could both envision independence from imperial rule and look beyond the nation-state' (p. 12). The authors do not negate the importance of nationalism in the twentieth century, but concentrate on three efforts to build political structures that 'cross[ed] large spaces without recreating the hierarchies of empire' (p. 20). Afroasia involved close cooperation among sovereign states; Eurafrica conceived of 'layering of sovereignty'; while Eurasia continues to feature 'a singular authority but a multi-ethnic society ... connected by cultural affinities and historical linkages' (p. 22).

The core theme of the book is the effort to organise structures around *both* 'vertical and horizontal solidarities', illustrated most explicitly in the advocacy of Léopold Sédar Senghor, the Senegalese philosopher and political leader who argued against the balkanisation of colonial territories and for combining federalism in French-controlled Sub-Saharan Africa with a wider confederalism in the French Union of the 1940s and 1950s (p. 25). Chapter 2 offers a detailed analysis of the effort to devise a post-imperial structure featuring both vertical relations with France and Europe, and horizontal ties among France's West and Central African colonies (and Madagascar). Various African and French leaders (notably including Senghor and Charles de Gaulle, though they had different priorities) supported some form of federalism or confederalism (p. 103). The Eurafrica project, Burbank and Cooper argue, 'appears inconsistent with conventional narratives of decolonization that oppose a militant African nationalism and a rigid French colonialism' (p. 143). In the end, however, key African and French counterparts failed in their efforts to structure a *political* Eurafrica due in large part to disagreement within France, and between France and its future partners within the European Economic Community over the inclusion of African voices in decision-making.

In a fascinating comparative note, the authors write that Kazakhstan's Nursultan Nazarbayev proposed a formal, legal framework for Eurasia in 1994 that closely echoed Senghor's (p. 234). The authors explore the early twentieth-century roots of Russia's anti-European ideologies and how its post-Cold War politics evolved toward official celebration of Eurasia as a political project, one developed by ethnologist Lev Nikolaev Gumilev and championed by conservative propagandist Alexander Dugin, who managed to insert his theories 'into the mindset of the Russian administrative elite' (p. 245). Vladimir Putin warmed to Eurasianism and spoke in 2013 of a 'state civilization model ... to flexibly accommodate the ethnic and religious specificity of particular territories, ensuring diversity in unity' (p. 254).

Chapter 3 explores the trajectory of Afroasia, surveying the debates and campaigns that marked the process of global decolonisation across multiple continents. As in previous cases, Burbank and Cooper argue that the 'goals of anti-imperialist movements have been more varied and more elusive than the empire to nation-state narrative implies' (p. 154). Debates raged across the decades from the Bandung Conference (1955) to the inaugural Non-Aligned Movement meeting in Belgrade (1961), leading to the creation of the United Nations Conference on Trade and Development (UNCTAD) in 1964 and the adoption of the New International Economic Order in 1974. Afroasia had cultural dimensions and featured impressive efforts to combat 'racialized imperialism' (pp. 191–3), but it essentially reflected political and territorial interests and rivalries and, increasingly, the demand for change in the global economic system. The authors appear impressed by the achievements, however limited and ephemeral, of the Afroasian movement, and leave us to ponder whether it represents 'a set of needs and aspirations that today remain to be addressed, in one way or another' (p. 220).

Rethinking the End of Empire: Nationalism, State Formation, and Great Power Politics
Lynn M. Tesser. Stanford, CA: Stanford University Press, 2024.
$30.00. 310 pp.

The central thesis of Lynn Tesser's book is that mainstream scholarship has 'been reading history backwards' (p. 176) by attributing the emergence of many of today's independent nation-states to bottom-up nationalist rebellions and revolts. On the contrary, she argues, states emerged from the ashes of empires because of decisions taken by specific actors: imperial policymakers who defined these territorial units, their great-power rivals who sought to exploit unrest in rival empires and states, and local colonial elites and activists who created narratives of nationalist assertion, often after the fact. As Tesser puts it:

> The persistent claim that nation-states came about largely because 'nations' desired them, an idea appearing even in recently published international relations scholarship, reflects the ongoing power of nationalist ideology that has long pervaded historical and social science research. The nation-state principle won out in multiple waves of state birth *only in retrospect* … The idea that a 'people' demanded and then won the right to self-government tended to develop *after* state birth, from state-led cultural and institutional policies designed to lead residents to imagine themselves as a distinct, singular people. (p. 177, emphasis in original)

Tesser supports this view by examining a wide range of regions and countries going back to the late eighteenth century. In the Americas, she argues that historical research 'undercuts stylized interpretations of US and Haitian independence as cases of self-liberating stateless nations', and that rebels in Spanish territories were 'even more reluctant separatists' because they sought other arrangements with both the metropole and their neighbours. It was the rivalrous interventions of France and Britain in both Spain and North America, as well as Spanish absolutism under Ferdinand VII, that created the conditions to foster local conflicts and transform local demands for home rule and representative government into demands for territorial separation (p. 39). In the case of Greece, Tesser suggests that 'few *indigenous* inhabitants in the southern Balkans would have thought of themselves as a people deserving of a nation-state' before the highly internationalised War of Independence. Major powers' preferences as to the conduct of fighting and the definition of territory dominated the outcome in a 'fractured' society where the act of external recognition proved decisive (pp. 62–3, emphasis in original).

Similar themes emerge in the case of the Balkans and Anatolia, where European pressures on the Ottoman Empire enhanced '(ethno-)religious polarization and identity-shaping' (p. 67). Tesser explores in some detail how the interaction of European diplomacy and Balkan autonomy led to the emergence of Albania, Bulgaria, Macedonia, Montenegro, Romania and Serbia. She concludes that recognition of these new states 'served great power preferences far more than the interests, needs, and likely preferences of the bulk of the affected populations' (p. 93). Empires and superpowers likewise played the central role in shaping and recognising the states that emerged from the Austro-Hungarian, Russian and Soviet empires in the twentieth century. Tesser argues that it is misleading to rely on nationalist histories to determine how the new entities established their identities, since it was the central imperial power that defined them geographically and conferred diplomatic recognition upon them – with the help of other major powers (pp. 96, 127).

Tesser's final cases explore decolonisation processes in Asia and Africa. She critiques social scientists' 'persistent tendencies to categorize the post-WWII clusters of state birth as due to self-generated (bottom-up) nationalism' (p. 130). Citing a range of recent historical research, she notes that critics of empire and political activists pursued 'multiple visions for change' right up until the final waves of decolonisation at the end of the 1950s. African and Caribbean activists imagined changing the world order and building new federal structures strong enough to avoid dependency and mitigate political fragmentation flowing from recognition of numerous small states (p. 131).

Brief discussions of India–Pakistan, Malaya, Myanmar and Vietnam underscore the evolving visions and ethnic diversity of protest leaders. The case of Algeria was uniquely shaped by France's Vietnam trauma, the sudden wave of francophone decolonisation in 1960, and the decisive role played by Charles de Gaulle in shaping the politics of the metropole. France's experience in 1958–60 of making systemic efforts that eventually produced formal but constrained independence in West and Central Africa is contrasted with British incrementalism. The francophone case well illustrates Tesser's core thesis.

Copyright © 2025 The International Institute for Strategic Studies

Closing Argument

The Managerial Revolution Rebooted

Joe Pesmen

I

In 2004, a CIA analyst writing under the name Zefram Cochran – certainly neither his real name nor his primary pseudonym – penned an article reflecting on how things might look if Jack Welch, the infamously ruthless CEO of General Electric, had been appointed deputy director for intelligence.[1] It was, on the surface, a fawning and uninspired thought experiment. But at its core, it was an earnest meditation on a question central to neo-liberal thinking: what if the government was run like a business?

Now, with Elon Musk's Department of Government Efficiency (DOGE) having conducted a devastating march through federal agencies, Cochran has gotten his wish.

Musk's role in the second Trump administration defies easy categorisation. Has he been a libertarian radical, intent on shrinking state capacity for its own sake? A conspiracist true believer, purging deep-state enemies in pursuit of some imagined equilibrium? Or has he simply seen a hollowed-out federal workforce as the prerequisite for centralising control – an opportunity to succeed where the first Trump administration failed in bending the apparatus of state to the executive's will?[2]

Joe Pesmen is a diplomatic fellow at Johns Hopkins University SAIS Europe in Bologna, Italy. He previously served as a Senior Advisor in the White House Situation Room and in various communications roles at the US Department of State. The views expressed here are his own and do not represent the views of the US government.

Survival | vol. 67 no. 3 | June–July 2025 | pp. 211–216 https://doi.org/10.1080/00396338.2025.2508097

Each of these interpretations has merit. Yet when trying to categorise Musk's impact on the conduct of government, the simplest answer may be the most accurate: Musk is a management consultant. Not in title, perhaps, but in function and philosophy. He has brought to government the same template he applied at Twitter (now 'X'), one forged in Silicon Valley and exported across industries. Today, it is being imposed on the American state.

When Musk took over Twitter, he didn't just cut costs. He staged a performance of executive dominance. He fired half the company's staff within days, eliminated entire departments and slashed core functions without a discernible plan for continuity. The remaining employees, many of them overworked and adrift, soldiered on under a regime of radical uncertainty, where the only constant was Musk's direct, erratic command.[3]

To outsiders, the chaos seemed imprudent – destructive, even. But to Silicon Valley executives, it looked like a master stroke. Musk had done what many had long fantasised about: stripping away what they saw as a bloated, coddled workforce and reasserting top-down control in an era that had, in their view, gone soft. Former Twitter CEO Jack Dorsey publicly praised Musk's decisiveness, former PayPal CEO Peter Thiel applauded the lay-offs as overdue efficiency, and Meta CEO Mark Zuckerberg explicitly endorsed the aggressive restructuring.[4] The lay-offs weren't merely budgetary – they were cultural. A statement of values. A return to dominance.

Other firms quickly followed. Alphabet, Amazon, Meta, Microsoft – each began their own rounds of mass lay-offs, often justified by market conditions but modelled after Musk's playbook.[5] In reality, these were less about finances and more about rebalancing power. Executives, having ceded authority during the boom years of flexible work and employee empowerment, were reclaiming their prerogative.

II

The return of this philosophy in tech – what John Ganz has aptly termed 'boss-ism', a managerial ideology premised on unilateral executive control – is no anomaly.[6] It's a familiar story, one that stretches back decades.

Drawing on Daniel Markovits's analysis, we see that American corporations in the mid-twentieth century were defined by dispersed managerial structures and stable middle-class jobs. Middle managers formed the connective tissue between executive vision and everyday work. Labour unions provided an external check on corporate power, and upward mobility was often built on long-term loyalty within firms.[7] Workers could, and often did, rise from the factory floor to the C-suite.

This changed dramatically with the emergence of management consulting. Firms like McKinsey pitched a new vision: leaner, more centralised, more efficient. Out went the middle managers, deemed redundant and wasteful.[8] In came the consultants, armed with spreadsheets and abstractions, slicing through the human infrastructure of the American economy. Lay-offs became a virtue, not a last resort. Cost-cutting was pursued not in response to need, but as a managerial ethic in itself.

These new managers excelled at cost-cutting and metrics, and they were lavishly rewarded for delivering higher returns to shareholders. But the rise of this managerial elite came directly at workers' expense: careers that once offered stability and advancement evaporated, and inequality exploded as labour's share of income fell. Whereas a mid-century CEO might earn about 20 times the pay of a production worker, today's CEOs rake in nearly 300 times as much.[9] What fattened corporate balance sheets in the short run also hollowed out the industrial middle class and exiled the manufacturing jobs that Donald Trump claims he will bring back.

This historical shift can also be seen as a fundamental reorganisation of corporate power. Management wasn't eliminated – it was concentrated. Planning and coordination, once spread across ranks, became the exclusive domain of a narrow cadre of elite executives. Those who managed nothing were dismissed; those who managed everything became irreplaceable. Thus, what began as a drive for efficiency evolved into a mechanism for power consolidation, cloaked in the language of innovation and meritocracy.

This logic, imported from the private sector, has found a bipartisan home in government. Democrats too have flirted with this managerial fantasy. Former transportation secretary Pete Buttigieg's stint at McKinsey was not a liability, it was a credential, a marker of seriousness in a party increasingly enamoured with technocratic mastery. The idea that government should be run by highly analytical, highly mobile elites, untethered from the messy specifics of any given institution, is not Musk's invention. It is the air the professional class has been breathing for decades.

III

If this logic risks corroding companies, it risks devastating countries. Government is not Twitter. The bureaucracy Musk now oversees cannot be slashed and reconstituted at whim without profound consequences. Civil servants are not advert buyers or product managers; they are the people who administer healthcare systems, environmental protections, disaster relief, food inspections, foreign assistance and veterans' benefits. The problems they face do not stem from a lack of will or competence, but from structural constraints that no amount of executive bravado can wish away.

The true dysfunction of the federal government lies not in its workforce, but in its design. Layer upon layer of congressional legislation, built up over decades without any serious effort to consolidate or reform, has created a system in which each action requires a gauntlet of approvals, compliance checks, reviews and sign-offs. The work is not slow because bureaucrats are lazy – it is slow because the rules are absurd.

Jennifer Pahlka's *Recoding America* provides a telling example: a Pentagon fiasco in which a next-generation GPS-software upgrade collapsed under the weight of a trivial technical mandate. In that project, an 'enterprise service bus' (ESB) – basically a redundant, labyrinthine software add-on no engineer wanted – was treated as holy writ by a cascade of overlapping rules, from a 1996 congressional tech law down through the Defense Department's own byzantine regulations. Engineers knew the ESB was pointless, but they were bound by contract to include it, and the result was years of delays and billions in cost overruns.[10] This absurd saga should give DOGE's efficiency gurus pause; technocratic wizardry can't save a project shackled by regulations that all but guarantee failure.

Privatisation is no escape hatch. Contractors must navigate the same thicket of regulation. They are bound by the same limitations, often at greater cost. Swapping a civil servant for a six-figure consultant may make the spreadsheet look cleaner, but it doesn't make the job easier to do.

What the federal government needs is not a purge. It needs empowerment. It needs systems that allow workers to solve problems rather than chase paperwork. It needs legal reforms that trust professionals to exercise judgement, not merely to follow process. It needs a public philosophy that values competence, not just credentials; diligence, not disruption.

Musk's tenure may, in the end, prove instructive, not as a model but as a warning. Twitter, under his stewardship, has not become leaner and more effective. It has become erratic, brittle and diminished. Its revenues have cratered, its user base has fractured and its cultural relevance has warped. And while Musk may still boast of building a new kind of platform, the old one is already a shell of itself.

That is what happens when institutions are treated as obstacles to be conquered rather than ecosystems to be tended. That is what happens when leadership confuses authority with capacity. That is what happens when we let management consultants run the country.

Until the United States reckons with the structural sclerosis that strangles its bureaucracy, no amount of genius, no volume of lay-offs and no reshuffling of organisational charts will restore the government's ability to function. We do not need a Jack Welch for the intelligence community. We need a public sector that trusts its workers, clears their path and lets them do their jobs.

That will not come from DOGE, and it will not come from a billionaire. It will come from a country that remembers that government, unlike business, is not about dominance – it's about service.

Notes

1 Zefram Cochran, 'Remembering an Imagined DDI: When Jack Welch Was Deputy Director for Intelligence', *Studies in Intelligence*, vol. 48, no. 3, September 2004, pp. 37–43, https://www.cia.gov/resources/csi/static/When-Welch-Was-Deputy.pdf.

2 The problem of excessive regulation and rule-bound processes causing endemic and wasteful delay has been a major theme of journalist Ezra

Klein's recent work. See, for example, Ezra Klein, 'Biden's Team Wishes They'd Moved So Much Faster', *New York Times*, 13 April 2025, https://www.nytimes.com/2025/04/13/opinion/doge-abundance-government-bulding.html.

3 See Matt O'Brien and Bernard Condon, 'How the Tactics Musk Brought to Washington Backfired at Twitter', AP News, 7 February 2025, https://apnews.com/article/elon-musk-twitter-takeover-x-doge-government-efficiency-e78ac431e7bbf2ae8513594078f1408b.

4 See Will Gendron, 'Mark Zuckerberg Praised Elon Musk's Push "to Make Twitter a Lot Leaner"', *Business Insider*, 10 June 2023, https://www.businessinsider.com/meta-mark-zuckerberg-praises-elon-musk-changes-twitter-layoffs-2023-6; Matthew Loh, 'Jack Dorsey Defends Musk's Twitter Leadership, Saying the Billionaire Slashed the "Critical Sin" of Its Business Model', *Business Insider*, 10 May 2024, https://www.businessinsider.com/jack-dorsey-explains-elon-musk-twitter-layoffs-free-speech-advertisers-2024-5; and Polly Thompson, '"You Should Never Bet Against Elon": Peter Thiel Says Musk Understands Risk-taking Completely Differently from Other People', *Business Insider*, 13 December 2024, https://www.businessinsider.com/peter-thiel-elon-musk-attitude-to-risk-business-2024-12.

5 See Maxwell Strachan, 'The Year Silicon Valley Bosses Reclaimed the Power', VICE, 21 December 2022, https://www.vice.com/en/article/the-year-silicon-valley-bosses-reclaimed-the-power/.

6 John Ganz, 'The Emerging Tech-lash', Unpopular Front, 26 April 2022, https://www.unpopularfront.news/p/the-emerging-tech-lash.

7 Daniel Markovits, 'How McKinsey Destroyed the Middle Class', *Atlantic*, 3 February 2022, https://www.theatlantic.com/ideas/archive/2020/02/how-mckinsey-destroyed-middle-class/605878/.

8 *Ibid.*

9 *Ibid.*

10 Jennifer Pahlka, *Recoding America: Why Government Is Failing in the Digital Age and How We Can Do Better* (New York: Metropolitan Books, 2025), p. 93.

Copyright © 2025 The International Institute for Strategic Studies

DETECT,
CONNECT,
PROTECT.
LOCKHEED MARTIN

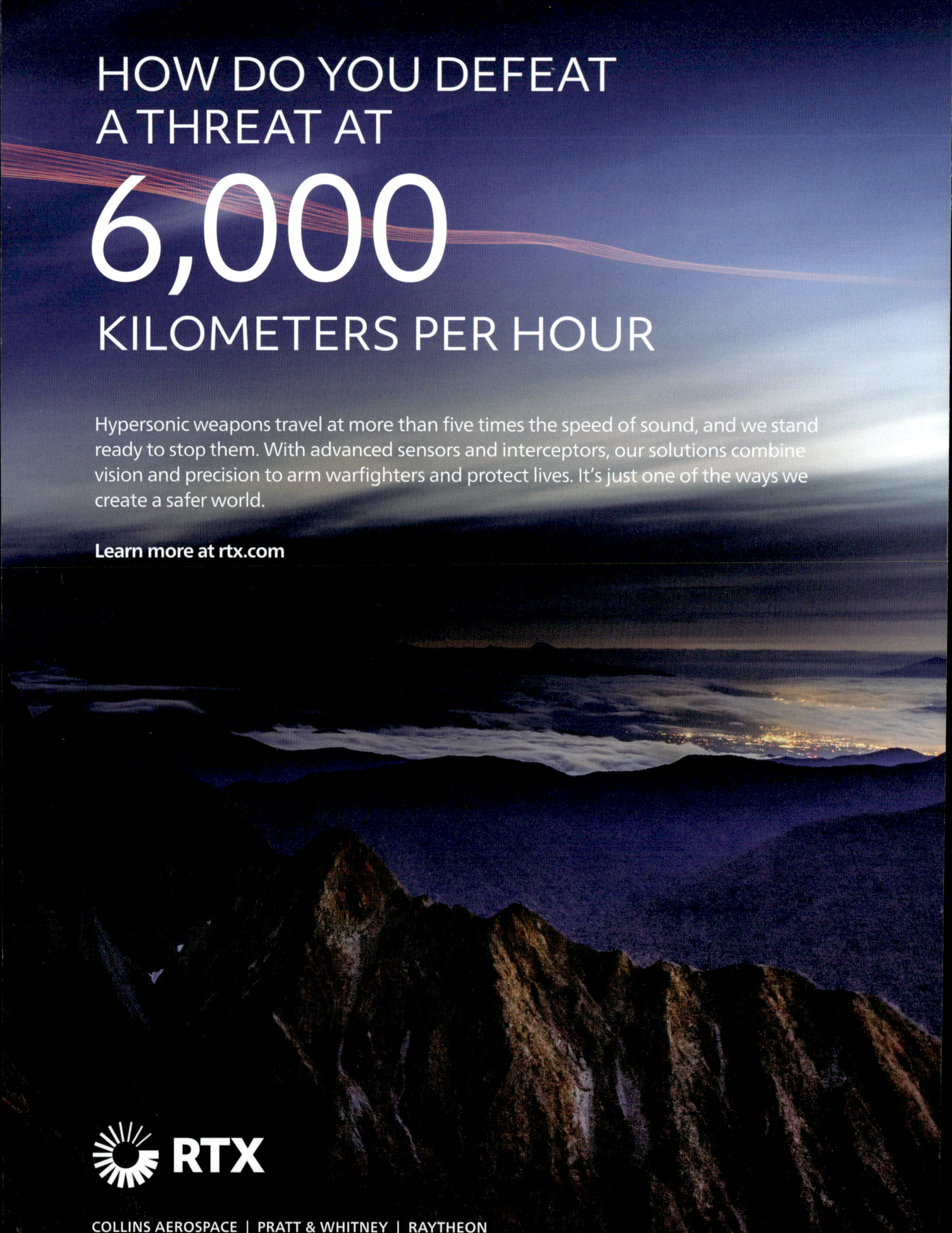
HOW DO YOU DEFEAT
A THREAT AT
6,000
KILOMETERS PER HOUR
Hypersonic weapons travel at more than five times the speed of sound, and we stand ready to stop them. With advanced sensors and interceptors, our solutions combine vision and precision to arm warfighters and protect lives. It's just one of the ways we create a safer world.
Learn more at rtx.com
RTX
COLLINS AEROSPACE | PRATT & WHITNEY | RAYTHEON

Creating hope together
Our cutting edge technologies deliver support to those who strive to create a better future.
Learn more at boeing.com
BOEING

MILITARY BALANCE+

THE ONLINE DATABASE

IISS

DATA AND ANALYSIS TOOLS

MILITARY BALANCE+, the online database from the IISS Defence and Military Analysis team, provides indispensable information for the private sector, governments, armed forces, academia, the media and more.

- **Perform your analysis on Military Balance+**
  Utilising seven search engines and three data tools you can ask complex questions of the data.
- **Save time and money**
  The Military Balance+ can do in seconds what would otherwise take hours of your researchers' time.
- **Data you can have confidence in**
  All data has gone through a rigorous verification process, meaning you can use it in your work without concern over its validity.
- **Original IISS insight**
  Military Balance+ contains a searchable library of original IISS analysis, charts and graphics.

A WORLD OF DEFENCE DATA TO DRIVE YOUR STRATEGY

Deployments
Exercises
Forces
Equipment
Economics
Procurements
Analysis and graphics

173 countries

Data tools

GSA® Contract Holder
Contract # 47QTCA22D000H

www.iiss.org/militarybalanceplus

CONTACT

For an online demonstration, trial and subscription information:

Robert Hopgood
Sales Manager for Military Balance+
Direct: +44 (0)20 7395 9911
Mobile: +44 (0)7548 217 063
Email: robert.hopgood@iiss.org